You Don't Have to Die of Disappointment

...but you can always die laughing!

To dear Lucia
with love,
Mina xx

You Don't Have to Die of Disappointment

...but you can always die laughing!

Memoir of a
Russian Yiddishe Yogini

Mina Semyon

First published by Mina Semyon 2021
publishingminasemyon@gmail.com

www.minasemyon.co.uk

British Library Cataloguing-in-Publication data
A catalogue record for this book is available from the British Library

ISBN 978-1-5272-9199-7

Designed and typeset by
Carnegie Scotforth Book Production

Printed and bound by Totem

About the Author

Mina was born in 1938 in the Soviet Union and has been working on her memoir and teaching Yoga for over 40 years. She was fortunate to become a student and friend of R. D. Laing, psychiatrist, poet, musician and spiritual teacher who, in the process of enabling her to transcend her harsh Russian childhood, initiated her on the path of awareness through the practice of Yoga and Mindfulness. This, combined with a determination to find her authentic voice, through the study of singing and sound led to a unique way of teaching and what has evolved is a way of practising and teaching which incorporates our whole being – emotional, mental, physical and spiritual, in daily life and relationships. This led her to transcending her traumatic past and expressing what happened without self-pity. Her aim is to liberate the mind and body of everything that obscures the spirit of joy, love, compassion, spontaneity and playfulness. Or in her own words, "The Royal Jelly of all my practice is the spirit of love!"

Mina appeared in the BBC television series *'Every Body Knows'* and the Yoga book *Body Life* written by her ex-husband Arthur Balaskas. Her piece, 'Take as Long as it Takes' – an excerpt from *You Don't Have to Die of Disappointment* – appears in *R. D. Laing Creative Destroyer* edited by Bob Mullan. Mina has also self-published two Yoga books: *The Distracted Centipede – A Yoga Experience* and *Yoga Stories for Healthy Living.*

Mina has also performed a number of one woman shows, based on excerpts from her memoir, Russian songs and songs written for her by Fran Landesman.

Endorsements for

'You Don't Have to Die of Disappointment...'

'A delicate, nuanced, sensitive, vivid evocation of a most unusual and yet strangely familiar childhood.'

– R. D. Laing

'The inner and outer horrors of life in Poland and Russia during the worst upheavals are here caught unforgettably, with a child's candid eye, and with a directness that is as refreshing as showers in a time of drought.'

– Elizabeth Smart, Poet and author of
'By the Grand Central Station I sat down and wept'

'I enjoyed her journey from the dark forest of her Russian youth to the light of R. D. Laing. It made me laugh with amusement and recognition.'

– Fran Landesman
Poet and songwriter

Contents

'The oyster doesn't fill with pearl until it is content. The pearl is the oyster's autobiography'

Federico Fellini

'My story isn't sweet and harmonious, like invented stories. It tastes of folly and bewilderment, of madness and dreams, like the lives of all people who no longer want to lie to themselves.'

Herman Hesse

'There is a way to look at the past. Don't hide from it, it won't catch you if you don't repeat it.'

Pearl Bailey

This book is dedicated to
my mother Dina Sher and R. D. Laing

Acknowledgements

I would like to express my deepest gratitude to everyone who has encouraged me on this journey of writing my memoir, through my many doubts and inner tribulations.

I am not embarrassed to admit that I started writing this memoir around 54 years ago in Johannesburg, just after I had left Russia and got married. My husband Arthur came out of the bathroom one morning looking a bit lost and worried and said to me, 'Don't worry ... but ...'

'A mouse!' I jumped.

'No, worse,' he said, 'a rat has just run over my foot.'

I put my hands over my ears, 'It's all finished, just as I was beginning to live this had to happen ... I don't know how I could ever let you touch me again!'

I am laughing now, but back then it was a different story. I won't pre-empt it by telling it here, but rather let you read it all in the coming pages.

Firstly, I want to particularly thank my dear sister-friend Mary Ann Ephgrave who stayed with me through years of writing and rewriting. Her enthusiasm never wavered, even after editing this manuscript three times, insisting that she was not bored at all. She kept my spirits up through the times when I was overcome by doubts that my story was any good, or of any use to anybody at all. Mary Ann really believed in me and my story, and without her I would not be writing acknowledgements for a completed book.

Thank you to beautiful Laura who came like an angel into my life, and after reading my manuscript, not only made a website for me, but insisted on including a crowdfunding page so that we could publish my book properly. With Laura came the gorgeous, encouraging and loving Maya and Izz, so I had three angels who gave me extraordinary support during the final steps towards publication, keeping my spirits up with singing, and playing music together.

I want to thank my lovely family Kira, Guillermo, Alexi and Luca for bringing much support and joy into my life, and my extended family, Janet, Kim and Ias.

I also want to thank everyone who generously donated to our crowdfunder, from the many friends to unbelievably, the people I didn't yet know. Thank you so much to everyone who contributed:
Adrian Oliver, Ana Seymenska, Anne Barnett, Danny Parashchak, Daphne Tagg, Dawn McCafferty, Diana Miller, Elena Sussman, Hagar Basis, Harriett Goldenberg, Janet Hanson, Jeb Walker, Kate Levitt, Lauren Liebling Davis, Lorraine Stirk, Luke Mullen, Malou Mella, Maud Gerritsen, Mishka Adams, Peter Walker, Rachel Close, Renara Akhoundova, Sarah Morgan and Sheryll Karpel.

A particularly special Thank You to:
Mary Ann Ephgrave, Esther Lopez, John and Lolly Stirk, Suzi Griffin, and of course, dear Bob.

In total we raised over £2,000, for which I am deeply humbled. Thank you.

PROLOGUE

All the things my mama called me

"Curses are closely related to blessings. Curses are blessings turned inside out. And if you can do one, you are capable of the other."

Rabbi Lionel Blue

Moscow 1945 – the war is over

My favourite scent, the scent of lilac, fills the air as I walk home from school in Khovrino, a suburb of Moscow. I am seven years old. It seems so easy to be happy, if only it wasn't for that tightness in my stomach and the dark worried shadow in my heart. I'm riddled with anxiety in anticipation of my mother's mood. A Jewish composer, Secunda, wrote a Yiddishe musical comedy in 1932: *'Men ken leben, nor men lost nisht'* ('You could live but they don't let you'), which became my mother's mantra.

It's not that my mother was not capable of spontaneous bursts of joy, it's just that they wouldn't last, they'd immediately get extinguished with a shrug: 'Akh, I could be happy but my bitter fate doesn't let me.'

My mind is in its familiar turmoil. Will she be up? Or will she still be in bed in our bleak little room, in communal block No. 1, with the covers over her head, complaining of backache, threatening that she is going to die any time now and that without her I am nothing? Will she get all worked up and start pouring her whole life's frustrations over me, cursing and shouting that I'm the worst of the worst; stupid, selfish, unaffectionate and unlovable; stubborn as a ram; that she likes me less than yesterday's shit in our hole-in-the-wood communal lavatory; that her bitter fate sent me to her and if she had her life over again she would never have children? And I'll end up rolled into a little ball under the table with my hands over my ears and stay there till I feel numb with pain.

I open the door timidly. Surprise and joy! A white embroidered tablecloth on the table; a vase with lilacs in the middle; the window is open into our little garden, a mild breeze gently blowing the lace curtains, which were left behind when we had to flee the Nazis advancing on Poland and after the war were returned by our Polish landlady.

My mother is dressed; her hair combed in her special forties style that takes her forever to get right in a frenzy of frustration and fury, hairpins flying all over the place – a ritual I've dreaded and witnessed, holding my breath too many times. Now, to my relief, she smiles as I come in, a touch of lipstick brightens her beautiful face. She kisses me and instead of the familiar curses, pours her blessings over me: "My treasure, my joy, my goodness, may you be with me forever, may my eyes always see you, my beauty, my only one, *moya umnitza,* my clever little girl."

She opens *pechka* – the Russian oven and brings out a plate of crumbed veal with roast potatoes and cabbage and a delicious smell fills the room. Now that the rationing is over and we have more food, she loves to watch me eat, lamenting all the while: "Do you think it is easy not to have any food to give to your child?" She sits down at the table opposite me, keeping a close watch over every mouthful disappearing down my throat and showers me with more blessings: "May joy and strength fill your precious heart and may God give you happiness for all your deprivation and suffering."

Being blessed and being cursed throughout my childhood, created the blueprint I worked with all my life, swinging from 'I'm the best' to 'I'm the worst', till I realised later in life, when I came across Buddhist scriptures, that there was a middle way to be found. My journey toward the middle way is what this book is all about.

PART ONE
A Russian Childhood is Hard to Beat

'Don't be sad; don't be angry if life deceives you!
Submit to your grief; your time for joy will come,
believe me.'

– Alexander Pushkin, Russian Poet

Life before and during the Second World War

I was born on a stormy February night in a little snowed-in thatched roof house on the Polish Russian border, one year before Russia and Germany invaded Poland and divided it between them. We ended up on the Polish side. A story went around about a guy whose house was bang in the middle, so when the Russian authorities came to mark the border and asked which side he wanted to be on, he replied: "In Poland, I couldn't take another Russian winter." A story like that, if overheard by the wrong person, could land you in a Siberian *gulag* [forced labour camp] for a lifetime, labelled 'anti-Soviet agitator and enemy of the people'.

My entry into the world took twenty-four hours during which my father paced up and down in the snow to get away from my mother's screams. My mother told me over and over again: "Your birth was the worst experience of my life, if I had my life all over again I would never have children," and in the same breath: "When I first saw your big blue eyes and long eyelashes, I felt such love I had to restrain myself from squeezing you to death."

A week after my birth our neighbour, who was bitter and resentful because she couldn't have children, came to see the newborn me. Casting covetous glances into my pram she exclaimed: "Who did you give birth to? The whole *shtetel* is talking about her eyes! And have you ever seen such eyelashes?" My mother immediately spat three times over her shoulder, *tsfu, tsfu, tsfu,* according to the Jewish superstition to ward off the evil eye. All the same, the next day I turned green. I stayed green until she took me to the doctor. The doctor, trying to detect the cause of my colour, asked if she'd had a fright recently. She said she'd heard screams in the middle of the night: "Fire, fire! I ran outside in my night gown, a whole row of thatched roofs was on fire. Ours was next!"

"That's why your baby is green," concluded the doctor, "your milk has gone off. Start feeding her with cow's milk."

"I got up and thanked him. He kissed my hand," my mother recollected with pride, as if the custom of kissing married women's hands in Poland was invented especially for her.

"When we left, I said to myself, 'Aha! You say cow's milk? I'm going to give her cream and an egg yolk on top.' Within weeks your cheeks filled out and looked like ripe peaches." But I also broke out in bright red spots all over my body.

"One day we met the neighbour with the 'evil eye' in the street. She looked at you, asleep in your pram, '*Oy,* still sucking a dummy! If you don't stop her now you'll never get it out of her mouth.' Before that I used to dip your dummy in sugar water, put it in your mouth and not a peep out of you, but after what she told me, as soon as we came home, I took your dummy, dipped it in mustard and gave it to you. *Ugh,* what a face you made! You spat it out and never wanted it again. You were no fool."

I never did figure out why she took advice from the woman who, according to her, gave me the 'evil eye' and, after my tender taste buds got assaulted by mustard at the age of six months I became a child with eating problems. My mother took me to the doctor to find out why I wouldn't eat.

"You'd munch everything at our landlady's, and with such an appetite, but not at home ... strange child, I could never understand you."

"I never let you crawl. From my arms straight into walking," my mother would announce proudly while telling stories from my childhood. "I wouldn't let you crawl on the filthy floor, not that my floor was filthy, I used to get on my hands and knees and scrub till you could eat from it."

"So why didn't you let me crawl on it then?" her logic made my head spin.

"*Akh,* what do you need to crawl and get splinters in your hands? Only *goyim* let their babies crawl in filth."

"Filth? But you just said how clean your floor was?"

"I used to put you in a pretty dress, a ribbon in your hair and prop you up in the window. Passers-by would stop and stare in amazement because you looked like a doll. But once you learnt to walk you kept pulling your hand out of mine shouting, '*Sama, sama,* [myself, myself]' already self-willed and obstinate."

My first lesson in life came when I was eighteen months old: "One day I went to the post office, carrying you in my arms. You were no lightweight, *tfu,tfu,tfu.*" As usual, she spat three times in my direction to keep the devil away. "A big *tokhes* [bottom] ... *tfu, tfu, tfu,* may you be healthy." In the Jewish tradition you never said too exuberantly how good things were for fear of incurring the wrath of God; the spitting was a way of appeasing God.

"It was a warm spring day but I was wearing a winter suit. At the post office I put you down so you could stand, holding onto me while I bought a stamp. You started screaming. I said to you, 'Just stand for a moment, while I put the stamp on.' You screamed louder. I thought to myself, just you wait till we get home, I'll show you ... So I picked you up, sweat pouring off me. As soon as we got home I pulled your pants down and with your father's belt really gave it to you until you screamed, 'Mama! Mama! *ya nie budu,* Mama! Mama! I won't do it again.' After that I hung the belt on the wall and if you did something naughty, all I had to do was look at it and you would stop immediately." For the life of me I wouldn't know what it was that I wasn't going to do again. This is text book material. I was surely being groomed for psychotherapy!

To distract me from hunger my mother played cat's cradle with me and told me the following stories about her childhood and youth.

"During the Revolution the Bolsheviks, may they rot in the ground, came to arrest my father under suspicion of having a stash of gold tucked away somewhere. Gold, *shmold,* he melted down a few pieces of my mother's jewellery and hid it for a rainy day, thinking that the Bolsheviks could confiscate our piece of land, our bread shop, but not a sack of gold buried somewhere in the ground under a rock. When the militia came to arrest him he managed to escape through the back door. They took the rest of us to an interrogation centre and locked us in one room. Then an officer came in and took my mother away for interrogation. I started crying; I was five years old but I remember it like yesterday. The Red Army officer sat me on his lap. I peed on him. I wish I had done something more. The sound of gunshots came from the yard; with each shot all of us children cried out in terror, imagining it was our mother standing in front of the firing squad. After many hours of interrogation we were all allowed to go home, and my father reappeared."

"I was the youngest of seven children. Maybe you won't believe me, but my father was also my great uncle. Yes, when my mother was nineteen she went to a fortune teller who told her that she would marry a man of her own blood, much older than herself. *Nu,* what do you think? When she was twenty-one she married her own uncle, twenty years older than herself. *Akh,* I still get goose bumps when I think about it."

"My father died when I was ten. My older sister, Sonya, ended up marrying a crude mill owner. When he came home from work she had to help him pull off his dirty old boots ... such a refined creature, with a delicate little nose, not like my potato. My youngest sister, Feigle, died at sixteen; she was the beauty of the family."

"As a child, I used to look at the small sepia photograph of Feigle's face in an oval gold mount and wonder if it had that faded, faraway look because she was dead."

"Your great-grandmother had twelve children but she still had to work in the potato field. She even gave birth in the field, tied the baby to her body and continued picking potatoes. She left the other babies in cradles suspended by a rope from the ceiling, so that they rocked from their own movement. She hung *soskas,* rag pacifiers filled with chewed up food, above the cradles where the babies could reach and suck. One day, when her youngest was only one year old, she came back and found him standing up in his cradle, with a mouth full of teeth, talking to her like a grown up, 'why do you leave me all alone?'" My mother rolled up the sleeve of her dress and showed me her goose bumps, giving me one of her penetrating looks that said, 'Maybe you don't believe me, hmmm?'

"One day your great-grandmother went to a fortune teller. When she came out of the darkened candle-lit room, her hair, raven black before she went in, had turned silver grey. She never told anyone what the fortune teller told her; she took the secret to her grave."

The stories certainly did their job; my hair stood on end, shivers ran down my spine and I would forget about my hunger completely.

In the meantime it would start getting dark outside, bleak and miserable inside, with not a doll to cuddle or a thing to eat. I became an expert at gauging which way her mood was swinging; she could suddenly, without warning, get into bed with covers over her head and look like she could remain there for the foreseeable future. So I tried to keep the stories going, "Oh please, please tell me the one about my grandmother and her bakery."

She'd get up and light the kerosene lamp. To save on kerosene she had to keep the wick low, but when the gloom reached unbearable proportions she'd turn the wick up a little higher and carry on, "*Akh*, those were the days. Your grandmother got up at 4 a.m. to bake bread for the whole village, and on top of that she'd bring me breakfast in bed: two rolls, still warm from the oven, with a chunk of melted butter in them, an omelette with four eggs, and a hot chocolate with an egg yolk whisked into it. Believe me, I was something to look at!"

"Now tell me about Papa and how he played violin."

"*Akh*, your father was the love of my life. Semyon Fishel was born in Austria and graduated from the Vienna Conservatorium as a singer and violinist. We met at my younger brother Nathan's wedding where your father played violin in the band. When he sang the Polish tango, '*Oh at least a drop of happiness in love*', what do you think? Our eyes met and he fell in love; it was not difficult; I was the healthiest and the most beautiful girl in the village."

"Beautiful I was, but a dowry I didn't have, and a girl needed one in those days to make a good match. The girl's parents had to give for the newlywed's home," she counts on her fingers, "a goose down duvet, two pillows, two sheets, plates, cutlery and pots. But my mother couldn't afford to give me a dowry. *Akh,* I was the matchmaker's favourite girl; she brought me many suitors. But they were all too common, no *kultura*. One was the rich butcher with the red face who wanted me so much he didn't ask for a dowry. God spared me this fate and brought me your father, whose heart was with the music, not dowries, but it was not to be for long. *Akh,* who can argue with fate?" She raised her palms to heaven and dropped them despondently.

"Your father was one of seven children, each adopted by a different foster family after both their parents died. *Nu,* what's there to talk long? He proposed and we got married."

All through my youth my mother tried to make sure I understood how modest and reserved a girl should be with a man, "For two weeks after we were married I slept with my mother. Your father would stand in the doorway, like *a nebbish,* silently begging me with his eyes to come to bed."

Still, she must have given in pretty soon – I was born nine months later.

When my mother was six months pregnant with me her mother died. She often told me the story of my grandmother's death. She had a routine; she could have been trained by the KGB brainwashing methods. First she'd tell the story of how her mother died and how there is no life without a mother, and then sing *'My Yiddishe Mama'* in Yiddish, ripping my heart apart.

How cheerful and light is a home where there is a mother;
How grievous and bitter it is when she is absent.

She'd go on, "When your grandmother lay dying she pushed my face away so I wouldn't look at her, it was considered bad luck for a pregnant woman to look at a dying person. After she died I didn't want to live. What is life without a mother?"

I was so stunned I couldn't even cry, and that was one thing I was good at. Was she really telling me that, while I was growing in her womb, she didn't want to live?

When my mother's two brothers left Russia after the Revolution and went, one to America, the other, to South Africa, where the streets were 'paved with gold,' she stayed behind to look after her mother. Grandmother flatly refused to leave the *shtetle* and Mama couldn't possibly leave without her – what is life without a mother? "And that," she would say, "is how we got caught up in the war."

The Great Patriotic People's War

June 22, 1941

The Second World War, the Great Patriotic People's War, broke out and sank our world into chaos and terror. My father's violin hung silent on the wall; no more soulful tangos – just eerie silence, interrupted by Molotov's sombre voice on the radio announcing the German invasion of the Soviet soil: "Our beloved Motherland has been attacked by the forces of Nazi Germany. We must unite and defend our Motherland from the aggressor". Soviet composers were ordered to write patriotic songs with melodies so haunting that they made their way even into my three-year-old heart and played havoc with my proneness to melancholy for the rest of my life. One song, in a waltz rhythm with a beautiful melody, can still make everything inside me come to a standstill: "on the 22nd of June, at precisely four o'clock, Kiev was bombed and we were informed that the war had started."

My mother's sister Sonya's husband, the 'coarse and boorish' flour mill owner, jumped up and down in his dirty old boots, clapping his hands with joy: "The Germans are coming! The Germans are coming!" He thought he'd get back his flour-mill which the Russians had confiscated as private property when they took over Poland. But when the Germans invaded, he and his wife and five children ended up hiding in the forests with the partisans, rats nibbling at them in the night. He did manage to find the piece of gold he had hidden, which got the family to America after the war was over.

Unlike her crude brother-in law, my mother didn't cherish any illusions about Hitler's plans for the Jews. She got herself, my father and me, and another family with two children, onto a cart drawn by an emaciated horse, and we set off with the German planes advancing behind us, bombing the roads. The other family were neighbours whom my mother often invited for dinner before the war broke out: "He was a 'real man,' and with shoulders like this," she'd spread her hands beyond her own shoulders, "she, a mousy little thing on crooked legs, who couldn't cook to save her life. And believe me, I could cook. I would come in wearing a dress with a deep *décolleté* revealing my magnificent neck. Look at it now, there is nothing of it left, but then it was something to look at ... I'd be carrying a flaming soufflé dish. He'd bend down to his wife, with his eyes riveted on me, and say in a loud whisper, 'Learn, Sonya, learn.'"

"How we managed to fit all of us on that cart I don't know, we took nothing with us, we had to leave everything behind. I just grabbed you, a few clothes and our photo album; your father picked up his violin and we ran like from fire. You didn't open your eyes for three days, not drinking, not eating, just whimpering, 'I want to be in my own little bed.'"

"During a bomb raid everyone rushed into the ditches, except me. Your father begged me to run too, but I refused. He tried to grab you, but I held onto you and the reins. I thought, 'If I am going to be killed, you might as well come with me. What is life without a mother?' I felt as if made of bricks, sitting there holding the reins."

"Why did you just sit there when everyone else ran into the ditches?" I ask, bewildered.

"*Nu,* for what do I need to run?"

We travelled that way for a month, seven of us on the cart, stopping in villages where some people gave us bread and milk and hay for the horse. Finally we crossed the border into Russia, just escaping with our lives. If we'd left only a few days later we would have been caught and deported by the Nazis to a concentration camp.

Finally my father, mother and I managed to get away from the Nazi invasion in a cattle train going in the direction of Kyrgyzstan in Soviet Central Asia; our neighbour with the broad shoulders, his wife who 'couldn't cook to save her life' and their two children, escaped on another train and we never saw them again.

On the train:

> I catch my thumb in the door of the train and my nail turns black.
>
> My father gets off at a station to try and buy some bread; the train starts moving and leaves without him. My mother screams: "Stop the train; stop the train!" The train gathers speed. By some miracle he catches up at the next station by hitching a lift in an army truck.
>
> A woman gives birth, screaming and swearing.
>
> Somebody dies. The body is thrown overboard.
>
> A loud sombre voice comes through the black loud speaker at every station: "The fascist aggressors ... our glorious Red Army ... Comrade Stalin ... we shall defeat ..."

After a month on that and other goods trains, with one small window covered with barbed wire for air and 'sightseeing' we arrived in Frunze (now Bishkek) in Kyrgyzstan, thinking we were safe. But when my father went to register with the military militia as all able-bodied men had to, he got arrested for being a 'deserter and an enemy of the people'.

My mother left me with neighbours promising to be back soon and rushed off on a night train to put in an appeal to the prosecutor for my father's release. She was away for two days. I desperately wanted my mother, especially when it started to get dark and the sixteen-year-old son of the family told me that the Tatar tribesmen had cut my mother into pieces and eaten her. I sat motionless, staring at the ground, waiting – until my mother's bare feet, cold autumn mud coming through her toes, at last appeared. She brought me new shoes and a pair of brown ribbed tights.

After a few days the militia released my father. He brought me a pink box with tooth powder, a little blue and red boat and a little rubber goat that said, *'m-e-e-e'* when I squeezed it. He got a job in a sugar-beet factory and for 'entertainment' my mother took me to watch the sugar fall from a big machine like a waterfall.

But after two weeks Papa was re-arrested and sent away to a Siberian *gulag*, a hard labour camp. The day he left he picked up his violin, which had been hanging on the wall untouched ever since we arrived, and played the Schubert serenade, *'May my song fly to you through the night'*. My mother cried; my father hung the violin back on the wall, put on the *telogreika*, the body warmer issued by the Red Army for forced labour convicts, which looked very short on him, making him look even taller, and kissed my mother a long goodbye.

When he bent down to kiss me I turned away and just stood there with a vodka compress around my neck for my sore throat, refusing to look at him. He enveloped me in his arms, held me close, kissed me tenderly on the cheek and left forever.

Recently, after I discovered the Internet, I found out that during the Second World War we were part of a wave of more than 20,000 Jewish refugees who fled from the Nazi-occupied western regions of the Soviet Union to Kyrgyzstan, trying to save ourselves from the Nazi invasion. On arrival, a large number of the men were imprisoned for alleged 'counter-revolutionary activity'. My father was one of them. It only became known fifty years later that this was all part of Stalin's insane campaign to exterminate Polish citizens, amongst millions of others, even those who were devoted communists, which my father wasn't. He was just a romantic violinist and tango dancer.

My father's death

On a bright hot sunny day, with not a cloud in the sky and the scent of cinnamon in the air, my mother holds my hand as we wander through the stalls of an exotic Kyrgyzstan market, fascinated by the Kyrgyz women with their squinty, smiling eyes and hair in little plaits. They sit on brightly coloured oriental rugs, selling intricately embroidered garments and spices.

"Stand to the side, a camel can spit in your face," a big burly man shouts to me, his belly shaking. I stand there totally mesmerised by the magical animal next to him that I've never seen before. I find out years later that camels *can* spit, but normally at other camels, over food issues, like 'this is my food, go away ... spit, spit'; very rarely does a camel spit at a person, and only if it feels threatened. The camel man frightens me; he's a bully spoiling a magical moment. At that moment my mother recognises a man on one leg and crutches, who had been sent to the same labour camp as my father. Their eyes meet. His eyes fill with tears. He doesn't need to say anything. She knows. "He is dead?" she whispers. The man just lowers his head.

Suddenly, in a matter of minutes, the sky darkens; it's a total eclipse of the sun. People move about, whispering and praying in fear; in their culture a solar eclipse is attributed to supernatural causes and is regarded as a bad omen. My mother and I stand there, dazed with the shock that has just hit us. After a few minutes the sun comes out again and lights up the market. Jolted out of her trance, my mother takes my hand and slowly we walk home. We sit on a bench outside in silence till it gets dark. When we go inside my mother lets rip, screaming and wailing and tearing at her hair. I am in a panic, so I keep asking questions, wanting her to stop: "Why is Papa never coming back? Is it because he is dead?"

A solar eclipse became the symbol of my father's death. Only after I learned as an adult the astronomical explanation of the eclipse as a natural phenomenon, did I realise that the eclipse on that day in the Kyrgyzstan market wasn't something aimed at me personally by some supernatural power.

The man with one leg comes to see us the next day. He tells my mother that my father sold his coat to send us money and died of pneumonia in the bitter cold and that they threw his body onto a heap of other frozen dead bodies.

All that was left of my father was his violin and one letter he wrote from the *gulag* written in very neat, slanting to the left handwriting: "Life here is impossible; it's either escape or death."

When I opened my father's violin case, I found the cream coloured silk handkerchief he used to fold under his chin when he played and a sheet of music he composed that had gone all yellow. How could the sky still be blue and children playing and people laughing when my father was gone forever?

Soon after my father's death my mother fell ill with dysentery. The sugar-beet factory sent a woman to prepare food for us. The rest of the time I looked after her, giving her water to drink and taking the night pot to the river to rinse out. Sometimes I forgot myself and played in the sand; the sand was so hot I saw people baking eggs in it.

Mama stayed in bed for five weeks. "The day I got out

of bed I tried to hang myself," she told me. "You came in while I was standing on a chair with the rope in my hands. You cried, 'Mama I'm hungry.' There and then I decided to take my life into my hands. I dropped the rope and took up chain smoking."

She got a night-shift job, the only one available, which she had to accept or starve. So for three weeks she had to lock me up with my little rubber goat and the blue and red boat, from five in the afternoon, when it was still light and the sun was shining and I could hear children playing outside, till the following morning.

I wake up in the middle of the night, call for my mother ... silence. I'm all alone. I see my father's frozen body on the heap of bodies somewhere in Siberia, which the man on one leg described to us so vividly. I overheard a story about a woman whose son was reported missing in the war. The woman goes to see a clairvoyant who puts her in front of a mirror in a dark room with one candle burning and says, 'Your son is alive, look.' The mother looks in the mirror and, instead of her own image, sees her son with his head bandaged and blood seeping through the bandages. I'm crazed with terror till I fall, exhausted, into the oblivion of sleep.

Many years later my mother told me: "When I came back in the morning you'd be sitting there, dipping a piece of bread in sugar and chewing on it. You wouldn't come to me or talk to me. But what could I do? I needed to get some sleep; I had to get back to work in the evening."

"What did you do at the factory?"

"I was packaging bandages for the front, standing barefoot on the cement floor."

"Why were you barefoot?"

"I was barefoot because my shoes broke. The head of the factory, can you imagine, the head of a five-story factory himself, no less, told me, 'Give me your torn shoes.' I felt embarrassed, but he insisted, so I gave them to him. I can still see him walking away, holding my torn shoes by the laces and swinging them. The next day he brought them back repaired, the head of the factory himself, you can imagine ..."

I still couldn't get it into my four-year-old head that my father was dead and kept asking my mother: "Where is Papa?" One day I was playing outside when the postman arrived with a letter: "Give it to your Mama." I rushed in, waving the letter and shouting: "A letter from Papa, a letter from Papa." My mother opened it. It was a letter from the military office, confirming his death.

She tried to change the night-shift by appealing to the director of the factory: "My husband died at the labour front and I have to lock up my four-year-old daughter night after night, all alone. The heartbreak will kill me and leave my child an orphan."

Sitting at his desk, puffed up with bureaucratic power, he dismissed her appeal: "Your husband died there serving his Motherland, and if you die here, don't worry, we'll find an orphanage for your child."

A woman worker, who saw Mama coming out of the director's office sobbing, asked her what the matter was and my mother repeated what the director had said. Together they made an appeal to higher authorities. It turned out that the man had been embezzling money selling government medicine that was meant for the front. The penalty for this crime was capital punishment. The man was shot.

The little radish

When my mother was put on day-shift, she found me a place in a Polish kindergarten. The first day she took me there I screamed so hard she had to pry my hands away from her skirt and run out of earshot.

My mother walks away. I feel demented as I watch her disappear. I can't hold it together. I have no identity other than the kid whose father just died in a hard labour camp in Siberia. Girls in pretty dresses seem to know each other and are playing together happily. My dress is old and worn, my shoes are too big for me and I don't know whether I'll see my mother at the end of the day or ever again. So I run after her, screaming with all my might, but she disappears around another corner and the white-uniformed teacher grabs hold of me and tells me in Polish: "Come, come, we are going to do a little play, *'The Carrot's Birthday Party.'*" And all the children start singing and dancing:

On the day of the carrot's birthday
All the vegetables are gathered together
The carrot greets each one politely
And asks them about their health
The potato starts jumping around
The beetroot is already dancing with the
turnip
And the cauliflower is chasing the parsnip
The little radish is sitting in the corner
So sad she's turned pale

The little radish

She is crying because nobody invites her to dance.

"And who is going to be the little radish?" asks the teacher with a mischievous look on her face.

All the children turn to look at me, sitting in the corner, sobbing, ready-made for the part.

The 'little radish' alienation theme continued haunting me throughout my life; even as an adult and an outwardly independent woman, I easily fell back into fear of abandonment if I wasn't the centre of attention with all eyes on me. Perhaps that is where my desire to be on stage came from. It wasn't until London in 1969, when Dr R. D. Laing accepted me as a client in psychotherapy, that I got my chance to pour out all the hurt in my heart to someone who listened with tenderness and love and the traumatised 'little radish' began to heal.

My uncle and his family

Back in Kyrgyzstan, standing in a queue for rationed bread, my mother overheard one of her brothers' name mentioned and was told that he and his family were living in the Tatarstan Autonomous Republic, near Alma-Ata. She wrote to him and he sent us the special pass needed to travel in Russia during the war.

Once more my mother and I set out into the unknown, with all our belongings in two bundles, this time just the two of us saying good-bye to the misty blue, snow-capped Kyrgyz Ala-Too Mountains on the faraway horizon. Our whole world has changed but the mountains look exactly as they did when we first arrived here with my father.

Once again we are on a platform crowded with women and children and men injured in fighting, with their belongings tied up in cloth bundles. My mother asks a woman: "How long have you been waiting?"

"Two weeks? Maybe three?" she sighs, nursing a new-born baby with two more toddlers clinging onto her skirt, resigned to her fate.

Holding me asleep in her arms, as well as a couple of bundles containing all our possessions, my mother crawls under cattle trains to cross the rails to find the train to take us to our destination. I wake up and ask: "Why do other people have Daddies? Why don't we?"

When the goods train arrives, a sea of people rushes to try and get into the carriages, already packed with soldiers. My mother, unable to deal with her bundles and me in her arms, passes me onto the train, into the arms of a soldier. The train starts moving and gathering speed. She frantically runs after the train. I scream. Another soldier just manages to grab her hand and pull her up into the carriage. I clutch onto her and never want to let her go. Suddenly the train stops and we all have to get out and wait on the platform for the next train. When it arrives, in the struggle to get on, a big man with a sack on his shoulder comes between me and my mother, wrenching my hand out of hers. I'm lost. I shout: "*Mama, Mama,*" but I can't find her. I'm beside myself with terror.

I didn't realise just how deeply those traumas still lived on in me until forty-five years later, while as my daughter Kira was seeing me off to a Buddhist monastery in Thailand for a ten-day silent retreat, I had a panic attack on the platform at Bangkok railway station and refused to get onto the train. The platform, full of people carrying children and bags, triggered memories of the war and filled me with dread.

But unlike me, fortunate to have found a way to heal my childhood traumas, my mother never recovered from the shocks of the war years. She kept on asking all through her life: "Can you imagine? Someone stole our only piece of bread. I don't understand; how can anyone steal from a widow with an orphan?"

She went on repeating the story of this journey of thousands of miles across Russia on numerous cattle trains well into her old age; the same faraway look in her eyes that made me feel so frightened and alone as a child:

"... But there were some good people too, like the time when we tried to get onto another train and a soldier stood, blocking the entrance with his rifle, repeating like a robot 'Not allowed'. An officer grabbed him by the scruff of his neck and screamed into his face, 'How do you know where *your* wife and children are at this moment? Let this woman with her little girl get on.' The officer pushed that soldier out of the way, grabbed our belongings, and another soldier gave me a hand, just as the train pulled off. Can you imagine – the officer gave us his bunk and himself stood the whole night, leaning his head against the top bunk? I swear on my life. And when it turned light, he woke the soldier sleeping on the top bunk and said: 'Now it's my turn,' and went to sleep. Yes, there were some good people too."

After weeks and weeks on cattle trains we arrive at our destination. In the whole world there isn't a sight gloomier than that little snowed-in station in the Tatar republic: a large waiting room full of people asleep on their bundles on the floor; in the middle of the ceiling a dull naked light-bulb swaying in the draught. In the corner sits a man with no legs from above the knees, a pair of crutches next to him. He plays an accordion and sings '*Wait for me,*' the most popular love song during the war, written by Konstantine Simonov for the actress Valentina Serova, with whom he was madly in love and who didn't wait:

Wait for me and I'll come back!
But you must wait with all you've got!
Wait when snow falls,
Wait when wind blows,
Wait when others get tired of waiting
And doubt if I'm alive
They will never understand
How amidst the strife,
By your waiting for me
You had saved my life.
Only you and I will know
How you got me through.

Simply – you knew how to wait –
No one else but you.

The song won the hearts of the troops. It was published in *Pravda* and soldiers copied it and sent it to their wives and girlfriends. It was found in the breast pockets of the dead and wounded.

I lie on the floor, covered with my mother's coat, quietly crying to the sound of the song, wondering if *we* didn't wait hard enough.

My uncle arrives, covered in snow; he hugs and kisses my mother and grabs our things. Hurriedly we put on our coats and climb onto the sledge pulled by a horse. My uncle doesn't even look at me.

He lives with his wife, two daughters, Bella and Ida, and his son's fiancée, Fira. His son, Sioma is fighting, God knows where, at the front. My mother tries to think of a way to make some money for food. She walks ten kilometres in the frost to the market, to try and sell the silk stockings she managed to save from before the war, and gets frostbite on her toes. When she comes back she brings bread and butter, a chicken and some multi-coloured caramels all stuck together, so she has to use a knife to un-stick them.

After overhearing her sister-in-law complain that there wasn't enough space in the house and that I eat too much, my mother showed her pride and decided to move out. She rented a single metal bed in the corner of a room belonging to a Tatar family. The family slept on the floor and my mother and I on the metal bed. Tied to the bed was a new-born calf that chewed up my woollen hat one morning. I missed my favourite cousin Bella, who was ten years old and played cat's cradle with me, and now wasn't allowed to visit us.

When the daughter of the family got married, my mother

and I moved again. We rented another single metal bed in a tiny snowed-in house from a woman whose son had just been killed in the war. She lay all day on a narrow ledge behind the Russian brick stove wailing and my mother lay in our bed, sobbing. When occasionally they got up, made tea and gave me a lump of sugar, it felt like a party.

I was frightened when I first heard that the people we were living amongst were Tatars, I still hadn't recovered from the trauma of being told by the big boy in Kyrgyzstan that Tatars had cut my mother into pieces and eaten her. But when I met the people in the village, they were kind and friendly and invited me into their houses to eat buckwheat baked in a pot in the oven, and *toqmaç,* their traditional soup with noodles. Their son played Jew's harp, the *Kubyz,* and taught me how to play it. The Tatar people wore *lapti,* footwear they wove from the bark of birch trees. The old grandmother measured my foot carefully and, on my next visit, gave me the *lapti* she had made for me, helping me to put them on, tying them around my ankles.

And before I knew it I was speaking Tatar fluently. My mother kept throwing her arms up in the air, speaking about me in the third person, appealing to God: "Why does she want to wear these rubbish *lapti* when she's got perfectly nice shoes that I bought with my last rouble? For what does she need to eat their food and speak their strange language?"

She needn't have worried that there would be pork in their food, since they were Muslim. Maybe she was worried that speaking the Tatar language would turn me into a little stranger, no longer totally under her power.

My stepfather Grisha

1944

As the saying goes, 'if it wasn't for bad luck I wouldn't have any luck at all'. Throughout the war, some mysterious luck seemed to accompany my mother and me; at each stage of our journey an unexpected path opened out for us to follow.

In the village store an acquaintance of my mother's happened to mention a certain 'Grisha'. Miracle of miracles, he turned out to be the man from her *shtetl* who'd been in love with her since she was a young girl. In the good old days, she had considered him beneath her and was waiting for someone 'refined, tall and handsome,' but now, left alone with a small child, she writes to him, telling him of her predicament. Travel regulations were strict; a permit was required to travel from one town to another. Grisha replied and sent us the required pass to travel to Bryansk, where he lived, four hundred kilometres south-west of Moscow and eight hundred kilometres from the Tatar village where we were staying.

"Soon we are going away to live with Grisha," Mama tells me trying hard to sound enthusiastic.

"Who is Grisha?" I ask anxiously.

"He is a man I knew before I met your father. He was in love with me, but I didn't want to marry him; when he came to see me I'd run away with my girlfriends to the river, and when I came back hours later he'd still be waiting. He is going to be your Papa now."

"I want my own Papa."

Off we went again with our two bundles, a piece of bread and six hard-boiled eggs. It took three weeks on numerous goods trains and military trains full of soldiers, before we arrived at the station in Bryansk. Grisha was there to meet us.

He's short and his military coat goes all the way down to the ground. I whisper in my mother's ear: "I don't want this Papa. I want my own tall one." On the way to his place we stop and stare at skeletons of buildings and trucks, grim reminders of the bombing by the Germans.

The first night in Grisha's little room I lie on a mattress on the floor listening to them arguing about me. As I'm falling asleep, I hear him say: "She is like a little wild animal, an unlovable child." Mama cries and lies down to sleep next to me.

Next he finds a summer camp for children of war victims and says mother should take me there; the saddest thing is that she agrees. I beg her not to. She tries to make it better by promising to stay with me for one night. That night at the camp I fall asleep holding onto to her tightly, but when I wake up it is light outside and the place next to me is empty. I grab my clothes, put them on, inside out and back to front, and run outside. My mother is sitting in the back of an open truck just starting to pull off. I run after it, waving my arms, crying hysterically. She doesn't budge. The woman sitting next to her pulls me up into the truck. My mother sits motionless, like a statue. It's a relief when she suddenly speaks: "You stupid girl; there, you could have had white bread and chocolate and at home there's nothing to eat."

"*Mamochka*," I sob, clutching onto her, "I don't want white bread and chocolate, I want to be with you."

So for better or for worse my mother takes the 'little wild animal' back to Grisha and to the tiny room that comes with his bookkeeping job at the cement factory. That night Mama sleeps in Grisha's bed.

After a short time, he is transferred to Moscow and goes off on a night train to find a place for us to live.

I know my mother doesn't love Grisha because, while he's away, she looks more beautiful and flirts with men.

I wake up in the night and, in semi-darkness, see my mother dancing with an army officer to the music of a popular war song '*Dark is the Night*':

> *Dark is the night,*
> *Only bullets are whistling through the steppe*
> *Only the wind is wailing and*
> *Stars are faintly flickering,*
> *In the dark night, my love,*
> *I know you are not sleeping*
> *You are sitting next to our child's cradle,*
> *wiping a tear away,*
> *I know you'll greet me with love no matter*
> *what happens to me.*

When the music stops I hear breathless whispers coming from my mother's bed. In the morning, the man in uniform is still there and for breakfast we have white bread and American canned corn beef. My mother looks beautiful and distant.

Then Grisha comes back, we pack our few belongings and take a night train to Moscow. When we arrive in Moscow station in the morning a truck from Grisha's work takes us to the suburb, Khovrino, where we are allocated one room in a two-storied block built of wooden logs. Simply known as Tenement No. 1, it holds ten families, one family per room. This is our new home. Across the road is an identical wooden log block known as Tenement No. 2. Between the two blocks is dried-up mud in summer, squishy mud in autumn, snow in winter and not a tree in sight at any time.

There's one kitchen in the whole block where the women regularly collide with each other, fighting for a place at the one stove to cook their evening meal; the stove has a flat wrought-iron surface and is heated by coal, but the coal runs out before everyone manages to cook their food. One woman hangs nappies to dry over the stove and another screams at her, "Your nappies are dripping into my soup."

One toilet, a wooden platform overflowing with excrement that is used as 'art material' for limericks on the wall:

Shame and disgrace on all of us
Who with our fingers wipe our arse

Boys have cut out a hole in the toilet door just at the level of our genitals as we squat – they must have practised, one squatting while the other cut the hole – so we feel observed, even during the one potentially pleasurable and private activity left to us.

I develop a habit of gnawing the knuckles on my right hand till they bleed. My mother keeps threatening that if I don't stop it she'll dip my hand in the toilet, and one day she grabs me by the wrist, drags me to the toilet and shoves my hand in the communal shit. I hold my breath, run to the tap in the kitchen and wash my hands over and over with a big chunk of industrial soap till they're red and swollen.

After that I give up gnawing my knuckles and start biting the inside of my lip, until it bleeds. My mother is exasperated and keeps copying the way I screw up my face when I get into the biting. She threatens to wash my mouth out with that big piece of industrial soap, but she never does and I keep up the biting for years to come.

Grisha helps my mother get a job polishing aluminium toy pistols. I enjoy helping her; it's one of our rare peaceful times together as we sit on the floor, polishing the rough edges from the pistols from one big sack and putting the polished ones into another sack – and I get a shiny toy pistol as a reward.

On my first day of school I don't have a uniform, or a coat, or a satchel. My dress is made out of *portianki,* pieces of flannel cloth that soldiers wrap their feet with and wear inside their military boots. For a coat I have a *telogreika*, a dirty grey-coloured body-warmer, like the one my father wore when he left for the *gulag.* It is much too big, so my mother ties a rope around my waist and rolls up the sleeves. I carry a coarse old Hessian sack for my books. Mama can't take me to school because she has to return the sack of polished toy pistols to the shop. She says she's sorry, so I trudge off alone. When I arrive at school and join all the children standing in a queue waiting to check in their coats, the sour-faced woman who takes our coats and hangs them on rusty hooks in the wall, looks me up and down: "Who is this – a little Jewish beggar?"

A coat is being made for me, but it still isn't ready. My mother and I take the Metro to the tailor for the fitting of the coat, but are told 'not ready,' again and again. The Moscow Metro stations are like Palaces full of marble and bronze statues, chandeliers and mosaics of semi-precious stones from the Ural Mountains. Stalin ordered the best artists to create works of art to glorify the Soviet people for winning the war. I am feeling less than glorious in my oversized *telogreika* when a woman sitting opposite us nudges her neighbour and says, pointing at me: "Have you ever seen such eyelashes?" Finally, after many more disappointing visits to the tailor, I get my long awaited coat. It's made out of blue cloth and has a little brown fake fur collar and a matching fur-trimmed hat. I love the way the snowflakes land on the fur and on my long eyelashes.

In my first math lesson the teacher writes numbers on the blackboard, 1-10, making them big, almost the size of the blackboard. So I think I have to do the same and copy them into my notebook the size of the whole page. The teacher goes around checking our work. When she sees my large numbers she takes the notebook and shows it to the whole class. Everyone laughs. Tears begin to roll down my cheeks; I'm confused and ashamed and don't know what I have done wrong. My heart is thumping; is she going to tell me to stand in the corner, *postavits na ugol*, which you are told to do if you've done something wrong?

At the end of the first term my school report says, 'By nature requires a gentle and quiet approach'. My mother shows off the report to neighbours, as if the fact that I burst into tears at the first harsh word is something to be proud of.

On worker's pay day, women from our block stand outside the factory watching the line of men like hawks, waiting to get hold of the money because if a woman lets her attention wander even for a moment, her husband manages to sneak off and most of the month's pay gets spent on vodka, often followed by drunken rages.

Militia never interferes if a husband beats up his wife. To keep their spirits up the women sing:

Threats do not concern us,
if he kills you, come and tell us
If he doesn't beat you, he doesn't love you,
and he is not a real man

Sometimes fights break out on the stairs of Tenement No. 1: one woman stands at the top of the stairs, screams at another down below, lifting her skirt and exposing her naked bottom, shouting: "Here, you can kiss my arse." They are ordered to appear before the 'People's Court' to be shamed for such un-Soviet behaviour and come back reconciled, with a bottle of vodka, which they finish together, singing dirty songs and swearing. My mother puts her hands over my ears to stop me hearing the juicy swear words. I feel confused when she starts using the same words to swear at me when I am a bit older. That was my initiation into the next stage of growing up.

Fenia and her daughter Nina

We are poor, but Fenia Ivanova and her daughter Nina are even poorer. Mama considers them dirty and looks down on Fenia, and I am brain washed to look down on Nina, even though she is my best friend. They live in one half of a room, separated from the other half by a cardboard wall that doesn't reach all the way up to the ceiling. In the other half lives a bent, old woman with two pregnant daughters, without husbands. Fenia doesn't know who Nina's father is.

Because my mother always has a backache, Fenia does our washing – two sheets and three pillow cases. On washing day, it is so exciting the way our room, which is normally deadly quiet, becomes a hive of activity. Nina and I watch Fenia good-naturedly scrubbing the sheets in a tub, on a wooden washboard with metal ribs, while my mother laments: "Before the war I never heard of backache; I could wash our entire laundry myself in the river, even on the first day of my period, and in the evening get dressed and go out dancing."

Fenia's job is to clean locomotive engines at the Railway Depot which, after many years, has left soot embedded in the wrinkles of her face. Even scrubbing herself in the worker's shower room doesn't remove the grime. It's a special treat when Fenia manages to sneak us into the bathhouse, which is reserved for the workers at the Railway Depot only. We get well-scrubbed, taking turns hitting each other all over with a bunch of birch branches, and come out looking all shiny and pink, the chronic gloom dispersed for a little while; and it feels as if Mama and I, and Fenia and Nina are equal.

Fenia came to Moscow from a far-away village, taking a month to walk part of the way, and going down the Volga on barges and steamers the rest of the way. She was seventeen, sent out into the world by her father – one less mouth to feed – with some dried bread and a handful of salt tied in a bundle. Nina and I love to listen to Fenia tell the story of her arrival in Moscow and she loves to tell it, acting it out for us with movement and sound.

"The first day in Moscow I go into a tearoom. I sit down at a table. Suddenly I see a man looking at me. I think to myself, what do you want? That man, he was up to no good. So I get down on my hands and knees and crawl out of the tea room." We shriek with laughter as she makes funny sounds with her teeth, *tsok, tsok,* imitating the sound her shoes made on the cobblestones as she got up and ran.

Fenia is impatient for Nina to grow up and get married; Nina is seven but Fenia tells people: "From next summer she'll be going into her ninth year." Nina's shoes are always two sizes too big; Fenia ties them from underneath with a string, explaining apologetically: "They didn't have her size."

On payday Fenia staggers home carrying salami across her arm like logs of wood, a bottle of vodka that's already half empty, and fruit drops for Nina in a newspaper cone. When we see her swaying silhouette – her deep blue eyes and white teeth shining as she approaches – Nina and I run towards her. She puts the salami and the vodka down on the ground and enfolds both of us in her big, strong arms that have cleaned six hundred and eighty engines in twenty years. Besides a wardrobe with no clothes in it, the only piece of furniture in their room is a narrow bed, covered by a sheet as clogged with soot as Fenia's skin. She puts the salami, the bottle of vodka and the fruit drops onto the bed and the three of us have a 'picnic'. But my mother is disgusted and forbids me to eat at their place because she says it's dirty.

Nina comes to pick me up in the mornings to walk to school together. In winter it is pitch-dark outside when she arrives, crunching a chunk of raw cabbage for breakfast. I'm still in bed and my mother tries to get me up, exasperated, cursing the day she was born: "Look at your friend, eating her breakfast already, and you lie here like a princess."

Children run after Fenia, throwing stones at her and shouting: "Beggar, dirty beggar." Fenia turns around, fixes one of them with her blue eyes and says: "Don't spit into a well, you don't know when you might need to drink from it."

Fenia's neighbour, Ksenia, who lives on the other side of the cardboard partition with her two pregnant daughters without husbands, comes into the communal kitchen with a few rotten, muddy potatoes she dug up in a field. She puts them on top of the stove, which is lukewarm, because Tenement No. 1 has run out of coal again, 'cooks' them on both sides for a few minutes and eats them. My mother shrugs and looks away in disgust, proud that she has never stooped that low.

There is a type of Russian song called *chastushki,* humorous, irreverent, lewd limericks, on every possible theme. They are usually played by an accordionist dressed in a wide-sleeved, red shirt, with two pretty girls in long, colourful, embroidered skirts, one on each side, singing and dancing through the village streets. One of the themes of *chastushki* was the Soviet emblem, the hammer and the sickle, supposedly symbolising the unity of peasants and workers.

Fenia and her daughter Nina

On top – the sickle
Underneath – the hammer
But whether you reap or hammer
All you get is fuck all

So, after Ksenia goes home my mother starts singing *chastushki,* hinting at Ksenia's daughter's 'immaculate' conception, the meaning of which I'm not supposed to understand:

Eight years already without a husband
But Marina gives birth to a son,
Wonder of wonders!
A beautiful baby is born.

The Sanatorium

My mother took me to the doctor at the slightest provocation. All I had to do was sneeze and she'd bow down to me and say mockingly: "Congratulations, you've done it again". Holding my shoulders she'd tilt my head back and command: "Say Ah!" Looking deep into my throat she'd announce: "Each tonsil the size of my fist." And off we'd go to the doctor. I liked going to the doctor because it was the only time we went somewhere. I liked sitting on the cosy sofa in the waiting room, looking at the books with pictures of happy children, pretending I'm the little girl in the pretty dress holding a doll in my arms. I'd get jolted out of my reverie by the nurse calling us in.

On one of those visits, the doctor put my x-ray up to the light and pointed to a dark area, which apparently was a shadow on my lung. I'm surprised my mother didn't diagnose it herself since she was always telling me she could see right through me. The doctor suggested a sanatorium for children of war victims which I was well qualified for. He said it was on the outskirts of Moscow in a pine forest and was good for children with weak lungs. I started dreading it from that moment on and begged my mother not to take me there. But she said it would be good for my lungs to breathe fresh pine air and they would have chocolate there.

The sanatorium stood on a hill, surrounded by very tall pine trees – a square, white, two-storied building with lots of windows. Two prim women in white uniforms looked after the children. Panic gripped me as I took in the scene; I didn't know how to fit in, how to join in the games. I felt alienated, different, not part of the group – the traumatised 'little radish' from the Polish kindergarten whom nobody invited to dance.

My mother stayed till the evening, trying to settle me in but I remained glued to her side, crying: "Please don't go, please don't leave me". She tried her best to comfort me: "You must breathe the pine air for your weak lungs and eat all the food and come back healthy and strong. I'll come to visit you on Sunday, it's only six days, and if you stop crying, I'll bring you a wide red hair ribbon." It was my dream to have a wide red ribbon for my hair.

At dinner I sat at the big table with the other children. I sat and stared at the food while the woman in the white uniform commanded me to eat it all up. I put the food in my mouth but I couldn't swallow.

After dinner we went to the girls' dormitory and there I discovered I was in for an 'initiation ceremony'. Four girls grabbed me, threw a blanket over me and hit me all over with their fists; it was called 'the dark treatment,' after which I was supposed to be accepted as part of the group. I became even more withdrawn and hid in the toilet for a long time, wishing with all my might for my mother to come and take me home.

There is one vivid happy memory: walking in the forest I saw a wild strawberry peeping out from under a leaf and, in the delight of that moment, forgot that I was a poor little orphan; I felt I was me.

But when I came back the white-uniformed women were examining everyone's hair. When my turn came, I was the only one with lice. They took me to the basement, wrapped a white sheet around my shoulders and shaved off my thick wavy hair with cold metal clippers.

On Sunday, parents' visiting day, all the children ran to greet their mothers and fathers. I saw my mother approaching, smiling, triumphantly waving the wide red ribbon. I watched her face. When she saw me standing there bald and forlorn, apart from the other children, her smile disappeared and her expression changed to pity mixed with exasperation.

That day, a group photograph of all the staff and children was taken. I am the only one in the photo with a bald head, lying on the ground, holding a bouquet of wild flowers I've picked, because I saw the other girls picking flowers to hold in the photograph. I look awkward, as if there's a rule about the right way to hold flowers and I'm the only one who doesn't know what it is.

My mother looked at the photograph and fell about laughing: "Look at the way you are holding the flowers!"

Grisha's super idol

Eventually and inevitably Stalin's purges reach Tenement No. 1. My girlfriend's father told a 'political' joke over a beer after work: "This guy had a talking parrot and one day the parrot disappeared out of the cage. The guy rushed to the KGB headquarters, 'my parrot has disappeared but I'm here to tell you that I don't agree with what he says.'" The next day my girlfriend's father was arrested. A hush descended over Tenement No. 1. People were afraid to speak, living in constant suspicion of one another.

One of the 'pioneer heroes' of this tyrannical era was a thirteen year old boy, Pavlik Morozov who symbolised 'fidelity to the state being a higher virtue than to one's family'. He supposedly denounced his father to the secret police for 'hiding sacks of wheat in his cellar, while the workers were starving'. The local Commissariat gave Pavlik Morozov a medal for his bravery while citizen Morozov the elder was arrested and served seven years in a *gulag*. The Pavlik Morozov story was compulsory reading at school to instil in all of us the duty to expose the 'enemies of the people'.

We were taken on school outings to see the statue, erected in his mini-hero image in the Moscow Central Park of Culture and Rest and had to stand in a circle around it singing hymns to his bravery. But what they never told us at school, and I learnt again from the Internet many years later in London, was that Pavlik's Uncle, in total disregard of his nephew's heroic status, picked up an axe, hit the mini-hero over the head, and killed him.

For me, communism was embodied in the image of stepfather Grisha, this short, bald man, sitting on the only stool in our room, smoking endless Russian *papirosy,* coughing and choking, listening to Party political broadcasts coming out of the cone-shaped radio in the corner of the room, promising us 'a splendid future and liquidation of the imperialist aggressors and enemies'. Radios were pre-set so that we could only receive official government channels. When Grisha went to work my mother turned the volume up high – volunteer informers could denounce you for not listening; the Party leaders made sure that you listened to the propaganda continuously enough to become thoroughly brainwashed. So getting dressed in the morning, eating breakfast, doing my homework, was always accompanied by the drone of propaganda.

On the anniversary of the October Revolution, Grisha is in a state of agitation from the moment he wakes up until he goes off to the Red Square for celebrations and to catch a glimpse of his Super Idol. He comes back late in the evening, a mad expression on his face, eyes glazed. "I s-s-saw him ... I saw S-s-Stalin," he stutters.

"Is that all?" my mother mutters under her breath, with as much sarcasm as she can muster.

Grisha's mother died when he was a baby. His father remarried and Grisha grew up with a stepmother, a stepbrother, and a stepsister. Before the war in Poland, Grisha was an underground communist. When he managed to enter Russia, triumphant at last that he could openly be a communist, they arrested him for anti-communist activities – another part of Stalin's lunatic plan to liquidate the Polish element. In prison he was tortured by a huge sergeant standing on a chair, holding him upside down by his legs, while another poured dirty water into his nostrils to make him confess. Grisha had no idea what he was supposed to confess. Eventually he was freed. Still, he remained a fanatic communist for the rest of his life, true to the saying that people repeated at their peril: 'definition of a communist – you piss in his face, he says it's raining.'

Making pickled cabbage

My mother used to pickle cabbage for winter. She'd spend a whole day shredding it and packing it into a barrel in layers with salt in between and then put it into the cellar. It sounds like we had a house and a cellar but no; we had little room with a cellar underneath. How she got that heavy barrel into the cellar I don't know and I wish I'd asked her when she was alive. But anyway, after getting the barrel into the cellar she'd lie in bed for three days, complaining of back ache.

A parcel from South Africa

The war is over but the rationing and food shortages continue. Everybody is hungry, including the German prisoners of war working on road construction. One day my girl-friend Nina and I, both of us eight years old, stroll arm-in-arm sharing a treat – one apple. One of the German prisoners gestures to me to give him what's left of it. I stop in the middle of a bite and hand it to him. Nina whispers in my ear: "These are Germans, they killed your father."

The shelves in the shops are empty. People stand in queues for hours with net shopping bags, *avoska,* just in case; talking about people dying of hunger and relieving the anxiety with jokes:

"What's the definition of a Soviet amnesiac?"

"A guy standing outside a grocery shop with an empty shopping bag and he can't remember if he is going in or coming out."

I remember the actual taste of hunger, standing in a queue outside the local grocery shop that is empty of provisions, anxiously waiting to get our ration for the week: one piece of sour, damp black bread. On the way back my hunger gets the better of me and I start nibbling at the bread. By the time I reach home, there's only a tiny piece left. My mother starts crying when she sees what's left of it, but does not scold me.

She manages to save bits of bread, lets them dry and hangs them in a sack above the bed away from the mice.

This is our emergency supply. I have recurring dreams of all of us dying of hunger. I wake up anxiously in the night and stand on tip toes to feel the bag and check how many bits are left.

A parcel arrives from South Africa from my Uncle Isaac who is handsome and rich, "*Akh*, and such a *krasavets* – so handsome, I don't know how he ended up with a wife on bandy legs, who couldn't give him children and couldn't cook?" says my mother.

Uncle Isaac is my mother's older brother, whom she adored and who left Russia before the Revolution when she was sixteen years old. Ever since then she has cherished a wild hope that one day she'd meet him again: "I know it can't possibly be true but every time the wind blows the gate open, I think it's him. One day we'll go to South Africa and he will be a father to you; he'll buy you a dress the colour of the blue sky and when you grow up a sports car and a cap to go with it."

Mama is nervous about receiving parcels from abroad because of rumours that people have been arrested for just such an 'offence', and they are not only rumours or my mother's paranoia; just because you're paranoid doesn't mean they're not out to get you. The 'anti-cosmopolitan campaign' of 1948 targets Jews and other 'foreign' nationals with relatives abroad. I thought cosmopolitan meant citizen of the world, but in the Soviet Union it means rejection of Soviet values, deserving of serious punishment.

But we try not to think about this when we open the parcel from my Uncle and find it's full of goodies like a slab of chocolate, a packet of wafers, a tin of cocoa, canned beef, and at the bottom, the prettiest red dress I've ever seen, with forget-me-nots embroidered around the collar.

Holding my breath I beg my mother: "Can I wear the dress to school?"

She predicts: "You are a *schlimazel*, you'll spill ink on it."

All of us children carry our ink in a little bottle inside a cloth bag tied to the satchel and write with a pen dipped in the ink, so that our fingers are constantly ink-stained and not only our fingers; our mothers stand after school commiserating with each other, "How do they manage to get ink even on their bottoms?"

I plead: "No, I won't spill the ink. I promise I won't, oh, please."

She gives in: "Alright, alright already, wear it, another dress you don't expect. If your father was alive ..."

I wear the dress to school and for once in my life I feel proud. Nobody experiences new things more intensely than children. A shiver of delight goes through me when I swirl the skirt round and round and all the girls admire it. At the end of the day as I'm about to leave, Lena, the poorest and the palest girl in the class, asks to borrow some ink or she won't be able to do her homework. I take my ink bottle out of its little bag to pour some ink into her empty bottle and, fulfilling my mother's prophecy, spill most of it on my new dress. If, out of two unlucky people, *schlemiel* is the one who spills the chicken soup and *schlimazel* is the one on whom it spills, it turns out I'm both. We run to the toilet to try to wash the ink off, but the more we try to rub it out the more we rub it in.

I come home late, covering the ink stains with my satchel. "What are you hiding?" asks my mother, her X-ray eyes looking straight through me. She sees the ink stains and lets out a long-suffering, resigned sigh.

Before I go to sleep, I tenderly lay the dress on a chair as if it's been injured, and fall asleep dreaming that there's been a mistake and my father is alive; I see him walking towards me carrying his violin.

I wanted a doll

There was an old man who wandered through our suburb with an old nag and a cart full of homemade yo-yos: little balls covered in colourful paper with sawdust inside, attached to a long piece of elastic. "Milk bottles, old sewing machines, old clothes," he'd shout, "in exchange for a yo-yo." I'd run inside and beg my mother to give me something to exchange. But after playing with the yo-yo for as long as it took for the man and his horse to disappear around the corner, the paper started to break and the sawdust fell out. But the next time I'd do the same thing again, hoping against hope that this time it would last.

Every household in our neighbourhood possessed a certain kind of doll; you could see them standing on every windowsill. They were made of wood and had a heavy round bottom, which kept them in an upright position and, no matter how many times you knocked them down, they stood up again. They were called *Vanka-Vstanka; Vanka* – the most common boy's name, and *Vstanka* – get up. The doll was a symbol of bouncing back from being knocked down.

But I wanted a real doll that I could cuddle; one with eyes that closed and opened. My mother was forever promising to buy me one and I lived in constant expectation of getting one. "They had so many dolls," she'd say enthusiastically, as she came in empty-handed. "Blonde ones with blue eyes, dark ones with brown eyes; I didn't know which one you'd like" And carry on, "*Akh,* you are too young to remember, but before the war you had a room full of dolls." The truth was she didn't have the money and she believed that a promise with no hope of fulfilment was better than no hope at all.

A girl with a doll, with eyes that open and close, comes to play. I need to pee, but I'm afraid that if I get up and go out the girl with the doll will go away. So I sit, until a puddle appears on the floor under me. The girl with the doll gets sent home. I get put to bed and my only tights are put out to dry.

I draw a doll's face on my knee with a piece of coal, tie a kerchief around her, and rock her to sleep, singing the one lullaby I know:

Sleep my baby, bayushki bayu
When you grow up
Comrade Stalin will guide you on your path
And give you strength to follow it

Anyhow, one could make a doll out of cloth, out of paper, cardboard, something ... anything. But my mother didn't. She wasn't inventive in that way. But she sure was inventive in saving us, just in time, from concentration camps and gas chambers. My life was pervaded by the disjointed stories I overheard, like images from a nightmare, of large numbers of naked people led into the gas chambers under the pretext of taking a shower, and then gassed. The first time the reality of it struck me was fifteen years later in Israel when I saw a number tattooed on my aunt's hand and hear people whispering that she survived a Nazi concentration camp. But she herself couldn't talk about it. She screamed in her sleep from her nightmares instead.

The stories and images of human beings reducing other human beings to numbers tattooed on their arms and then to ashes became ingrained in my body and soul and manifested in a deep anxiety, suspicion and mistrust of other people. Although we escaped just in time, before being put onto trains to be incinerated in the gas chambers, I've always felt the horror of it in my blood.

When I arrived in London in the freedom-loving sixties, what I found to my amazement, was respect for and celebration of individuality, personal dignity, creativity and self-expression. I was astonished that people were allowed to question established values and speak out against leaders and government. There really *was* freedom of speech, but I still couldn't believe that a comedian poking fun at a politician wouldn't be shot the next day.

It was in that atmosphere of London in the sixties that my trust in life and in other people began to stir.

Tangerine segments

Back in Russia, I'm nine years old and my mother and I are going to Moscow on a train to see my very first film, *'David Copperfield'*. An ice-cream lady, with shiny red cheeks and a box full of ice-creams hanging from a strap around her neck and resting on top of her large breasts, walks through the carriage. I want an ice-cream. My mother says she can't afford to buy me one. I see the lady with the red cheeks cut an ice-cream sandwich with a knife and hand one half to a little boy, who is jumping impatiently up and down, so I venture: "Can I have the other half?" My mother says that she only has enough money for the cinema and the train tickets. I start crying. She starts shouting: "What do you want from me, my soul? Do you think it doesn't hurt me not to be able to buy you an ice cream?" I go and sit in an empty compartment by the window with my eyes shut tight, crying. Suddenly I feel something cold touching my lips. I open my eyes. It's a cool tangerine segment. A young woman in a military coat is sitting next to me, stroking my hair and tenderly putting tangerine segments into my mouth, one by one.

At the cinema, before the film starts, I forget and ask my mother for sweets.

"Do you have holes in your head? Don't you remember what I told you? I have no money for the film *and* sweets." She appeals to God, "She'll be the death of me." Again I go off by myself to sulk in another row.

The film is a Russian version of Charles Dickens'

semi-autobiographical tale of David Copperfield who is sent away by his father after his mother dies. The moment when the mother dies, I creep back to my mother, sobbing, begging her not to die and leave me alone in a world 'full of indifferent strangers', as she's threatened to do so many times. Through my tears I watch David Copperfield triumph over incredible adversities, but for me, life without my mother is impossible to imagine.

A girl in my class is absent for a few days after her mother dies. The day she comes back I notice, with a heavy pain in my heart, that her sandwiches are now bundled into a bit of old newspaper whereas before they were lovingly wrapped in a red checked cloth. I also notice her hair – one plait is thicker than the other and the parting at the back is zigzag; you could always tell by the look of the hair which girl didn't have a mother. My plaits look neat except for the days when my mother doesn't get out of bed in the morning.

Becoming a Pioneer

At nine years of age, all children must become members of the 'The Young Pioneers'. For the big occasion we have to learn by heart '*The Pioneer's Code*' – the goals and duties of a young pioneer, which is stuck on the wall in our classroom. I now have a uniform, a brown dress with a detachable lacy white collar and, over it a black apron gathered at the waist. The night before the big celebration, my mother takes off the white collar, which has been left on for so long that it looks grey and scruffy, washes and irons it and sews it back onto my dress.

On the big day we are lined up in a row at the Pioneer's Assembly and have to stand in front of a girl of fourteen, a member of Komsomol, (Communist Union of Youth) who solemnly announces, "Young Pioneer, be ready to fight for the cause of the Communist Party of the Soviet Union!" and we have to salute and say: '*Vsiegda Gotovy*, Always Ready!' Then she comes up to each of us in turn, ties a red scarf, the sacred symbol of the Soviet red flag, around our necks and repeats again, "Pioneer, be ready to fight for the cause of the Communist Party". When my turn comes I stand up very straight and don't breathe, I bend my right arm at the elbow, bring my right thumb to my forehead and respond in a barely audible voice: '*Vsiegda Gotova*!'

I run home from school as fast as I can, I can't wait to tell my mother about the salute and show her my new red tie. She is cleaning fish when I fly in.

"Mama, Mama, look! I'm a Pioneer."

"*Hak mir nit kayn chainik,*" which means 'don't bang the teapot, don't get on my nerves'.

"Look at my tie," I say proudly, bending my arm in a Pioneer salute, "and we had to say altogether, "Always ready!"

Without looking she says, with bitterness in her voice: "Very good ... will it bring us more wood so I can cook this fish? *Sol zei gein in drerd,* may they rot in the ground," she concludes and gets on with cleaning the fish.

So I tell her all over again because I can't understand why she isn't sharing my enthusiasm. And after she slaps me across the face with a damp hand covered in fish scales, I don't understand it any better.

Surviving starvation

In the Soviet Union there is no Christmas. The Soviet version of Santa is *Dedushka Moroz* – Grandfather Frost who carries a long staff and a bag full of presents for the children. He is accompanied by his daughter *Snegurochka* – the Snow Maiden. Stalin ordered that all *Dedushka Morozes* must wear blue coats, not red, so they would not be mistaken for Santa Claus. On New Year's Eve children of all ages from all over Moscow gather at the Pioneer's Palace to celebrate New Year, not Christmas. I go with my mother. In the centre of the Pioneers Palace stands a decorated pine tree, reaching up to the ceiling with a huge red star on top. Holding hands all the children dance around the tree and sing the New Year Song to a piano accompaniment:

Little pine tree, you were born in the woods,
You grew and grew straight and green summer and winter
Frost wrapped you tightly in snow: 'Take care; don't freeze!'
Until an old man came and chopped you down
And now you are here at this celebration with us
Bringing us lots and lots of joy.

We dance around the tree three times and then join in the queue to *Dedushka Moroz*, who sits on a decorated sledge with his blue bag full of presents. We each receive a little paper bag with two tangerines and two red lollipops in the shape of roosters. And then mama and I go back home on the train.

Mama tries to be as strictly *kosher* as total absence of kosher food in Moscow allows. As for pork she won't even *touch* it, never mind eat it. But one time, out of despair, she buys a piece of pork because there is nothing else, and she has to cook it in our one and only pot. But she doesn't eat the pork, although she is weak with hunger; she only serves it to my stepfather and me. Afterwards she scrubs and scrubs the pot with sand. So can you imagine how far she is driven by hunger and despair when she goes to the market and buys a little pig to fatten up and sell for a profit? My stepfather puts a board across a corner of our room to make an enclosure so the little pig won't run everywhere but eventually they have to give him away because there isn't enough food and he's getting thinner rather than fatter.

Grisha has a job as a bookkeeper in a shoe factory. Once a week we sit up till late, waiting for Grisha to bring home his extra ration of bread. My mother tries to keep me awake so that I won't fall asleep hungry. But of course I do fall asleep so, when Grisha comes back, she wakes me up: "Come, come *Minochka*, you must eat something." She gives me a piece of soggy black bread and I fall asleep while chewing it and she wakes me up again to finish it. We develop a disease called *kurinnaya slepota*, which means 'chicken blindness'; night blindness caused by extreme vitamin deficiency.

Then my mother thinks of an enterprise; she'll go to buy a sack of flour in Riga, Latvia, where it is rumoured to be cheaper; come back, bake buns and sell them for a profit, which is strictly against Soviet Law.

She leaves me with my stepfather's step-uncle Solomon and his wife Sonya, in a suburb of Pushkino. In contrast to us they always have plenty of food. When they had invited us to eat with them once, my mother said I made her proud: I'd inherited my father's *eidelkayt*, refinement, because I said no to a second helping even though I was still hungry. Another time I overheard my mother telling the story, which showed my father up as a *nebbish*, a pitifully ineffectual person. Unable to get a job as a violinist, he had to carry sacks of flour at the flour mill; on payday the boss's little boy ran up to him, twisted the money out of his hand and ran away; instead of catching the boy, boxing his ears and getting the money back, my father just stood there with tears rolling down his face. So I was confused: was he *eidel*, gentle and refined or was he a *nebbish*, weak-willed and ineffectual, and which of the two did I inherit?

Uncle Solomon and Auntie Sonya are old. His eyes look in opposite directions and I wonder if he can see me when I stand in front of him or if I should be standing in front of just one eye. She wears the same cardigan with holes in the elbows and complains of being poor. Their house is also old and there are old wooden trunks in a dark corner that smell strongly of mothballs. It stands in a spooky overgrown garden with an old hammock tied between two trees. Auntie Sonya swings me in the hammock until I feel like throwing up, but I am too shy to say anything till it's too late.

In the basement lives a young woman with two daughters. I have just begun to get close to the younger one with lovely dark curls and soft brown eyes, when she's taken away to a sanatorium because she has tuberculosis.

As a fish doesn't know that it's in water, I didn't know

that I was in a state of constant nervous tension. Children can hear adults think. I knew that Uncle Solomon and Auntie Sonya were hiding something from me even before I overheard them whispering that my mother could be arrested in Riga. After that I had recurring dreams of my mother barefoot, on her knees, washing floors in prison and woke up every morning in tears.

The big red pencil

After what seems like forever my mother suddenly appears, carrying a big sack of flour over her shoulder. She seems so young, her hair in two plaits. It's time to pack my things and go 'home' to Grisha. There's only one thing in this old house that I covet – a long thick red pencil, lying untouched on a dusty antique desk. So I climb up on a chair while no one is looking, take the pencil and wrap it in layers and layers of newspaper until it doesn't look anything like a pencil, but more like a big round newspaper ball.

As we are saying our goodbyes my mother nudges me: "And what are you going to say?"

While I mumble something resembling 'thank you', she notices the parcel.

"What's that?"

"Nothing ..."

"What do you mean – nothing?"

"Nothing ..."

She makes me unwrap it in front of Uncle Solomon and Auntie Sonia and the long thick red pencil is revealed. They don't say, '*Akh*, let her keep it.' They take it from me and put it back on the desk where it had been gathering dust since the October Revolution.

But Mama has brought me a present from Riga, my first crayons! She tells me to be careful because they break easily. They do. I try to make a drawing but the crayons keep breaking, so I'm afraid to touch them.

With the flour from Riga, Mama bakes cinnamon rolls

and buns to sell, and with the money from the buns, she buys cabbage to pickle for the winter, and with the pickled cabbage she makes *shchi,* a soup boiled with beef bones. After all that she lies in bed for a week with a sore back.

Rumours spread that the rouble is to be devalued. It makes no difference to us, we have no money, but it turns out that Uncle Solomon has lots of money hidden in those trunks that smell of mothballs. Urgently he calls my mother to help use up the money by buying sable coats and hats to sell later. A couple of days later she comes home with a bag full of money and lets me peep inside; in there, mixed up with the money, is a whole packet of my favourite sweets, *Mishka kosolapy* (pigeon-toed bear), which she could never afford to buy me before. I finish them off at once, and in the night come down with a high fever, which my mother puts down to the sweets.

Auntie Sonya doesn't survive the money devaluation; she dies of a heart attack. Nephews and nieces arrive, like vultures at a death scene, with empty bags for the inheritance, expecting the old man to submit to loneliness and a quick death. But Uncle Solomon doesn't even wait for the end of the customary mourning period before marrying a 'young' woman of sixty-nine, who wears low *décolleté* dresses and paints her nails and lips bright red. She opens the trunks, airs them of mothballs, and starts wearing the pre-revolution silk dresses, lace shawls and furs she finds inside.

My name

My name at birth was Mina-Rivka. I was named after my grandmother who, my mother told me, lived with this name for sixty-five years and was proud of being called after *her* grandmother. I was *not* proud of my name – I hated my name. Mina in Russian means 'land-mine' and Rivka means you are most definitely Jewish. It means that boys shout, 'Get out of the way! Mina will explode!' Interspersed with, 'Beat the Yids, save Russia!'

Little sparrows were called 'Yids' or '*kikes*'. Our history teacher said: "What Jews, Gypsies and sparrows have in common is that they can be found in every part of the world." Since I was the only Jewish girl in the class, all the children turned to look at me with sneers on their faces.

I decided to change my name to Zoya, and begged my mother to call me by my new name in front of other children. She tried, but 'Zoya' sounded like pork in her mouth. Otherwise she never really called me by my name; I was either *dochenka,* or *mamochka* – 'little daughter' or 'little mother'... No wonder I didn't know who the hell I was.

I come home from school, stand in the doorway and cry, letting gusts of freezing air into the room.

"What are you trying to do," asks my mother, "warm up the street? My back is breaking from carrying wood from the shed, trying to keep this room warm. What happened, did you lose the money I gave you?"

"No."

"What then? Did you see someone play the piano? I told you I'll buy you a piano as soon as the rationing is over."

Silence.

"What is it?"

I burst into sobs: "They call me 'explosion' at school. I want to change my name; I want to be called Nina." I decided Nina was a little closer to Mina than Zoya.

"You let those *drek,* little shits, upset you? Your grandmother was the most honoured woman in Glembokie, when the Rabbi was ill people came to her for advice."

"Nobody at school cares about my grandmother and how clever she was."

"Don't talk like that about my mother. Alright already, before you tear my soul out alive, let's go to *Zags (*Registry of Acts of Civil Status), and we'll change your name. You want to be a *shiksa,* it's up to you. *Oy,* if your grandmother knew, she would die a second time."

We walk through snow and frost to *Zags*. I want to run, anxious that my mother might change her mind. All my thoughts are on that office with the miraculous power to make me like everybody else.

We enter a gloomy room, where people get married, divorced, register births and deaths. Portraits of Lenin and Stalin hang on the wall. There's a man sitting at a desk, writing. I pull my mother closer to the desk.

He looks up. "Yes?"

"She wants to change her name," says my mother pointing at me in exasperation.

The man looks at me: "What is your name?"

"My name is Mina."

"Mina? What kind of name is that?

"What kind of name?" exclaims my mother, "It's not good enough for her? My mother lived with this name for sixty-five years and was the most honoured woman in her village ..."

"*Grazhdanka*", the man interrupts, "do you or don't you want to change your child's name?"

"I? Of course I don't want to change her name; she should consider it an honour to be named after her grandmother."

"Then let's not waste each other's time."

My mother grabs me by the hand and storms out; so much for my dream of being like everyone else.

I eventually changed my name many years later after I got divorced, and, not wanting to be called by my husband's name Balaskas, nor by my father's family name Fishel, chose to drop Rivka, took my father's first name and became Mina Semyon. Many years passed before the guilt about it subsided and before my mother's voice, telling me that I'm self-willed and obstinate for daring not to be like everyone else, to step out of line and go against tradition, lost its power over me. Tradition!

Pasha Zuev

Pasha Zuev was a thief. He was sixteen years old. He raped and stole and was put in jail. He had served his sentence and had just been released. I'd heard women in our block talk about him but I'd never seen him, so when, one morning on my way to school, I see this young hooligan standing in the doorway, rakishly blocking the exit, an oversized checked cap on his head slanting to one side with *chubchik*, a forelock falling onto his left eye and shoes that are too big, their toes curled up, I know it's him. A cigarette is hanging from the corner of his mouth and he's singing a song by Esenin, the poet:

I cherish a secret dream that I am pure at
heart
but I still might stab someone
to the sounds of the autumn's whistling wind.

A neighbour on the way to work trying to get through the door, says to him: "I see jail taught you nothing, huh? Still a hooligan, smoking at your age?"

Pasha takes the cigarette out of his mouth, holds it between his thumb and index finger, and spits on the ground. He grins, revealing a row of gold teeth, and says, looking out into the distance, "I smoked and I will smoke. I stole and I will steal."

I tremble with admiration at his defiance, wishing I had

the courage to throw off all the restraints put on me and be what I really am – wild and free.

At the school toilet I hear Pasha's sister, Tanya, saying to another girl: "I know my brother fucked you."

The girl shouts back: "I know he fucked you too."

Tanya sniffs: "Only standing."

Nina and I confess to each other that we both secretly wish Pasha would 'rape' us in a dark corner of the corridor and then we could forget all about it. Then we wonder: how do we know that it hasn't happened already and we've forgotten?

Pasha's father dies. The dead man is going to be carried out in an open coffin at any moment. Nina and I hang around outside their room, frightened and curious. Pasha stands in the corridor, tap dancing on one spot. Tanya, who has seen me naked at the public bathhouse and now knows all about my latest pubescent developments, sniggers: "Come on, tell him where you've started growing hair."

I am about to run for my life when Pasha gives me a lecherous wink and continues tap dancing in his oversized shoes.

Stalin's death

> "Stalin's greatest crime was the brutal humiliation of human dignity."
> – Evgeny Yevtushenko

I hope the ghosts of the millions Stalin murdered passed before his eyes as he lay dying in his *dacha* on March 5th, 1953. A grave announcement came over the radio: "The heart of the comrade-in-arms, the upholder of the genius of Lenin's cause, the wise leader and teacher of the Communist Party and the Soviet Union, has ceased to beat."

I was fifteen years old and didn't know who I was or what I was supposed to feel. What a luxury now to be able to say freely, 'I felt nothing!' I just thought, 'On a day like today, I can get away with not doing my homework.' In the anatomy lesson the teacher asked me: "How many teeth does a human being have?" I didn't know exactly; these sorts of facts would always go in one ear and out the other. With feigned tears in my voice I answered: "I was too upset to do my homework."

This propelled her into a passionate sermon: "Now that our Leader and our Teacher is gone," her voice got shriller, "we have to unite and work even harder," and in my notebook she gave me 1 out of 5, writing it big and in red ink. 2 out of 5 was already bad enough – it meant failure, but '1', we kids called it *kol*, was the most humiliating grade to be given. The word *kol,* a stake, comes from Tzar Ivan the Terrible's favourite way of dealing with disobedience; torturing and impaling his victims on a stake. In Russian, *sazhat na kol* literally means 'to be put on a stake'.

Stalin identified with Ivan the Terrible, except that, according to Stalin, Ivan the Terrible wasn't 'terrible' enough; he was insufficiently cruel because *he* repented his deeds; after ordering executions he'd feel sorry and pray. Stalin, being an atheist, had nothing to deter him.

And to think that all through my childhood I wanted a Daddy like Stalin, with his oriental doe-like eyes and cosy moustache, holding his daughter Svetlana in his arms, with a bow in her hair, like the one I always longed for.

During the war Stalin's hero image reached its zenith; soldiers went into battle and died 'For the Motherland, for Stalin!' A typical scene from a Soviet war film of those days: Stalin stands on a podium surrounded by an ocean of people. One woman from the huge crowd steps forward and hands him a letter folded into a triangle, which is the way letters were sent because there were no envelopes, to pass on to her son who is fighting somewhere in battle, God knows where. The close-up of the woman's face emphasises total trust in Stalin that the letter will get to her son. Such was people's faith in Stalin ... our leader, our teacher. Portraits of him dominated my childhood; they hung in schools, hospitals, libraries, and even in bathhouses.

Stalin, who destroyed art, science, literature and everything personal in Mother Russia, whose infamous midnight purges inspired the nickname: 'Genghis Khan with a telephone'. When he gave a speech no one wanted to be the first to stop clapping, so a mechanical device, a loud bell ringing, gave them permission to stop.

On May 1st, International Worker's Day, all the children from my school joined school children from all over

Moscow marching in step in the Red Square Parade, getting worked up into a frenzy of sentimental solidarity, shouting in unison: "Thank you, comrade Stalin for our happy childhood!"

For Stalin's seventieth birthday we were taken to the exhibition of gifts he had received from all the Soviet Socialist republics, where we had to bow to his gigantic portrait and again shout altogether, "Thank you comrade Stalin for our happy childhood!" and then take turns looking under a microscope at a grain of rice with a homage written on it to Stalin: 'Our beloved Yossif Vissarionovich, all the people of the Soviet Union are wishing you a long life'. In spite of the atmosphere of terror, people still made up jokes – like this one:

> *On May Day Parade a very old Jew carries a slogan, 'Thank you, comrade Stalin, for my happy childhood!'*
>
> *The KGB man approaches him, 'What's this? Are you deriding our Party? Everybody can see when you were a child comrade Stalin was not yet born.'*
>
> *The man replies, 'That's precisely what I'm grateful for!'*

Most people, brainwashed by propaganda, saw Stalin's death as a tragic event. Heart-rending funeral music blared from the loudspeakers on the streets of Moscow day and night. The railroads and trains had to be stopped so that Moscow would not be flooded by a sea of people. I heard two women at the well outside our house whispering indignantly, 'And, imagine, she was wearing bright red lipstick on a day like today.' Propaganda had created the unquestionable belief that Stalin was irreplaceable to our safety and salvation.

Stalin's body was placed on temporary display in the

Hall of Columns. Many years later in London, I read in a newspaper article that around five hundred people were crushed to death while trying to get a glimpse of Stalin's corpse. The brilliant Russian composer, Sergey Prokofiev died on the same day as his oppressor Josef Stalin. For three days the crowds, gathered to mourn Stalin, made it impossible to carry Prokofiev's body out for the funeral service at the headquarters of the Soviet Composer's Union. Paper flowers and one single pine branch were put on his coffin and a taped recording of the funeral march from his *'Romeo and Juliet'* had to be used, as all real flowers and musicians were reserved for Stalin's funeral. Of course we were in total darkness about all this at the time.

My mother, in a haze of panic, kept repeating under her breath: "Now it will be the end for Jews. Stalin was our father and protector." Then the news came that Stalin's death saved all the Soviet Jews from deportation to *Birobijan*, the Jewish autonomous republic in the Far East of the Soviet Union. The plan of deportation was linked to Stalin's plan to execute leading physicians, mostly Jews, accusing them of a plot to murder members of the political elite, including himself. Fortunately for us Stalin's attempt at the final act of terror was cut short by his death.

I hated lessons in history; deadly boring and saturated with Soviet propaganda and ideology, they made my ears wilt. The Second World War was made up of quotations from Stalin and praise to him for winning the war, which we had to memorise, word for word, and recite, "This war is not an ordinary war. It is the war of the entire Russian people, not only to eliminate the danger hanging over our heads, but to aid all people groaning under the yoke of Fascism."

Six years later in 1956, after Stalin was dethroned and

publicly accused of 'the cult of personality', the whole of the Second World War disappeared from the history curriculum for a year.

At the twentieth Party Congress in February 1956, Nikita Khrushchev made the famous 'secret speech' accusing Stalin of 'the cult of personality'. Suddenly Stalin was a murderer, a coward, a criminal. It turned out that Khrushchev, having been one of the people closest to the increasingly paranoid tyrant, had his tactical reasons for denouncing him; he was trying to obscure his own culpability in Stalin's war on his own people. He himself sent thousands to torture and death; he supervised deportations and executions in western Ukraine after Hitler and Stalin divided Poland in 1939. It was only two years after that that my mother saved us from the Nazi invasion by entering Russia from Poland, naively ignorant of the internal persecutions and killings which were going on in Russia at that time.

Malenkov succeeded Stalin as premier in 1953. During his short rule as prime minister he sought to reduce the arms build-up, tried to decrease the power of the secret police, lessen heavy industry in order to increase consumer goods manufacture, and give more rewards to the farmers on collective farms. He also opposed nuclear armament, as he believed that 'a nuclear war could lead to global destruction.' Two years later he was forced to resign because of some misdemeanour and finally was expelled from the party.

During the time when Malenkov was prime minister, I remember standing in a queue and hearing two women talk 'politics'; one said to the other, pointing at a portrait of Malenkov's chubby round face with admiration and awe: "He is as handsome as he is merciful."

My mother and the mirror

My mother's relationship with the mirror was a major part of my childhood and adolescence. She looked in the mirror a lot, mostly with regret that she didn't look the same any more as the buxom young girl she was before the war, who sang songs in the big hall in her village, to standing ovations. "Even the Chief of Police used to come to me on the stage to kiss my hand." She examines herself in the mirror and concludes mournfully: "He wouldn't now. I don't recognise myself. Are those my eyes? Is that my neck? *Aaagh* ..."

Occasionally she puts a smudge of lipstick on her lower lip and brings both lips together to smudge a bit onto her upper lip. I try to figure out whether it is to economise on lipstick or out of modesty. Mascara is unheard of so she puts some soap on the ends of her eyelashes to make them stand out, and suddenly her face lights up. She puts on one of her two coats – she has a grey, loose fitting coat and a maroon one tapered at the waist – and looks in the mirror this way and that, obviously pleased with what she sees. Then, suddenly and abruptly, she turns away, throwing her arms up in the air in a despondent gesture: "*Akh* ... and for whom, and for what?" Within minutes she's lying in bed with the covers over her head and gloom descends on our only room once more.

When Grisha, very occasionally, goes away to visit his brother in Gorky on the River Volga, my mother's friend, Galya comes to visit, stays the night and sleeps with my mother in her bed. I lie in my bed and listen to them reminisce about those days in the Tatar republic when fate threw them together.

"Remember, how we borrowed the horse and cart from the ancient Tatar with the squinty eyes to go to the market?"

"It was a good fifty kilometres away and that horse, just like me these days, had seen better times; he kept stumbling."

"I decided to sell the silk stockings I'd been saving and buy food. Where would I wear the stockings, in the *lapti*?"

"And the swanky *pani* with the bouffant hair-do and the nose that reached down to her lips bought the stockings and your blouse. With that money we bought meat, bread, even a small piece of butter."

"Potatoes ... cabbage ..."

"I found some caramels for *Minochka*, and with the money that was left we bought the can of kerosene that saved our lives. On the way back we took a short cut through the forest, *nu*, it turned out not so short."

"By the time we reached the forest it was dark, suddenly the horse shook his head and neighed in fear. *Oy gevalt*, then we heard the eerie howling. What's there much to talk, we were surrounded by wolves."

"I still get goose-bumps when I remember the eyes of the wolves glowing in the dark." She pulls up her sleeve and points.

"And the howling ..."

"We threw the blankets and boxes off the cart, made them into a pile, poured the kerosene all over and set it on fire to frighten them off."

"*Oy*, as the glowing, red eyes of the wolves got closer we threw whatever else we could find on the fire, even the clothes off our backs."

"All through the night we huddled together on the cart with the cabbages and caramels, shivering and trying to calm the horse till it started to get light and the wolves ran away."

"We looked at each other and started howling ourselves."

"'Dina,' you said 'your hair has turned grey'"

"... And I said to you, 'do you think yours is raven black?'"

To change the mood my mother brings out of her apron pocket a piece of crumpled paper with a lewd joke scribbled on it. She reads the joke in a low voice, as I lie still, pretending to be asleep, perking up my ears, trying to hear.

A husband draws a duck inside his wife's thigh before going away on a business trip. While he's away the wife sleeps with the next-door neighbour, so when the husband comes back there's no sign of the duck.

'What's happened to the duck?' he demands.

'I don't know; it must have swum away?'"

Through gasps of laughter my mother reads out another story:

"A husband puts a chastity belt on his wife, and gives the key to his best friend in case he dies while he is away. The husband is just riding out of the village when his friend catches up with him, shouting, 'Hey! Stop ... stop! You gave me the wrong key.'"

Dina and Galya turn red with laughter, tears streaming down their faces. Holding onto their bellies, they rush outside to pee. Their laughter is raunchy and erotic, uncontrolled and spontaneous: the laughter of two women with nothing to lose.

On those rare occasions, warmed by the good-humoured sensuality oozing out of my mother, I get a chance to relax and feel cosy and safe like other girls I know, whose mothers get out of bed every morning, get dressed and have friends, with whom they joke and laugh.

Grisha's illegal enterprises

To make ends meet Grisha goes into illegal partnership with a woman photographer, Maria Borisovna. His part of the deal is to go into small villages and talk people into having photographs of their ancestors enlarged. One week later Grisha comes back, with a pile of old sepia photographs, each photograph has one face encircled in red pencil for enlarging. Maria Borisovna does the printing. The original photos are so old and faded that when the faces are enlarged they lose all their individual features and look more or less the same as each other, with cheeks, lips and eyes touched up in fluorescent pinks, reds and blues.

Then Grisha goes off to the villages to return the portraits and comes back with a pile of money. This is *comandirovka*, a Soviet business trip. Such a 'capitalist enterprise' has to be kept highly secret; if caught the sentence would be at best, the rest of his life in a *gulag*, at worst, capital punishment. My mother bitterly regrets ever reading Chekhov's short story, *Ward Number Six*; the vivid description of Ivan, a sensitive, educated man, liked by everyone, who one day meets two men in the street wearing foot irons, escorted by four soldiers with rifles. He has met convicts before but this time the meeting makes a strange impression: he starts imagining how he too could be put in irons, *zakovan v kandaly* and led into prison. Gradually his slide into acute paranoia begins, as he suspects people everywhere of spying on him, planning to arrest him, eventually leading him into a 'mad house', where he dies. My mother can't get these images out of her mind and becomes haunted by scenes of Grisha being arrested, flung into prison, or even shot. She trembles every time she hears footsteps outside. It doesn't help matters when we see a neighbour being led away with his hands tied behind his back for selling Czechoslovakian shoes under the counter.

But Grisha comes back safely every time, and with pockets full of money. Then he and Mama go to Moscow together to share out the loot with Maria Borisovna. It is a big event for my mother. It gives her a chance to dress up in one of her two smart coats, pluck her eyebrows so they arch over her big black eyes, do her lipstick routine, put some soap on her eyelashes, pin her hair up and, *ura,* hurrah, have somewhere to go.

Late in the evening when they return, I hear them arguing outside, my mother's voice screeching: "Maria Borisovna, Maria Borisovna, I'll show you Maria Borisovna; I saw your face when you were calling her name."

"She's mad," Grisha appeals to me as they barge in.

"Mad?" shrieks Mama, "maybe also deaf?"

"I just thought, to save time, while I telephoned you could use the toilet."

"Save time? What's the hurry suddenly? Where do you need to go in such a hurry? You send me to piss? I'll piss when I want to piss. Don't tell me when to piss."

Next, Grisha, as usual, loses his temper and slams his fist on the table so that all the unwashed dishes jump. I'm glued to mother's face watching which way her mood is drifting. She shouts, with the veins in her neck looking like they are about to pop, that she wishes she had died before she ever set eyes on Grisha, and resorts to one of her fainting fits. It means I have to run to the clinic to fetch a nurse to give mother an injection.

The road is thick with mud – too slippery to run fast. I fall, get up and continue running. On the way back the nurse marches ahead, muttering, "Jews, hypochondriacs," with me behind her, trying to catch up, pleading, "She's not going to die, is she?" The nurse gives my mother an injection and she lies in bed for a couple of days, depressed.

Eventually, with the money he has made from the portraits, Grisha buys one room in a private house and we move to another suburb, Khimki. Only one room but it is ours; to get out of communal living is the dream of every Soviet citizen.

Like a proper family

Khimki is only twenty minutes by train from the centre of Moscow but it's like a village – two parallel rows of wooden houses with thatched roofs and wooden fences, no street lights and lots of geese sticking their necks out and hissing at you as you pass.

There's a well outside our gate for the whole neighbourhood and, now that I'm fifteen, it becomes my chore to go and fetch water. As I walk towards the gate, the yoke on my shoulders with two empty buckets hanging from it, my mother always shouts, "Don't fall in!" I like leaning over and looking down into the well, but it's so deep and dark I can never see the water. I have to turn the handle of the well and lower the chained bucket until I can hear it splash, then I turn the handle with both hands to pull the full bucket up and then do the same with the second bucket. I do a kind of dancing walk carrying the two full buckets balancing from the yoke with water splashing all around me.

In winter the days are short; it's dark when I walk to school in the morning and it's dark when I come back from school in the afternoon. I am not afraid of the morning dark, but I'm terrified of the evening dark; it feels crowded with menacing presences. My galoshes, which are too big for my shoes, get stuck in the deep snow and I have to stop to put them back on. Then I run, crazed with fear, feeling as if someone is trying to grab me by the heels. On the way there is a long row of barracks. There's always a light burning in one of the windows. People say that an old woman, who lost three sons to tuberculosis, lives there alone and sits all night staring at the kerosene lamp.

In our new home, once again I'm sharing a room with my mother and stepfather. The room is only just big enough for their bed, my bed, a wardrobe, a clay oven, and a table mostly covered with dishes. I do my homework on the edge of one side of the table and they play cards on the other, if they're not arguing. My mother wants me to call Grisha 'Papa', but I refuse and call him 'he'.

'He' hit me only once. While the three of us were having lunch, I boasted that I'd fooled the physical culture teacher by running down the hill with my skis under my arm and putting them on at the bottom of the hill without being noticed. Grisha said something disapproving. I burst out, "What do you know about skiing anyway?" He leaned over the plate of *gefilte* fish and slapped me hard across the face.

I once saw Grisha's genitals; they sort of fell out of his pyjamas as he got out of bed. He noticed me looking and quickly scooped all the bits back in.

There were a few occasions when my heart was at peace around my step-father, like when he'd peel potatoes without breaking the skin, all in one go, and I'd jump and clap my hands, which would put him in a good mood and give me a break from their never-ending rows. Or, when I helped him saw a log of wood in half outside our garden shed, one of us at each end, pulling the saw back and forth rhythmically and the saw dust falling on the ground in soft piles. Then he'd chop each half into small pieces with an axe for our wood-burning stove and I'd carry them inside for my mother and both of them would be pleased with me and we would be like a proper family for a little while.

When his stepsister died it was the first time I saw a

grown man cry; I thought that only women and children cried.

When Grisha and my mother spoke Yiddish in front of my friends I held my breath, aiming pleading looks at my mother to answer him in Russian. She'd nudge him with her elbow and speak in Russian, but he'd exclaim in Yiddish: "I believe in the equality of all nations and so does the Soviet government and her people and I'll speak what I want to speak." Then he'd add in Russian, for the benefit of my gentile friends: "And anyone who doesn't like it can kiss my arse."

Equality or not, I couldn't go outside without being called a dirty Yid, or having stones thrown at me in summer and snowballs in winter. There was 'no official anti-Semitism in Russia' but everybody knew that there was a quota on how many Jews could enter academic institutions or the Bolshoi Theatre for that matter. And even that was the subject of a joke: 'A Jewish guy goes for an audition at the Bolshoi for the part of Boris Godunov in the opera. When he comes back his friend asks, 'Did you get the part?' The guy replies, 'N-n-no, they are a b-b-bunch of a-anti-s-s-semites'.

In Khimki, Grisha gets a new job in a building materials shop. Although he is a proud member of the rank-and-file march 'forward to the international victory of communism, mankind's brighter future', it doesn't prevent him from under-measuring each customer 'ever so slightly' and coming home with his pocket bulging with money.

With that money he builds an extension onto our room; one part of it is a small space just about big enough for a Russian brick stove and the other part is my first room of my own. Privacy is a concept that didn't exist in the Russian language, so having my own room doesn't come naturally. However, I am just beginning to adjust to this unknown luxury when my mother tells me that she caught

Grisha peeping through the gaps in the wooden partition when I was getting undressed. Did he specially ask the builder to leave those gaps? It seems that I have suddenly become a 'loveable child' overnight, when he starts pulling me onto his lap and giving me pocket money from his bulging pocket.

The banya

Now we are coming up in the world; we have our own private toilet! It's outdoors but it's a grade or two above that toilet in 'Tenement No. 1' with the lewd limericks written in shit on the walls. This outdoor wooden toilet becomes my mother's pride; she scrubs it and cleans it and announces, "You can eat in it." There's no such thing as toilet paper; my mother cuts up *Pravda* into squares and nails the small pile neatly on the toilet door.

In the corner by the brick stove hangs an *umyvalnik,* a wash-stand, a small aluminium cylinder filled with water, with a basin underneath. Grisha washes his face and neck in the mornings, making loud noises and spraying water everywhere. My mother warms up water on the stove, fills up a small wash-tub, and washes first under her arms, then her private parts, and ends up with her feet. But I refuse to wash; Grisha is always hovering somewhere. To lure me into washing my mother tells me to smell her armpits and compare them with mine. I have to admit hers smell better, but I still refuse to wash, except for a splash of cold water on my face.

On Sundays we go to the *banya,* the bathhouse, which is situated on the outskirts of our suburb on the other side of the railway line, where a cargo train, stretching so far in each direction that you can't see where it begins or ends, always blocks the railway crossing. In order to cross we crawl under the train. I see people climbing through the train to get to the other side, but my mother insists we crawl underneath. Maybe she feels compelled to re-live the war traumas and I've learnt not to ask questions that won't be satisfactorily answered. I hold my breath in terror in case the train suddenly starts to move – for some unknown reason goods trains in Russia move without a signal.

We also have to go past the cemetery. Any reminder of death plunges me into the same lonely gloom that has followed me since the day my father died. When one of the Party Comrades dies, they carry him through the streets in an open coffin with brass tubas and all those big wind instruments playing a thunderous funeral march that tears at my guts. My mother spits three times, *tsfu, tsfu, tsfu,* and says under her breath, her usual prayer at the sight of death: 'it shouldn't happen to us'. Knowing how it sinks me into gloom and trying to protect me, she rushes to shut the windows at the first note of the funeral march – as if it makes any difference – those tubas make our windows shake.

By the time we arrive at the *banya* I'm even more unhinged than usual. There's barely space to enter the packed waiting room; one woman sits in the corner darning a sock stretched over a glass, another is reading; a little boy does his homework; an old woman sits on the floor plucking a chicken, putting the feathers into a potato sack; others just stand and wait. Finally, after about an hour, it's our turn to go inside. We take off all our clothes in the communal changing room and hand them to the uniformed attendant who gives us a paper ticket on a string with a number written on it in ink. Where does a naked person put a paper ticket on a string? Even now, at swimming pools in London, I never take for granted being given my locker number attached to a rubber band that fits neatly around my wrist or ankle.

We enter the hot steaming room full of naked bodies of

all shapes and sizes, sitting on wet wooden benches side by side separated by small aluminium basins. If we are lucky we get one basin each; sometimes there's a whole stack of them piled up, but at other times there are none left and we have to wait and be very quick to snatch at least one to share.

Suddenly a fight breaks out because one woman is seen using two basins. She has her feet in one and washes herself in the other: "Hey, where do you think you are, in the Tzar's palace? Who do you think you are, spreading out over two basins, like a princess?"

"Shut up before I pour the dirty water from my feet over your head."

Holding the basins we stand in a queue for water: two taps – one for hot, one for cold. We soap ourselves with industrial soap the size of a brick; it's rough and gets stuck in your hair no matter how hard you try to rinse it off – I swear it must have had glue in it. Sometimes the water supply is cut off, leaving everyone covered in soap. Finally, if the number on our ticket is not altogether washed off, we get our clothes back without too much trouble. Then out we go into the frost. It's dark outside, Sunday is nearly gone. We walk back past the cemetery and crawl under the goods train, feeling scrubbed and tingling clean.

I refused to go to the *banya*, after the women started stealing glances at the darkening area of my pubis and at my budding breasts and pointing out to my mother that one breast is bigger than the other, getting her sufficiently wound up to take me to one doctor, who said it was normal, then to another for a second opinion.

A life-threatening level of sadness

My mother and stepfather Grisha never married, which was pretty wild in those days. When the three of us went for a walk together, Grisha walked ahead, smoking and coughing, with my mother and me walking behind. If we met a couple strolling by she'd say to me: "Look at her, a dried out fish on crooked legs, and next to her a Prince, and look at me ... what bitter fate sent me this?" She'd point in the direction of Grisha, walking in front in his military Stalin-style coat, coughing, choking and spitting: "And this is what I have to go to bed with?"

Many nights I'm an unwilling witness to the laborious toiling in their bed. It starts with her sulking and him begging: "Please, give it to me, let me, oh please let me, give it," his voice getting more and more breathless, and then the moving, sighing heap in the dark, grunting and whispering in a breaking voice: "*Oy, a mmmekhaie, oy,* delicious, *oy* what a pleasure, *oy, oy,* is it g-g-good for you? Yes? *Oy, oy, ai* ... grunt, grunt... and you? *Oy, oy.*"

Eventually the heap collapses, satiated, with him crying out, "*Mmmama!*" and her whispering: "Sh-h-h ..." and in a gently scolding, still breathless voice: "*Ty slabun,* you're my weakling."

I am rather ashamed to admit that their goings-on in that bed aroused me sexually, but they did. Although I couldn't imagine Greta Garbo in the '*Lady of the Camellias*' doing it with Robert Taylor when I walked through the park after seeing the film, feeling mysterious and imagining my shoulder blades in a *décolleté* dress, as delicately bony as hers.

And besides, Grisha and Mama's sex life takes my mind off the squeaking mice and the chronic terror that there could be a knock on the door with the secret police barging in telling us to get dressed and come with them. Everybody knows that 'they can come for you at any time in the night'. Pasternak spoke in *Dr. Zhivago* about the Russian's 'cursed capacity' for suffering, humour being the one means of survival: 'A knock on the door woke a family in the middle of night. All family members, shaking in terror, jumped up, thinking it was the KGB. "Take all you can carry with you, and get out at once," a voice sounded, "but don't panic, it's just me, your neighbour, it's nothing serious, just our house is on fire."'

Another of Grisha's step-uncles, Uncle Liova, is married to Berta and they have a little girl Bielochka – little squirrel, late in life. Berta is fat. I have nightmares after seeing her in the nude when I stay over with them; her long hair hangs down to her breasts, which hang down to her knees, and her stomach covers her pubic hair. By contrast, Uncle Liova is like a skeleton with a mop of white hair. Bielochka is skinny and pale with fine blue veins showing through the skin on her cheeks.

When finally the rationing and starvation come to an end and food begins to appear in the shops and at the market, my mother invites the three of them for Sunday lunch. For starters, she makes chopped liver and chopped herring to eat with thickly cut chunks of black bread, followed by chicken soup with *kneidlekh,* matzo balls, and for the main course *cholnt,* a chicken dish with onions, potatoes and carrots stewed in the oven for hours. For dessert, prunes and ice-cream, and ... after a little break, my mother serves tea and brings out her homemade chocolate cake, which, she says, rises higher than any other chocolate cake she's ever seen.

Berta eats with enormous appetite, praising the food with her mouth full. After tea and cake she says: "*Oy*, I need to lie down." She collapses on the couch, half her body hanging over the side. Holding her stomach with both hands she moans: "*Oy, oy,* my stomach. It's a bit upset; I don't know what could it be? I think it's that second cup of tea, I shouldn't have had that second cup of tea."

After this leap in her entertainment skills, my mother decides to have another luncheon and makes her special beef on the bone, with horseradish that takes the top of your head off. This time, to add to the party, she also invites Uncle Liova's sister, Marsha and her son Boris. Boris is thirty-eight years old, tall, pale and thin, eats very little and gives the general impression of being ill. He studied science at University but got expelled for not attending lectures. I like visiting them in their flat in the centre of Moscow. It's the only flat I've been to that has a telephone and an indoor toilet, and not only that; Boris has fixed the light in the toilet to go on and off when you open and close the door.

"I like Boris," I tell my mother.

"Boris is mad," she says, "He still lives with his mother ... at his age? You know what he did? He booked a ticket to go on holiday to Odessa, and just managed to get to the station before the piss hit his brain, so he turned around and came back. Why? Nobody knows. He's *mishuge. Akh*, he makes his poor mother suffer."

Boris is the only person who makes me feel that I have a brain. He asks me mathematical riddles, plays chess with me, reads poetry and asks me to sing him a song. Sometimes when he visits us, he walks up and down observing the people in the room as though he is trying to figure out if it is worth saying anything at all, and, deciding against it, sits quietly with his head in his hands.

Then suddenly he gets up, starts pacing the room fast, with his hands clasped behind his back, and bursts out, his speech jerky and feverish, "hypocrisy ... meanness of spirit .... forces that hide the truth ... the time will come when truth will triumph on this earth ... no tyrannical dictator will have the power to crush the individual soul by destroying art and beauty ..." Everyone gets agitated trying to calm him down, but I want to hear everything he has to say.

Russians have more words for 'sadness' than Eskimos for 'snow'. If there was such a thing as a 'sadness-ometer', it would have registered a life-threatening level on me. But I felt even sadder after Boris hung himself in the toilet with the light that came on and off when you opened and closed the door.

One orange from Odessa

It's a special festive occasion when my glamorous cousin Sioma, who is married and has a reputation for being a bit of a lecher, comes on his yearly visit on the way back to Lithuania from his holiday in Odessa. For me Odessa conjures up images of boulevards lined with chestnut trees, of merchants and sailors; poets reading their poems and musicians singing *blatnye piesni*, the bawdy songs of thieves and ruffians. Odessa is where everything fine and sordid mixes effortlessly together in my imagination.

Sioma arrives, sun-tanned, relaxed, dressed in a stylish light grey suit with an open-necked white shirt. He brings us a precious gift – one orange from Odessa.

My mother, Grisha, Sioma and I sit around the table watching my mother carefully peel the solitary orange and divide it into segments. The ecstasy of those translucent segments, bursting their luscious juices in my mouth, magically disperses the chronic gloom in our dreary room and stirs hope in my heart that a brighter life is waiting somewhere for me.

But the next morning, when Grisha goes off to work and my mother to the market, leaving me alone at home with Sioma, he tries to shag me with a penis as limp as a wilted banana, not that I'd ever seen an *erect* penis, except on the snotty little boy who lived in Tenement No. 1 in Khovrino, running around naked from the waist down, with his little penis sticking out, stiff with cold. I'd also never seen a banana for that matter, except in pictures. While all this is running through my mind, Sioma explains to me that he can't 'do it' because of my body odour. So, after all, refusing to wash preserves my chastity for another couple of years.

Sexual awakenings behind the Iron Curtain

One day, playing our own version of cricket with my girlfriends, I felt something wet and sticky in my knickers. I ran home, looked and found blood. I was in shock, asking my mother "Does it mean I'm not a child anymore?"

She replied, "Don't worry; you'll be a child forever."

Sanitary napkins haven't caught up yet with the 'Soviet Union leading the world to paradise', so my mother cut up an old piece of cloth and made me two menstruation rags, which had to be washed and used over again. And I went back to play cricket with my girlfriends, my passage into womanhood complete.

I've just turned fifteen when a boy from my class invites me to join two more couples to practice kissing. It feels weird, but just to be included in any team activity is a big deal for me, so I say yes. After school the six of us squeeze into his small bedroom where he switches off the lights to let the kissing rumpus start. The aim is to see who can hold the kiss the longest. I've never kissed a boy before; my neck feels like it's about to dislocate and I'm close to asphyxiation. After a while to my relief he gets up and puts the lights on: "Let's go to the ice-cream cafe on Gorky Street for ice-cream and cognac."

Off we go by train to Moscow. Outside the café, looking bedraggled and feeling awkward with each other after the embarrassing kissing competition, we stand in a long queue in the snow in –30C temperatures, before we are allowed into the café – another first time experience for me.

I'm wearing my one and only winter dress made of thick wool with a very tight polo neck which I keep pulling at, trying to stretch it. The dress already has big sweat rings under the arms and now they are damp and even darker after all the sweaty kissing. Inside the café it is hot and my first taste of cognac sends hot flashes all through my body. I sit there sweltering in my woollen dress, keeping my arms tightly pressed to my sides. Deodorant is unheard of. The Russians explode the hydrogen bomb long before they introduce deodorant, while in America roll-on deodorant is introduced the same year that the bomb is exploded.

When the film *Tarzan and his Mate* comes to Moscow the queues outside the cinema are longer than the endless lines of 'faithfuls' to the Mausoleum of Lenin in the Red Square. Within days all the girls at school are singing a refrain:

For a hut with Tarzan
For wild Negroes, jazz
I'd give up an apartment
With telephone and gas

The girls in my class think that our technical drawing teacher, Mr. Troubliov looks like Tarzan. When he comes into class we start singing the Tarzan refrain, thinking he'll be amused, but his handsome face remains expressionless. Still, he does look the part, even if he doesn't have a sense of humour; he is tall and muscular, with a mane of wavy hair and wild dark eyes, and seems misplaced in his role as a teacher. I'm not a bit interested in technical drawing;

I just wish Mr.Troubliov would kidnap me and swing me up into a tree-house in the jungle like Tarzan and Jane.

I imagine I look really romantic when snowflakes settle on my hair and my long eyelashes, so one day I deliberately come to his class late, hoping to bewitch him as I make my entrance, fluttering my snow-covered eyelashes. But he just throws an annoyed glance in my direction and says, looking down at his technical drawings: "Go out and shake the snow off and next time, don't be late."

Why, oh why, isn't life like a Tarzan film?

I was a 'good girl' at the Secondary School No 2 in the suburb of Khimki, I was too terrified not to be. Our headmaster, who was also our astronomy teacher, was an ex-major in the Red Army. He wore military trousers and an army jacket studded with war medals *a la* Stalin and taught us astronomy as though all the stars in the sky were under his command. No one had ever seen him smile. Out of terror of his militant disapproval, we memorised everything parrot fashion so that not a trace of wonder about galaxies and stars and the infinity of space was allowed to awaken. We were far too inhibited to ask any questions. When your voice is silenced your soul is stifled. It took a lifetime for my soul to sing.

We had ideological courses in History of the Communist Party and its philosophy. Even the characters in pre-revolutionary literature, like *War and Peace*, were scrutinised from the point of view of Soviet ideology, drumming into our heads that the life of nobility was without direction and purpose. There was no space for inspiration, being whipped into shape doesn't leave much room for creative thought. Only one touch of encouragement stands out in my memory, when my literature teacher patted me on the head for reciting a poem.

My favourite subjects were reading, writing and English. Our English teacher was the only one in the whole school with a sense of humour. She introduced her first lesson: "In English you write *Manchester* and pronounce *Liverpool*." When I first came to the West I boasted, "English my best subject was." But my most enjoyable times were when exams were over and I could read any book I liked. I devoured books by Emille Zola, Maupassant, Balzac, Theodor Dreiser and Mark Twain. My inner world started to wake up and be validated by the ideas in the books. They captured how I felt, awakening my imagination and my dreams of love.

I am sixteen in my last year of school and I'm given the part of the young gypsy Zemphira in the play in verse '*Gypsies*', by Alexander Pushkin. Our literature teacher directs it and does our makeup. I wear a long flowery skirt, an embroidered blouse and large gold earrings, all borrowed from a girl at school. My face has dark make-up and my lips are painted scarlet red.

Our parents are in the audience. The curtain rises. My soul soars at being on stage, doing what I want to do more than anything else in the world. I am Zemphira, the young fiery gypsy, who is travelling with her father in a caravan through the planes of Bessarabia: "Their camp at night is gay as freedom, They sleep at peace under the skies."

She is married, but falls in love with a young gypsy and keeps taunting her husband Aleko, with a provocative song her own mother sang to her husband before running off with her young lover: "Freer than a bird is love. Who has the power to hold it back?" Soon Aleko catches the lovers and kills them both. She sings, "I die loving."

The play ends with the narrator reciting:

> *The stars shine above,*
> *The gypsies depart across the steppe*
> *and leave Aleko behind, alone in his wagon,*
> *just as a flock of cranes rises and flies away,*
> *leaving behind one with a broken wing.*

The lights go on, the audience applauds and we take our bows; I'm swept away by the play and the applause and, still in the part of free-loving Zemphira, I run, beaming, to my mother. She says: "Very good, now go and wash that paint off your face, it can soak into your skin and remain there forever."

Leaving school is a distressing end of an era for me, leaving behind the childhood that never happened and going out into the world: ready or not. I am not ready.

Our radio has only one station, mostly Soviet rhetoric, but there are also cultural programs and I try to give myself a crash course in music by memorising names of operas and composers and training myself to recognise arias. I want to educate myself so that I won't appear ignorant and will have things to say, but now school is over I can't even begin to imagine myself out there in the world.

More than anything I wanted a piano, if only I could play the piano I would be popular. Just to touch the piano keys felt like magic. Hearing a girl at school play the piano made my eyes prickle with tears of envy. I drew a keyboard on the windowsill and practiced the pieces I'd learnt. My mother kept promising me a piano; every time I heard a truck outside, in my mind it was my piano being delivered. My mother doesn't have the money and, besides, there is a five year waiting list for pianos, or at least that's what I'm told.

For my school graduation party I paint my nails with colourless nail varnish for the first time ever and stand by the wall, hiding my hands behind my back, occasionally stealing a look at them.

A young man invites me to dance.

"I don't dance," I say, immediately realising how lame that sounds; he smiles in a puzzled sort of way, shrugs his shoulders and walks off and I instantly fall in love with his nonchalant air and curly hair.

I cry all night after the graduation party; bitter tears all through the night without stopping. Where could so many tears come from?

I cry because I'm not a child any more, not because being a child was such a ball, but because the next step feels even worse.

I cry because I didn't dance with the boy with the curly hair.

I cry because I have low marks in my matriculation certificate, even in English, even though 'it my best subject was'.

I cry because I feel I'm a failure. I'm on that threshold between leaving school and not knowing what the hell it means 'to step out into the world.' What am I supposed to be now?

My mother, alarmed that I might never stop crying, says: "Silly girl, why are you crying?" as though everything's fine and my crying is childish and there's no good reason for it. It's tempting to believe her, only deep inside I know that something isn't right.

Soon after the graduation party I hear from a girlfriend that, while I was standing by the wall hiding my manicured hands behind my back, Volodya Tarasov, who graduated from school three years earlier and was studying art, told her how beautiful he thought I was and how he wished he could meet me.

A couple of days later, crossing the railway bridge, I come face to face with a tall young man with hair the colour of corn flopping over his forehead and know, without a doubt, it's 'him'. He smiles and I smile back. He has blue forget-me-not eyes and sensuous, slightly chapped lips. We start going for walks together in the evenings. He carries a tattered little book of poems, *Loves of a Hooligan* by Sergei Esenin, one of the most beloved poets in Russia, who managed to survive the Stalinist regime when his rough, melancholy and fiery poetry was considered 'in conflict with socialist realism'. It's exciting the way Volodya, the artist, sings the same rogue song by Esenin that Pasha, the gaol bird, sang in his oversized shoes years earlier:

> *I cherish a secret dream that I'm pure at heart*
> *but I might still knife someone*
> *to the sound of the autumn whistling wind.*

Volodya calls me *'ma Boheme'*. My mother calls me 'whore' when I come back from a romantic walk in the park, in the snow, in the moonlight.

He asks me to sit for him and does a portrait of me, eyes extending beyond the limits of my face. I feel embarrassed. I don't know what to say or what to make of it. He asks: "Have you heard of Picasso?"

"No," I've never heard of *anybody*.

He invites me to the art exhibition of impressionist paintings looted by the Russians at the end of the war and exhibited before being returned to Dresden. It's my first art exhibition and I have no idea what I'm supposed to think, feel or say. While Volodya is in another hall I take out my notebook and frantically write down the name of the artist and the painting, and, as quickly, hide the notebook when I see him enter the room. I didn't yet know the freedom of not being embarrassed by what I didn't know.

I can feel it is the gypsy in me, the outsider from conventional society that he is attracted to, but can't figure out why this 'gypsy' is so timid. One dark night, as we stroll through the snow, he recites another of Esenin's poems, 'As I was born a poet, I kiss like a poet' and kisses me passionately. To this day I remember those sensuous, slightly rough lips, so warm, in contrast to the frosty air around us – twenty-five below zero. My lips disappear in his but I don't know what to do with them, feeling rigid with inhibition; my mother is always watching. He stops suddenly and says, "How long am I going to kiss these rubber lips?" Oh, my God.

On another romantic night, with the crescent moon in the clear winter sky, he says: "I want to see longing in your beautiful eyes, look at me with longing." I try, he laughs and I never see him again, except in the summer, when I stand hiding behind our pre-war lace curtains, choking with tears, watching Volodya with his friend Sasha from next door, and a pretty girl in a bright flowery skirt, walking down the narrow path fringed with daisies. I can't hear what they are saying but I can hear their laughter. They seem so at ease and I feel so tied up inside on this balmy summer evening with the smell of jasmine in the air. I am not allowed the thrill of falling in love, so I disappear into fantasy: my father is alive; I'm relaxed, confident and popular and can sing and play the piano. One good thing about fantasy is that it puts me in touch with the place of confidence and grace that I will one day feel for real, at least some of the time.

My dreams of romantic love are shaped by my mother's stories of an elegant Polish man bending down, lifting the edge of her kid glove and kissing her hand, all the while not taking his eyes off her. Being a sentimental *klutz,* I am seduced by the slushy, idealistic melodramas of Socialist Realism films: a collective farm where the hero and heroine are working together making haystacks for the glory of our Motherland. The erotic tension between them is intensified by a misunderstanding: she mistakenly thinks he is in love with the girl who drives the tractor. But when our heroine accidentally falls off a haystack into his open arms, all her doubts are dispelled in the sexual *frisson* between them and they sing, "Together we are strong and confident, ready to rebuff our enemies".

I remember my first *frisson*; watching the film *Terese Raquen* based on Emile Zola's story, with Raf Vallone and Simone Signoret. Terese is married to a sickly hypochondriac whose mother makes her cater to his every whim. A handsome young traveller passes by and stays with them for the night and the four of them play cards in the evenings. She goes into the kitchen to make coffee and, after a polite pause, the stranger follows her. He approaches her as she stands with her back to him, trembling in anticipation of his touch. The moment his big hairy hands touch her shoulders, I feel a warm, powerful, current shooting from the base of my spine right through the crown of my head. Oooo, what was that?

Tatyana, in Pushkin's novel in verse, *Eugene Onegin* is my dream heroine. I stand in front of a hand mirror propped up on a chair and recite, with a lot of feeling, the letter sixteen-year-old Tatyana wrote to Onegin, declaring her love and baring her soul.

I write to you, what can I say?
I know it is in your power to punish me with your disdain,
but if you have only a drop of pity for my unfortunate fate,
you won't abandon me.
At first I kept silent.
Believe me, you would never have found out my shame
if only there was hope of seeing you in our village,
only to hear your voice, to say a word to you,
and then, just dream and dream ...

She allows that letter to fly out of her heart like a wild bird of love, without stopping to consider the implications of what she is doing... the disgrace of it, for a young girl in those days in Russian society to write to a man confessing her love. Only when she has given the letter to her faithful nanny to deliver to Onegin does she become tormented by doubts and fear of humiliation. Tatyana's courage and tenderness in Pushkin's beautiful verse touches my soul and melts my heart.

From early childhood I was mesmerised by the magic of the movies. I adored the Soviet film actress, Tamara Makarova, to tears. I collected post cards of her, tried to walk like her, talk like her, wrote letters to her, but never got a reply. I even fell in love with my physics teacher because she looked like Tamara Makarova. I stayed after lessons with my heart practically jumping out of my chest in order to see her one more time and say one more good-bye.

After graduating from school I dreamt of going to the

Institute of Cinematography in Moscow to become a movie actress.

"Don't even dare to think about it," said my mother, "or the door to this room will be closed to you for ever. An actress she wants to be? Why don't you just become a whore?"

I want to sing, dance and perform! You shouldn't need to justify why you want to do something with all your heart. It's simple. I feel a pull towards cabaret, being outrageous, glamorous, telling *risqué* jokes, making people laugh. But since I lack the guts to go for what I really want, Grisha steps in, bribes the examiner and has me admitted to the Library Institute. I, like a *shlemil,* give in and thinking it is expected of me as a librarian, cut my hair short. And I cut it myself so it looks as if I've escaped from an asylum.

For some weird and unknown reason. we have lectures in agriculture and learn about different kinds of manure and about the 'heroic soviet sow' who broke the world record by giving birth to a litter of fifteen piglets. I fail the agriculture exam five times in the first semester.

It is compulsory to attend political meetings and read newspapers. There is a joke going around about the two main newspapers *Pravda* – Truth, and *Izvestia* – News: 'There is no truth in the News, and no news in the Truth.'

The one time I remember being free of anxiety is when the Library Institute sends my class to a *kolkhoz,* collective farm, to help pick potatoes. My mother considers work in a *kolkhoz* too coarse for her fragile daughter and tries to have me exempted because of my painful periods, but luckily her excuses are not accepted. I am in heaven; not to have to sleep in the same room as Mama and Grisha for a couple of nights, for one thing; feeling the bliss of spending the whole day in the fresh air digging in the mud for potatoes, joking and laughing; and in the evenings baking potatoes in the fire and dancing the tango to the music of *Leshchenko* – and then falling asleep in the hay.

Zhanna is the only girl in our year at the Library Institute who is married and the only one with a clear complexion; the rest of us have pimples. All of us girls decide that she has no pimples because she is having sex. My mother also hints that the spots on my face will disappear as soon as I get married. When Zhanna comes back after a three day absence, one of the girls sends her a note 'How was it?' to which she replies, 'At first it was tight and then it got sucked in'. The note is passed around making us all giggle, but leaving us no more enlightened on the subject of sex. I keep staring at her, trying to discern any signs of wisdom or maturity, but can't see any significant change.

After failing the agriculture exam for the fifth time, Mama and Grisha decide that my only hope is marriage. I have a close brush with an arranged marriage when my cousin from Lithuania sends a 'nice Jewish boy', Aaron the lawyer, to stay with us. I can't even bear being in the same room as him so I promise my mother that I'll try and pass the agriculture exam so long as I don't have to marry him.

She lets me off the hook, but doesn't give up altogether; she takes me off to Lithuania to find a husband there. I expect that, coming from Moscow, I'll be a big hit in a small town like Vilna, but it turns out that the young people I meet are actually a lot more hip and in the know than I am about the latest fashions and dances from the West. In fact I'm not hip at all, except somewhere very deep inside.

I fall under the spell of Misha, the sexy jazz pianist of Vilna, who shows an interest in me; he invites me home and introduces me to his father. I feel awkward, tongue tied and couldn't have made much of an impression on him since he goes to bed straight after dinner. Misha sits down at the piano and plays *'Lullaby of Birdland'* beautifully. I sit on the couch, overflowing with emotions, desperately wanting him to like me, wanting him to know how much I love his playing; wanting to sing, to play the piano; in other words going berserk.

After he finishes playing he sits down next to me and puts his arm around my shoulders. I feel like a coy sixteen year old from a remote *shtetle,* transfixed by the explosion of new impressions and feelings. Going a little further he puts his hand under my dress and withdraws it looking at me quizzically. My mother makes me wear thick flannel underpants with tight elastic at the knees that leave permanent red marks and turn out to be an effective chastity belt. I also wear a bra, coming all the way down to my waist, like armour.

Walking me home, he asks: "Tell me, I'm curious, why is it you walk as if your legs don't belong to you? You are a beautiful girl, be proud of it."

The next day, in the public bathhouse, my cousin's wife points out a slim, graceful girl with beautifully cut straight blonde hair and a flat muscular belly. "She's the jazz player's girlfriend, a *shiksa;* she gave his father a heart attack." Getting dressed in the communal changing room, pulling on my flannel underpants, I notice her teeny-weenie, snow-white lace panties the likes of which I've never seen before and won't see again for a long time to come.

I am puzzled; why is he interested in me if he has this gorgeous girlfriend? Maybe he is trying his best to be a dutiful son and please his father by trying to marry a Jewish girl? Or maybe he really likes me? Either way, I am so inhibited and unable to relate that he gives up.

Grisha is dead

In 1959 Russia and Poland make an agreement to allow former Polish citizens to repatriate to Poland. This includes Jews who had Polish citizenship on September 1939, when Poland was split up between Nazi Germany and the Soviet Union. Being eligible, my mother decides she is going to take the opportunity to leave the Soviet Union and realise her dream of reuniting with her beloved brother Isaac in South Africa.

After many quarrels, during which Grisha says he isn't going and my mother says: "*Minochka* and I are going, whether you come or not," he concedes reluctantly: "We'll see."

All *I* can think of is being discovered by a film director in the West.

My mother puts in the application while Grisha is in hospital having his stomach opened and closed with a fatal diagnosis. Everyone knows he has terminal cancer except him. There is always something going on that everyone knows except the person in question.

I overhear Grisha say to my mother: "When I get better I'm going to take her in hand. You are crippling her, she never washes a dish."

But I knew he was dying.

The day before he died he asked me to make him an omelette. I was so thoroughly brainwashed by my mother that I was 'helpless' and 'useless' that the very idea of making an omelette was veiled in deep mystery, not to be probed by the likes of me, but I decided to give it a go and approached the task with reckless confidence. He tasted it, shook his head and declared: "It's no good!" but ate it anyway. Then he asked me for the bedpan, did an enormous black shit and said: "It's a sign that I'm getting better." That was his last shit.

The next morning I wake up feeling guilty; as usual 'my soul was not in place', as the Russian proverb says. My mother comes into my room whispering: "Come to the market with me, you'll help me carry the shopping." Why is she whispering? I can feel something strange in the air but then there was always something strange in the air, so it is hard to tell when it is for real. Coming back from the market, as we are about to enter the house with our basket of food and a *bidon,* a three litre aluminium cistern, filled with milk at the market by the peasant woman from a *kolkhoz,* my mother announces: "Grisha is dead."

She had confided in me enough times that she didn't love Grisha and found it disgusting to go to bed with him, so I assumed she'd be relieved he was dead. But she cried and cried about her 'bitter fate' that once again deprived her of a husband. Or maybe she was fond of him in spite of herself. I was not sorry that he died. Guilt-ridden as I normally was, I felt ruthlessly guilt-free about it. I was sick to death of their quarrels and having to tiptoe around them, anxiously testing the level of tension between them, and if that's what it took to stop it, so be it.

Grisha lay in state on the table in their bedroom for three days before being buried; I don't know why, something about a truck not being available to take him to the cemetery.

On the third day, two plain-clothed KGB men come to arrest him and confiscate his belongings for doing the illicit deals in the building materials shop. KGB – *Komitiet*

Gosudarstvienoy Biezopastnosti, subversively renamed Kommunist Gangsters and Bandits.

"Comrade Ginsberg?" they demand sternly.

My mother points to the room where Grisha lies on the table. The men go inside and come out with their hats in their hands. These 'guardians of law and order' are powerless to confiscate his property since my mother has had the foresight to put the rooms in her name in order to sell them before we leave for Poland.

My father's violin, in its worn case, used to hang on the wall in my room till my mother got fed up with me opening it from time to time and crying my eyes out, so she'd hung it up in the woodshed and I never touched it again. As we close the door of our home forever, I am aware of the violin, which has travelled with us all through the war, hanging on a rough wall in the woodshed – delicate and abandoned.

Leaving behind the shores of childhood

Before our final departure from Russia we spend a month in a Lithuanian village by a lake waiting for our repatriation documents. We rent a room in a house where an old man is dying of cancer. For once I am not touched by the gloom; we are on our way to a new life. The country air and the lake fill my heart with promises of romantic love.

It isn't long before the twenty-three-year-old local sports teacher, with the body of a young stallion, spots me carrying Jean-Jacques Rousseau's *Essays on the Common Humanity of Men* under my arm. My mother, of course, notices him cock his eye at me and gives him a menacing 'don't you mess with my daughter' look. But, she can't exactly lock me up since she's brought me here to breathe the fresh air, which, she does her best to convince me, is for my 'weak' lungs.

The village teacher and I spend days rowing in his boat and bathing in the lake and evenings walking in the forest by moonlight, breathing in the aroma of wild strawberries. There and then I'm prepared to say *"To hell with what my Mother told me"*, and give in to the wildness in my heart and limbs. But as I lie in his arms on the grass in anticipation of passion, to my surprise the young stallion's body is limp. At the time I thought he didn't find me attractive and ended up crying all night about it. Now, I think he was even more frightened of my mother than I was.

In the summer of 1959 we left Moscow. It was the time when Stalin was posthumously accused of the cult of personality. Posters, creating an idealised heroic image of the dictator: 'Beloved Stalin – the people's happiness', or 'Our Leader – symbol of friendship', were destroyed, and all the monuments of him were demolished.

Khrushchev came to power. Nikita Khrushchev initiated liberal reforms; he formally rehabilitated many individuals and groups repressed during the Stalin regime in an attempt to demonstrate how different he was from his ruthless predecessor and to ease ever so slightly the internal conditions for people living in the Soviet Union. Fear of police and authorities was no longer as great as before and two thirds of the labour camps in Siberia were dismantled. People felt freer to speak with foreigners and to discuss problems and difficulties. That's what the papers said but, from my experience, it takes a lot more than the same old indoctrinating rhetoric to overcome the emotional aftermath of terror and persecution and begin to find trust in life.

But still, to us repatriating to Poland, Khrushchev made a significant difference: we were allowed to send all our belongings in a wooden crate by rail to Warsaw free of charge. Now we had a few valuables; to invest the money from selling our one-and-a-half rooms my mother got up at the crack of dawn to be first in line to buy a refrigerator, a washing machine, a vacuum cleaner, four hair dryers, and four boxes of *sevruga* caviar from the Caspian Sea, to sell at a profit in Poland. We heard rumours that refugees from other eastern European countries, on their way to Israel, were allowed only one small suitcase each. But maybe it was Khrushchev spreading that rumour.

We did have to surrender our internal passports and our nationality and we could never return, as we were now classified *vrag naroda*, enemy of the people. I was also supposed to surrender my *Komsomol* badge but, since we already had our documents, I dared, as an act of protest, to throw my 'Always Ready!' badge across a field, as far as I could throw, and, ashamed of my low marks, also threw away my matriculation certificate, pretending I had lost it. When I came to London some fifteen years later, I was astonished to see *'Vsiegda Gotovy!'*, 'Always Ready!' *Komsomol* badges, depicting a bust of Lenin on a red star with a flame coming out at the top, being sold at Portobello market. I wondered if mine was amongst them, pilfered by some capitalist entrepreneur selling Soviet relics for a profit, which, ironically, is what we were always brainwashed to believe would happen.

After three days of quarantine on the border of Russia and Poland, where all of us hundreds of refugees, men, women and children, are examined for lice and disinfected, we continue our journey to Warsaw.

My mother and I have been given the address of a man called Shmuilovsky who has recently repatriated to Poland and has already established himself as an advisor in black market dealings in Warsaw: the best place to change money; where to find somewhere to live; how to sell the goods we have brought. We contact him as soon as we arrive and he helps us sell all the goods and suddenly we have more money than all the money we had put together throughout in our life in Russia.

He helps us find a room in a one-roomed flat rented out by a Polish widow to make ends meet. She and her two daughters move themselves into the kitchen and all three of them sleep on a mattress on the floor. For the first time in my life, I'm living in a flat with running water, a bathroom, a flush toilet, a telephone and gas.

As the story goes I, at nine months old, wouldn't sit for the camera, so my father ended up holding me. It is the only photo of the two of us together.

My father in Vienna before the war.

Mother holding me, four months old.

Mother holding me, four months old.

My mother and father fell in love while dancing to the Polish tango 'Maybe in a bar or in a cafe'.

With mother, five months old.

Two years old in our garden, in a pretty dress, self-willed and obstinate.

At school in the suburb, Khovrino. I am on the top row, second from the right. I remember clearly the bottom left corner of this photograph being chewed by mice, to my horror.

At a sanatorium, I am very pretty and very sulky, in the top row, third to the right from the teacher.

With a friend at a sanatorium, wearing my red young pioneer tie.

The group photo from a sanatorium, at which my mother laughed, "Look at the way you are holding the flowers!" I am in the bottom right, holding a bouquet of flowers self consciously. I am not at all like the other girls lying on the ground, relaxed and with their hair intact. My hair had been shaven off with a cold metal shave upon my arrival, because they found lice.

Fenia's daughter, Nina and I.

My school graduation photo: I am on the second row from the top, fourth in from the left. My technical drawing teacher who we thought looked like Tarzan is second from the left on the top row. My ex-Red Army Major astronomy teacher is in the top right corner.

My mother with her prominent widows peak, which I inherited and was trying to pluck, despite wearing a hat because my hair still hadn't grown back after being shaved at the sanatorium.

In my new winter coat
and matching hat.

Last year of school in
the suburb Khimki.

With my mother, in the village in Lithuania, waiting for documents to leave the Soviet Union for Poland.

Reading Jean Jacques Russo (I don't know why) in the village.

With the village school teacher on his boat. I remained a virgin even after my tempting posturing, because he was even more intimidated by my mother than I.

PART TWO

Goodbye Mother Russia
Hello Sexual Confusion

'You have the right to experiment with your life.
You will make mistakes. And they are right, too.'

– Anais Nin

Deflowered in two stages

I lost my virginity in Warsaw, at the age of twenty-one, not out of love or even infatuation, but to spite my mother. As soon as my breasts developed she became obsessed with my losing my virginity before marriage and falling pregnant, so she tried her best to intimidate me. She would spread her hand in front of my face: "You are open to me like the palm of my hand; I will know immediately if you dare do anything with a boy; I can see through you."

I had had real feelings for Volodya Tarasov, the artist with forget-me-not eyes and slightly chapped lips. When I came back from a date with him in the frost and snow, where you'd freeze your arse off if you took any one of your garments off, she'd turn me around to check if I'd been lying somewhere untoward and throw in 'whore', for good measure.

She succeeded in making me feel embarrassed about my sexuality. Having to restrain the flood of powerful erotic feelings coming from the mysterious feminine depths, I became self-conscious and behaved in a weird way. Suppressing my feminine power and my capacity for joy led to despair and depression. And Volodya, puzzled by my behaviour, stopped seeing me, which broke my heart. I was angry with my mother and the only way I was capable of getting back at her was to become self-destructive.

So now we are in Warsaw and here is Shmuel, a middle-aged repatriate journalist from Russia, with a wart on his nose. Whenever he comes round, I assume he's come to visit my mother and I'm baffled when he asks me out. My mother nudges me to go: "*Nu,* who knows, maybe he'll propose."

He proposes we go to his place on the tramway, where he bumps into an old friend of his who asks casually: "Where are you going?" and Shmuel gives him a wink and says he's taking me to his place to *yentz*. I don't believe my ears. *Yentz?* That's Yiddish for 'shag'? Maybe he's joking? Some joke.

But I say nothing; I'm lost in my fantasy of being a film star waiting to be discovered. In my mother's eyes I'm either 'the best' or 'the worst', and mostly 'useless and helpless', so I'm well on my way to confused, self-destructive relationships with men.

When we get to his place I start giving Shmuel confused, double messages; I take off my clothes, get into his bed, tell him I'm a virgin and play hard to get. He ignores my game, gets on top of me and pierces me with his penis. Blood appears on the sheet and makes him realise that I am, in fact a virgin, which stops him in his tracks. All he needs is for my mother to find out. He puts his sheet in a bucket of water to soak, in case it remains stained forever, and takes me home. After that we never see him again and my mother, puzzled, keeps repeating: "I wonder what happened to Shmuel?"

'Aha,' I thought, 'if *that* passed her by, then she can't really see through me. And since he did nothing more than rupture my hymen, I can get away with letting her think I'm still a virgin.'

Because of her diabetes my mother panics if she doesn't have a doctor to call in case of emergency, so, on our arrival in Warsaw, she immediately registered with the local clinic.

Soon her doctor comes on a home visit and spots me,

spilling out of my only cotton dress. My mother, in her romantic euphoria about Polish doctors and the chivalrous custom of men kissing women's hands, offers her hand to be kissed and, loosening her hawk-eyed watch over me, allows him to take me out on a date.

Doctor Lekh Kovarsky, baby-faced and podgy with beady eyes, lives with his parents at the age of thirty-nine, around the corner from where we live. He takes me to a nightclub where, in semi-darkness, a few couples are dancing to a band playing pre-war Polish tangos. Maybe it's because my mother and father fell in love dancing the tango, or because I heard a lot of tango music while still in the womb and for the first three years of my life, that I am instantly transported into the alluring world of glamour and romance at the first sounds of the music.

In the meantime, the doctor keeps filling my glass with vodka to lure me into his bedroom in his parent's flat. There I recklessly lose the rest of my virginity, engrossed in romantic notions about the older and wiser man who knows me and understands me so deeply that even hurt from him is mixed with sweetness. I tell the doctor that it's my first time, discarding the journalist with the wart on his nose and all my virginal blood left on his sheet. The doctor doesn't believe me and, technically speaking, he has a point.

I learnt to speak Polish by reading movie magazines, so when his mother bangs on the door while we are making love, shouting hysterically: "Get your Jewish whore out of my house ... she's got you by the balls, you can kiss your balls goodbye, she knows how to move in bed, *dobrze tylek daje...* I'd rather see you dead than marrying a Jewess; I married a Jew and that made me hate Jews," I have no trouble understanding every word.

Nevertheless, on one of his professional visits to my

mother, Lekh Kovarsky asks her if he can take me to a ski resort in Poland's Tatra Mountains, and my mother, still in her ivory tower about Polish doctors being courteous and honourable, lets me go with her blessing and money for my own room. We don't ski even once. When I tell my friends this story, they smile, in a nudge-nudge, wink-wink sort of way, imagining a week of raunchy sex. It is nothing of the sort.

Sleeping next to my mother and stepfather for fifteen years and hearing their shenanigans in the night, I was witness to a pattern that I began to associate with erotic feelings; she'd sulk, he'd beg and then they'd shag, and that's what I found exciting. So at the Tatra Mountains ski resort I find endless reasons to sulk. At first he follows my cue: sulking, wooing, coaxing, shagging, but after a few days he reckons: "You're a very strange girl." I sort of know, through a fog in my mind, I am putting on an act, but I can't help it, I've been programmed to follow a pattern – sulk, coax, shag.

On the way back on the train I feel something new and strange in my body; my breasts are bursting and I feel nauseous but I try to pretend nothing out of the ordinary is happening.

Back in Warsaw Lekh Kovarsky does a pregnancy test and my fears are confirmed – I am pregnant. There's no question in his or my mind about keeping the baby. The only way I know how to deal with the situation is to cut off and cry. My mother says: "You see, I told you you'll get attached to him, that's how it works."

She goes off to a soviet 'health spa' on the outskirts of Warsaw for her back pain, and Lekh Kovarsky gives me an injection to terminate the pregnancy. It works; I lie in bed bleeding and sending the landlady's younger daughter to the pharmacy for huge packets of cotton wool every few hours. The landlady keeps coming in, looking at me suspiciously and shaking her head. My mother sends me a postcard of herself with a group of women at the spa, all wearing striped pyjamas, looking like convicts.

By the time she comes back, two weeks later, the bleeding has stopped. Seeing how pale and thin I look, she doesn't miss a chance to rub it in: "You see, I told you, you'd be lost without me."

The whole experience of the previous two weeks is wiped right out of my mind when I read in one of my movie magazines that Roget Vadim's *'Une Parisienne'* is showing at the cinemas in Warsaw. I can't wait to see it. I go alone in order to savour every moment and because I don't have any friends. My whole being is in ecstasy watching Brigitte Bardot sparkling and flaunting her beauty and charm without a hint of inhibition, so carefree and fearless; I have never seen anything like it. On the way home I try to walk like her with a confident stride, swinging my hips.

I snap out of it fast when I come in and see my mother, standing in the middle of our room, looking like an admiral ready for battle, furiously holding out a packet of big round tablets.

"What are these?" she demands.

Were there no condoms in Poland? Why did Lekh Kovarsky give me those circular spermicidal vaginal tablets that I never used because they foamed like mad? Why did I 'hide' them in the drawer of the table in our room? Good questions.

"They are pills the doctor gave me," I say, trying to sound confident like Brigitte Bardot.

"What for?" my mother shrieks in a voice, which I know is a prelude to her losing all control.

"For a sore throat," I mumble now with less assurance.

"This size?" my mother screeches, her black eyes piercing through me, "You slept with him."

"Yes," I reply, as though under hypnosis.

A slap like lightning strikes me across my face. "Whore!" screeches my mother. "Who will marry you now? You could have married a millionaire in South Africa, and now? Who needs you? How could you?"

And she tells me again as though it's the most valuable lesson I need to learn: "I was already married to your father and I couldn't bring myself to go to bed with him; he stood in the door silently begging me with his eyes to come to bed but I couldn't. I slept with my mother for two weeks ... and you, you whore, how could you?" And she lies down on the bed and spreads her legs wide open: "Like this? You open your legs? How could you? What's the hurry? *Pospeshish – ludei nasmeshish* – if you do things in haste you'll make people laugh. I have no daughter. It's all finished. You made your bed, you lie in it; you don't want *manna* from heaven; eat shit," she repeats the same thing in Polish, proudly enunciating the words: *"Nie chtzesh manny, yesh guvne,"* and in conclusion quotes another of her proverbs: *"Shto imeem nie khranim, a poteriavshi plachem* – What we have, we don't cherish, then cry when we lose it."

She lies in bed not washing and not cooking, grieving the loss of my virginity for one whole week, forbidding me to go out. After she gets up from her mourning she summons the doctor for a *tête-à-tête;* he tells her that he isn't the first, which lets him off the hook of having to marry me and confirms that I'm a whore. I'm forbidden to see Doctor Lekh alone ever again.

For two weeks my mother continues being distant and cold. I feel as if I don't exist; it's a familiar feeling from my childhood when she would stop talking to me for a whole day and I'd feel like a little lost stranger in the big world. It made relationships with people a mystery to me for a very long time; I literally couldn't understand how other people communicated with each other and seemed to have so much to say; what did they talk about? I was not capable of maintaining a real connection with another human being, nor a dog or a cat, or a teddy-bear, for that matter.

I still remember the day when she started talking to me again. We were out on a busy street in Warsaw when we passed an attractive young man. He looked at me and smiled, but I felt as if my mother was holding the strings to my smiling muscles. As we walked on my mother said: "Did you notice the way he devoured you with his eyes?" sounding as though it's a good thing. I burst out crying from having the tension released and being taken back by her. But the chronic humiliation of being controlled by her and restricted from spontaneously being myself I can't forget.

It is 1959. Poles are marching in the streets with slogans – "Jews to Palestine". I feel furious and frightened, raging and helpless I want to shout: 'OK, relax, that's where we are going!'

After a year in Poland our documents arrived and we left for Israel, our transit stop on the way to my mother's dream: reunion with her beloved brother in South Africa.

As the Warsaw-Vienna train starts to move out of the station, Doctor Lekh, whom I haven't seen since the big ban, suddenly appears on the platform and runs alongside, waving. My mother and I are sobbing to the sound of the haunting song from the station loudspeaker, bringing back memories of other departures:

As I run alongside the moving train
I know how dear you are to me.
Please take care and don't forget me.

But as soon as the doctor's podgy silhouette retreats into the distance, out of sight out of mind – my tears stop. As if touched by an angel of hope, my heart lifts with joy and confidence that all my dreams are not just *mishugene* fancy. Losing my virginity and learning to speak Polish were the most significant events of our one year in Warsaw.

Vienna

The compartments of the Warsaw-Vienna train are stuffed with refugees and their luggage. I remain in the corridor looking out of the window, wanting to be alone with the new hope in my heart. A young man introduces himself: Kzystof is a journalist, also travelling to Israel with his mother. We stand together silently, watching the passing scenery, both of us shy and awkward in our refugee status. Then my mother comes out and orders me back into the stuffy compartment to be squashed between her and the journalist's mother. Since I am not a virgin any more, according to her the tollgates are now open and there's no stopping me. I cringe, flinch and squirm in helpless fury and shame.

But just the sound of the word 'Vienna' elevates me into the world of glamour and elegance, waltz and romance, inspired by the tiny photograph of my father before the war, looking dashing in a stylish suit and a fedora hat, carrying his violin outside the *Konservatorium Wien*. And here am I, in Vienna, the city of my dreams, wearing a cotton dress that has seen better days and black clunky shoes, in a refugee camp under strict orders not to leave the campground.

Somehow Kzystof manages to sweep aside my terror of authority and we ignore the orders. I walk on clouds as we go wandering through the streets, trying to imagine how my father felt walking through the same streets all those years ago. As it gets dark the window displays of fabulous dresses and elegant shoes with fine, delicate straps, looking like exotic insects, are suddenly ablaze with light and, like them, all my dreams light up. Once more I feel that anything is possible.

The next day we are transported to Naples, on another crowded train, to board the ship for Haifa. The ship is called *Artza* and is full to the brim with refugees from Hungary, Romania, Egypt, Iran, India and Ethiopia; hundreds of people have to sleep on deck. Rumour has it that *Artza* has capsized a number of times already; God only knows how it manages not to sink this time, with all of us aboard. The Hebrew word for immigration *(aliya)* means 'to go up', or 'spiritual ascent' but, at the moment, it feels like basic physical survival to me. I don't feel I'm coming home to Israel. I wish I did, but I am too busy rejecting my Jewishness. I felt unaccepted as a Jew in Russia and I don't want to be accepted now in Israel, just because I am Jewish.

My mother and I are given a cabin below the water line and have to share it with Kzystof and his mother. Both mothers are bursting with indignation,

"Whoever heard of a boy and a girl in the same cabin? Unacceptable! Unheard of!"

"Who around here can speak English?" asks his mother through the noise of the ventilating fans.

"Go and speak to the captain," orders my mother.

I get as far as the good looking Italian purser, who bursts out laughing at my mother's request: "Look around you," he says, "look how many people have to sleep on deck; you'll have to make do with what you've got; tell your mother she has a beautiful daughter."

In the evening *Artza* begins its voyage to Haifa, gliding slowly and smoothly out of the harbour, leaving the lights of Naples in the distance. I am euphoric as I stand on deck looking out to sea for the first time in my life, caressed by the soft, gentle Mediterranean air. Joy and certainty are in my heart that I am going to be discovered by a film director, meet my soul mate and wear beautiful dresses and shoes, just like the ones in the Viennese shop windows. The sea is calm, the ship is moving smoothly and I naively expect it to be like that all the way to Haifa. To my surprise the sea becomes choppy and the ship starts rolling from side to side and nose diving. We are now in open sea, exciting and scary.

I want to stay out on deck all night, drink in the sea air and flirt with the journalist, but my mother insists I come down to the airless cabin, where the roar of the ship's engines, combined with the racket of the massive ventilation fans, is deafening. Anticipating being seasick, both mothers choose the bottom bunks to have easy access to the bucket provided, leaving the top bunks to Kzystof and me. For the whole journey all he can do is reach out and touch me while I move seductively under the covers, imitating Brigitte Bardot in '*Une Parisienne*', accompanied by seasick groans coming from our mothers.

And so we pass our four days and nights at sea. On the last morning, standing on deck, we see land emerging in the far distance, coming gradually closer and closer! This is Haifa, the sea port in the north of Israel, at the point where the Mediterranean Sea touches Mount Carmel. The view is breath-taking, like pictures of heaven; the air unfamiliarly warm and humid.

There's no time to dwell on the new impressions in the hustle of having to gather our belongings and joining the long queue stretching to the desk where a clerk sits, allocating people to different jobs in the city or to a *kibbutz*, before we disembark. I have a vague idea that a *kibbutz* is a collective community and once you live there you become a *kibbutznik*, you don't own anything and children belong to everyone.

Queuing with all the other refugees and waiting to be allocated, instantly deflates my joyful mood and my dreams of a glamorous life. My mother notices it and whispers to me: "Don't worry; I'll say that we are going to stay with relatives, they'll let us through." And they do. Kzystof and his mother go their own way; we exchange phone numbers, promising to meet in Tel Aviv, but we never see each other again.

Mother and I move in with cousin Bella and her family; Bella with whom I share childhood memories of hunger and of wolves howling in the night in different tones and varying pitches, during the war in the Tatar Republic.

Being a Jew amongst other Jews doesn't change anything for me; I've been repressed and manipulated as a human being by the Stalinist regime and my mother's anxious efforts to inhibit any spontaneity, so I've become incapable of relating to myself or to others whether they are Jews or Eskimos. I feel an outsider. I fantasise about being 'discovered' and becoming rich and famous; my main drive is 'to show them', 'them' who don't respect me, don't recognise me for who I am. I myself don't know who I am. Although the free spirit in me is always ready to burst into song and dance, in my mother's mind this is associated with promiscuity, so it takes a lifetime to let go of the guilt and fear and claim my right to joy and freedom, approved or not.

When I pass a group of young men in the street of Tel Aviv, instead of throwing snow balls at me and calling me 'dirty Yid', like they did in Russia, they give me wolf whistles and call out *'Eizo Khatikha!'* – 'What a piece!' It sounds like a compliment but it doesn't make me feel like I belong in Israel any more than in Russia, or anywhere else for that matter. I still lack confidence and walk 'as if my legs don't belong to me'; I still press my arms tightly to my body because I am so self-conscious of my body odour and have never heard of deodorant. When Bella takes me aside and discreetly tells me that I most certainly need it, to cover up my embarrassment I obstinately refuse to believe that rubbing something sticky under my armpits can possibly stop me from being smelly. I give in eventually and, to my astonishment, it works!

At the South African Embassy, where we go to apply for our visas, a young man takes the opportunity to chat me up by offering to help with our immigration forms. His name is Jacques Politi. He is an Egyptian Jew and he has dark skin. My mother's exasperation at her cruel fate goes into overdrive: here we are in Israel, where the chances of meeting 'a nice Jewish boy' are higher than anywhere in the world, and I go and meet a Jewish boy who turns out to be black. And this after I've already lost my virginity to a *goy … oy*! She whispers in my ear in horror: "He is a *schwartze*!"

Jacques' family are Egyptian Jews. His father is a doctor so they are housed in a temporary settlement for professional immigrants. Jacques takes me there one day when his family are out and, in spite of anxiety that his parents might come back at any moment and that my mother is forever watching me, I have my first orgasm.

Drifting aimlessly, I accept an offer to model a bikini for a fashion photographer that Jacques introduces me to. Having to keep it secret from my mother, I lock myself in the bathroom to get the hair off my legs and make a bikini line. An overwhelming stench of depilatory cream, like rotten eggs, fills the whole flat. Mother, who never lets me lock the bathroom door, starts banging and demanding: "What are you doing in there? Why is the door locked?"

Absurdly the bikini factory's manager is a little orthodox man with a long beard and sideburns tucked under his skullcap. His eyes pop out when I appear from behind the curtain in a bikini, exuding whiffs of depilatory cream. He comes up to me, his head on my breasts and his glasses sliding down his nose. I move back and say: "Aren't you afraid God will punish you?"

"Not if he punishes us together," he giggles, leering at me.

The photos appear in some obscure magazine and are so grainy that I'm barely recognisable and, anyway, my mother doesn't get to see them.

After a year we receive our visas and at last we are on our way to South Africa. I cry all the way from Tel Aviv to Cape Town. Losing my father and being constantly uprooted all through the war has made me unable to deal with change and separation. I'm twenty-two, suffocated by my mother's control and, at the same time, clinging to her for security. I do feel pangs of remorse that I haven't told Jacques the date of our departure.

In Nairobi, where we stop for refuelling, I walk by myself in the waiting lounge, and have a moment of feeling free, like a proper international traveller. It is the first time I see black African people except for a Russian propaganda film we were shown at school, where Paul Robeson walks arm in arm with a blonde Russian actor singing together:

Wide is our beloved country
Many forests, fields and rivers it contains
I don't know another land in the world
Where a man can breathe so freely.

If we could breathe so freely why were we in a state of constant fear and anxiety? In those days we were so submerged in fear that we didn't know we were in it, like a fish doesn't know that it's in water.

The uncle of my dreams

As the train pulls into Cape Town station, my mother hangs out of the window, her eyes, like two search lights, looking out for her beloved brother. Suddenly she whispers breathlessly: "Isaac" ... and there on the platform is 'the rich and childless Uncle of my dreams', who my mother said, was going to be like a father to me, was going to buy me a dress the colour of the blue sky and, when I grew up, a sports car and a leather suit and a cap. One look at him and my heart sinks. He does look handsome and distinguished, but his face has an empty, vacant expression. He recognises my mother and puts his hand up in greeting, like the Queen.

My mother and I carry our suitcases off the train onto the platform and at last my mother is embracing her favourite brother. I suppose, like the Queen, he doesn't carry money either, because we have to walk about a mile from the station to his house, *shlepping* the suitcases, containing a few clothes and the two sheets and pillowcases that have followed us all the way from Moscow. My mother and I left Israel with four jersey suits; we each had a black one and a purple one. For our arrival in Cape Town she's wearing the black one and I'm wearing the purple one. We totter along in our high-heeled shoes; the heels on mine are loose, so they wobble, and the sweltering Cape Town sun is definitely not for jersey suits.

In Moscow I was proud to receive postcards from my uncle and be able to read them in English. One was of

Muizenberg Beach on the Indian Ocean, with a line of colourful bathing huts; an arrow, pointing to a yellow hut, said 'our hut', another arrow, pointing to a house, said, 'our house'. And then followed the heartening words: "You'll forget all your suffering and deprivation when you step onto our land of sunshine and plenty". The wide steps to the International Post office in Moscow were studded with pigeons and Georgian men eyeing the passing women. I enjoyed being the object of the Georgians' flashing eyes when I went, full of hope for a bright future, to write a reply to my Uncle.

On the way to his house I recognise the view from the postcard: the ocean, the white beach with tiny figures of swimmers dotted here and there, the multi-coloured changing huts and my uncle's house on the main road, overlooking the sea. As soon as we enter the house a gloom hits me that can only compete with the Mausoleum of Lenin and Stalin in the Red Square, which I visited for the first time before leaving Russia for good. I was just in time to have a look at Stalin lying side-by-side with Lenin in their glass tombs, before Stalin's body was taken out of the Mausoleum in the middle of the night, cremated and the ashes buried near the Kremlin wall along with the 'lesser mortals'.

A few minutes after arriving, my uncle asks me: "How is your English?"

"English my best subject was," I proudly announce.

He corrects me, peering at me over his glasses: "In English you have to put the verb after the noun – 'English was my best subject.' You and I are going to speak English together; you need to practice." He continues, enunciating each syllable very carefully for my benefit: "My wife and I in-tend to leave all our prop-er-ty to char-i-ties ... be-cause we don't want rel-a-tives eag-er-ly a-wai-ting our death."

For a moment, my pride in understanding English overrides the fact that, after two years of travelling thousands of miles, and a lifetime of dreaming of my rich Uncle, here he is informing me that he's made sure I have no vested interest in his death.

At dinner they talk about the rising price of tinned sardines; for dessert tinned peaches in sugary syrup are served. I wonder what has happened to all that exotic fresh fruit he promised in the postcards. My uncle and aunt fire their black maid, *'can't trust dem, zee drunken rubbish ...'*, and my mother takes her place in the kitchen. They put a lock on the telephone to stop me, who doesn't know a soul in Muizenberg, from making too many phone calls, and my Aunt locks the fridge and carries the key in her bra.

"Don't worry, we've been through worse," says my mother, "Everything is going to be all right."

"Vie should shpeek Einglish together," suggests my aunt, in a garbled mixture of Yiddish, Russian, Polish and English, *"Hau oild arr ye?"*

"Twenty-two," I say.

"Not mutz taim to bee tzoozy," she says, raising the crookedly painted eyebrows zigzagging over her milky-blue eyes. She trots off into the bedroom on her platform heels and returns with a handbag made of transparent plastic with crisscross embroidered cloth showing through. She holds it enticingly in front of me, *"if yu shud get merid soon I giv ye dis bag for ai presint, I boit it in Bruklin."*

I rush into the bathroom, look in the mirror and, scrutinising the area around my eyes, notice a tiny new line in the corner of my right eye that wasn't there before. That's when I start lying about my age.

Out of the frying pan – into the fire

Before I came to South Africa I had never heard the word 'apartheid'. Having been forced to read newspapers at school and attend totalitarian political meetings, I didn't want to have anything to do with politics. And now, here I was, living under the apartheid regime and unable to avoid seeing the cruel injustice of it all around me; out of the frying pan – into the fire. There were signs: 'Whites Only' – in English and Afrikaans – painted on the park benches and on train coaches and buses; all the banks and post offices had separate entrances. The vast beautiful Muizenberg beach on the Indian Ocean was for whites only, the blacks and 'coloureds' were only allowed to walk through with a box around their necks shouting 'lolly-pop, ice-cream, lolly-pop, ice-cream'. After being part of the oppressed minority in Russia, I'd become 'the privileged white minority' in South Africa; well, at least until some jerk at a party told me that I had 'Jewish legs'. Jewish legs?

I was embarrassed by my 'white' status and yet, I have to confess to the initial relief of not being the one who is oppressed. That is how a crazy policy of segregation gets under one's skin insidiously and becomes passively accepted as part of everyday life. Fortunately I just could not become a white South African 'Madam'; like Groucho Marx, 'I would not belong to a club that would have me as a member.'

Besides the black and white divide, people were segregated further into Black, Coloured and Indian, with a perversely dehumanising variation in the degree of their oppression. I watched how 'Cape-coloured' people were bunched together into a police van with bars on the windows, arrested for hanging out in the streets and getting drunk, telling jokes, falling about laughing and being jolly.

The day after New Year I stand on the balcony of my Uncle's house, watching in amazement as a wave of Cape-coloured men, women and children in dazzling costumes, singing and playing penny whistles, dance past. My Aunt comes out and says: "*Akh*, what do you need to watch these drunken *shwartze* thieves?" She makes me go inside and locks the door of the balcony, as if these people, with every fibre in their bodies swinging to the rhythms of the music, have nothing better to do than try to steal her miserable belongings.

The dream of a lifetime turns out to be an instant disappointment. Thank God for the mercy of tears. Besides bringing immediate relief from stress, tears also release toxins; tears from sorrow have a different chemical content to tears from peeling an onion. Experiments confirm that emotional tears help the body regain its balance after stress, which in turn allows the systems of the body to maintain the state of wellness. I don't know what experiments they did to arrive at that conclusion but I could have told them that from personal experience.

Cape Carnival – A sea of colour

One day life unexpectedly changes for the better. Libby, the chair lady of the Liberal Women of Muizenberg, involved in refugee charity work, makes me one of her charity cases and, to help me enter the Muizenberg social network, introduces me to her nephew Etienne. While walking with him along the seafront one evening, he points out a house with a red light in the window and sounds of an accordion playing. I say dreamily: "I wish I knew people like that." Etienne makes a theatrical bow: "Your wish is granted!" dashes up the steps and knocks on the door. A woman in her late forties, with dark, expressive eyes and grey hair framing a vivacious face, opens the door and exclaims in a strong French accent: "Etienne! Come on in. Introduce me to your charming friend."

Charming? Does she mean me?

We enter a softly lit living room with men and women sitting on cushions on the floor. My mother's voice in my head is saying, 'What sort of people sit on the floor? Only dogs sit on the floor.' A man is playing the accordion and a slim, striking woman all dressed in black, with short, straight, dark hair, is dancing seductively to the haunting French tune, *'Petite fleur'*.

Simone and Charles are Belgian Jews who, after hiding in cellars during the four-year occupation by the Nazis, immigrated to South Africa and opened a quaint little jewellery shop in Fishhoek, where they made and sold jewellery.

The next day the phone rings and, surprise, surprise, it's for me! Simone inviting me for dinner: "Charles is on his way to pick you up." Feeling too shy to accept an invitation so soon, I try to find an excuse: "I can't, I must wash my hair."

"You can wash your hair tomorrow, or you can wash it here."

I start seeing them nearly every night, wishing I could move out of my Uncle's mausoleum of misery and live with them. Besides being a French gourmet cook, who makes the finest *coq au vin* and *pomme fritte*, Simone loves life and people. Just to go with her to Kalk Bay harbour on the False Bay coast to buy fish from the Cape-Coloured fishermen is an adventure. She explains to me that the term Cape-Coloured refers to the modern-day descendants of slave labourers imported into South Africa by Dutch settlers; they are of mixed race, their mother tongue is Afrikaans, but they also speak English.

Simone and I stand at the harbour watching the fishermen returning from their hard day's fishing trip, pulling in their brightly coloured boats, unloading their catch. As soon as they see Simone, quick-witted banter starts flying from both sides. She buys *snoek* – which couldn't come any fresher – prawns and crayfish, all the while exchanging jokes and pranks. Then we go back to her place to prepare the evening meal.

Through Simone and Charles, I discover what the Cape Coon Carnival is all about. Every year, on the second of January, known as the Second New Year, this unique festival explodes onto the streets of Cape Town. It's an opportunity, once a year, for the Cape Coloured and other mixed race people to be unreservedly jolly and express their talents and exuberance without being arrested. They sing songs originating from their fathers and forefathers who came here as slaves from Indonesia. Song and dance is the way they can release their indignation.

The Carnival is inspired by the American minstrel shows; like them white face make-up is worn. The atmosphere of anticipation for the Carnival is in the air for months. Despite the poverty the 'coons' live in, every spare penny is saved for expensive satin fabrics and frills to make their costumes glamorous and impeccably coordinated in dazzling primary colours. They write new songs about contemporary issues and create new dances with intricate footwork.

They dance through the streets, turning Cape Town into a sea of colour and rhythm, splendour and gaiety. I go with Simone and Charles and other friends to watch the procession. These brilliant, graceful, imaginatively dressed people are so much more alive and stylish than us whites. I wish I could look and move like them. I'm so inhibited and they're so free and yet, they're considered inferior and have to call us 'madam' or '*baas*'.

Simone and Charles, having been victims of persecution themselves, are outraged about District Six, the suburb where the majority of coloured people lived, being declared a white area under the Group areas Act of 1950. All the houses in District Six were flattened by bulldozers and sixty thousand people were forcibly removed to barren outlying areas, which became known as the Cape Flats. District Six was situated within sight of the docks and one of the reasons for removal given by Government officials was that the district was a vice den, rife with gambling, drinking and prostitution. But most people knew that they wanted the district because it was close to the city centre and the harbour.

In London in 2004 I was deeply moved when I read that Nelson Mandela had handed the keys of new homes to the first returning residents of District Six: Ebrahim Murat, 87 and Dan Ndzabla, 82. Later 4000 families returned.

Simone's little jewellery shop in Simonstown becomes my refuge. It has a constant flow of people coming to hang out and drink her very special *café-au-lait*. One of her friends, a camp, elegant young German hairdresser, works in a salon next door and in his lunch break comes to talk to Simone about his love life. Like me, Ralph Krall is twenty-two, a refugee and a Pisces. Eventually he also meets my mother and becomes our hairdresser and a close friend, endlessly amused by my stories about my mother, which is what I mostly talk about, and by my mother's stories about me, which is all she talks about.

This reminds me of the one about the two Jewish mothers sitting in a café; one says, 'My son really loves me, he bought me a condominium, he takes me to the theatre once a week and to the opera once a month.' The other woman says, 'Ah, this is nothing, my son pays two hundred dollars an hour to the best shrink in New York and what does he talk about all the time? Me!'

I'm from Russia and I want to make a record

I always loved singing, performing and making people laugh. In our one room in Russia, when I was left on rare occasions, alone at home, I'd prop up a hand mirror on a chair and stand in front of it singing gypsy songs to an imaginary audience. It was new to me the way Simone and her friends unreservedly encouraged all creativity, cheering and applauding and laughing at my antics. This gives me the *chutzpah* to walk into a recording studio in Cape Town, straight from the beach, with my dress clinging to my body over my wet bathing suit, hair full of sea and sand, and announce: "I'm from Russia and I want to make a record."

"Have you made a record before?"

"No."

"Do you have an accompanist?"

"No."

"Do you have the music?"

"No."

"So how do you propose to make a record?"

"I thought you might have someone here who plays the piano and can improvise. Oh, please I have to make this record."

The guy looks at me as though I'm crazy, but seeing that I'm not about to give up says: "Come to think of it, one of our recording technicians plays the piano," and the receptionist adds: "I'll do the cover."

So they do the whole thing for nothing in one afternoon. I sing six Russian songs, three on each side. *'Do not awaken my memories'* is the title of the album, printed dramatically in black next to a large black treble clef on a plain white sleeve.

Hugging the record close to my heart, I run out of the studio, onto the train and to Simone's jewellery shop. Without saying a word I go straight to her record player and put the record on. Even though it never makes it beyond Fishhoek's bohemian community, watching Simone's face at that moment light up into the most surprised and loving smile is a treat worth every bit of this outlandish effort. Life has never been better! Until...

A parade of men

My uncle and aunt demand that I stay home to meet a parade of men, as they start introducing my mother to the widowers they play bridge with, and me to their sons and nephews. It doesn't take much to figure out that, having done the *mitzvah* of bringing out 'the poor widow with the orphan' from Russia, they are most eager to marry us both off. I suppose that's fair enough; having 'saved us', what are they supposed to do with us next? According to them I am 'fussy and difficult', but my mother, like a martyr, heaves a deep sigh, accepts widower Beni's proposal and tells me she is doing it for me.

Since I still believe that 'only my mother will take my shit', I follow her, like a sleepwalker, into her new husband's home in Vredehoek. It is not more than thirty miles away from Kalk Bay, but when I say goodbye to Simone and Charles I cry bitterly, as though I'm going back to Russia and leaving them forever. The spell, that I am useless and helpless, hasn't yet lifted. After that I rarely see Simone and Charles.

In the new home with her third husband my mother takes me aside and starts whispering.

"Why are you whispering? We are alone." I'm barely able to hold back my fury,

"*Akh*, you never know, the walls have ears. Listen to me carefully. I told Beni that I was only married once before – to your father."

"What about Grisha?"

"Don't ever mention him."

"What about all the photographs of the three of us together?"

"I burnt them."

"Burnt them? What about me and you in them?"

"I cut Grisha out and said mice ate them."

"Why?"

"Why? Don't be a fool. He doesn't need to know about everything. Believe me, you listen to me, I was married only once before."

"What do you mean? How can you pretend Grisha never existed?"

"*Akh,* you don't understand; you are still young."

My room overlooks Table Mountain with the Jewish old age home at the foot of it. My mother comes into my room in the mornings to take her insulin tablets, cursing the day she was born.

"What's the matter?"

"*Akh, in drerd,* I have to hide the insulin tablets from him."

"Why?"

"You listen to me. It's better he knows nothing."

Beni keeps asking me: "What's the matter with your mother, why does she never eat a cake, a chocolate? When we go to *bioscope* I want to buy her an ice cream. She always says no, *akh,* a strange woman."

The phone never rings. If it does, it's Beni's lawyer or the wrong number. The doorbell never rings. If it does, it's the milkman.

I ask: "What happened to *Chazzen* Kusevitsky?" Nobody answers.

Cantor Kusevitsky from the local synagogue came on many occasions to visit with his wife Zelda. My mother would serve tea and her special homemade apple cake.

They would sit on the sofa, the plastic cover of which would be removed for the occasion, but the lamp shade remained covered in plastic, God forbid some dust should settle on it.

Then they would ask my mother to tell her story about two Jewish guys listening to the beautiful voice of the cantor in the synagogue: the one guy says, 'What a magnificent voice.' The other guy says, '*Nu*, if I had his voice, I would also sing like him!' And no matter how many times they heard the story it always made them laugh.

"So what happened to *Chazzen* Kusevitsky?" I insist.

"Till my dying day," Beni darts a hateful look in my direction, "I am not speaking to him."

"Why?"

"When I went to Israel last Passover, I asked to borrow a suitcase. Do you think he let me have it? I might need it, he said. *Ay*, till my dying day may my eyes never see him again."

There is one painting in Beni's flat. It is of a blue windmill, surrounded by green trees and it hangs on the wall above the couch. I keep looking at it, trying to figure out why it is so flat and boring. My mother notices me looking and whispers: "Beni's son, the lawyer from Johannesburg, sent it; he did it himself. It's painting by numbers. But don't tell anybody."

There's a Russian proverb: 'Grass perishes, iron rusts, and secrets and lies devour the soul.'

As for her brother Isaac, after a lifetime of longing to see him again, they end up not speaking for the next fifteen years. My mother keeps shrugging her shoulders in disbelief: "*Agh*, he's gone *mishuge* ... it's all because of his wife; he's gone mad; he thinks Frank Sinatra has nothing better to do than read the film script he sent to him. A film script he wrote – *agh*, totally *mishuge*!" The next time brother and sister speak is when he phones to tell my mother that he is seriously ill.

"Shall I come and visit you?" she asked.

"That won't be necessary," he replied.

He died the following month.

Despair

> 'Suicide was not in my nature. I was too completely swayed by the sense that I was in the grasp of unknown forces to believe in my power of self-release.'
>
> – George Eliot in *The Lifted Veil*

I cry every day. I thought that crying every day was the most normal thing to do. I cried every day begging God for help. Not that I knew anything about God, or about prayer. God was a forbidden word at school in the suburb of Moscow. Campaign against religion was at its height in the Soviet schools. A girl in my class, whose grandmother was seen to cross herself, was rejected by the other children who wouldn't play with her anymore.

The vague resonances of Jewish religion reached me through my mother when she'd cover her head with a handkerchief and light candles for Shabbat in an atmosphere of fear, muttering something under her breath, her face in her hands. She'd emerge from these prayers optimistic for a few minutes: "God will help us." I wanted to latch onto those moments, to feel that everything would be all right, but the heavy oppressive atmosphere was always waiting, robbing me of my natural right to joy, leaving me disconnected from my inner world and the guiding voice within. So when I said, "Please God," it was only a figure of speech.

My tears and supplications came from sheer despair and

frustration at my predicament: feeling utterly miserable living with my mother and second stepfather, and at the same time unable to move away, my mother's words, 'you are helpless and useless', ringing like tinnitus in my head. I even went on holiday with them, feeling like I was being driven to my execution.

My stepfather Beni, my mother and I are in the car on the way to Muizenberg. I can see from the back seat that Beni's eyes are only just above the steering wheel of his Oldsmobile, even with the extra cushion under his bottom. There is a deadly silence in the car interrupted only by, *'sonofabitch, luk ver ye goyink, dont know hou to draiv'.*

I sit in the back, contemplating opening the car door and falling out, but Beni drives too slowly for me to die; I probably would just become crippled and be condemned to live with them forever. I don't really want to die but thinking of death is my only consolation.

Every morning I get up before sunrise and go to the beach; I can't swim yet so I splash in the shallow water and then run in the gale force south-easterly wind, hoping to catch pneumonia and die. Even in my suicidal state I can't resist picking out my uncle's house and my uncle's yellow changing hut on the beach that were, not so long ago in Moscow, the source of hope for a glamorous future.

I don't catch pneumonia but I do get a hell of a fever and my recurrent sore throat, which at this stage provides the only relief from my constant, tormenting anxiety: when I have a sore throat, my mother temporarily suspends her customary criticism. While I'm lying in bed a memory from childhood surfaces: high fever, constricted throat, vague images of my father, my mother's worried face, hovering over me, and her hand putting a damp cloth on my burning forehead.

My mother, in her usual panic whenever I get ill, calls a doctor. I don't want a doctor. I want somebody to come over to visit, like other people have visitors, to lighten the atmosphere, talk, and tell stories and jokes.

I don't die and Beni, mother and I drive, in the same old Oldsmobile, back to Vredehoek. Soon after that I find a job as a switchboard operator at the Jewish Board of Deputies, which all of us working there call 'The Jewish Boredom of Deputies'. I spend days trying to figure out how to operate the switchboard and connect the phone calls to the right person, while dreaming of being discovered.

One day the phone rings and when I manage to connect the call, after furiously fumbling with the wires of the switchboard, it's my mother, her voice sounding unusually elated: "Don't worry, it is good news. I found your father's sister in New York. I didn't tell you but I put an advertisement in the *Jewish New Yorker* in the column, 'Looking for relatives lost in the war'. *Nu*, we have to believe, miracles do happen; your Aunt Dora saw the advertisement and replied. She said it was so small she needed a magnifying glass to read it, but she read it. It's fate."

I wrote to my Aunt Dora, telling her about my father's death in the Siberian *gulag*, and our journey from Russia via Poland and Israel to South Africa. Two weeks later I received a letter from her with a return ticket to New York. I knew nothing about America; I remembered a documentary propaganda film we were shown at school called '*San Francisco, Chicago, New York*'. Decadent night clubs with jazz bands, lavishly dressed 'capitalist women and men' dancing, laughing, smoking cigarettes and drinking champagne; prostitutes hanging out in dark doorways; long queues of unemployed, beggars in the streets, emaciated men and women standing in breadlines while the sombre drone of the commentator emphasising 'the total lack of unemployment in Russia, and the absence of prostitution and crime.'

Going to New York to get discovered

I was forever trying to conjure up my father out of the stories my mother told me, 'if I take myself, subtract my mother, then what is left should be my father.' I kept looking at the few photographs we had of him with my mother before the war, her head resting on his shoulder, eyes a combination of longing and suffering, with him looking rather absent; another of him in Vienna, wearing an elegant suit and carrying his violin, and the one where I'm nine months old and he is standing behind me and holding my hands – the only photo of my father and I together. I often tried to imagine the sensation of his musician's hands holding mine. I've never seen a picture of him smiling. Did he ever laugh? Did he play with me? The prospect of meeting my father's sister in New York was the stuff of fairy tales. My imagination went wild, 'my Aunt will be like my father, glamorous and musical, with connections in artistic circles. I'm going to be *discovered* and be in movies.'

So here I am – on the plane to New York. This is my second time flying, and my first time alone, since the flight with my mother from Tel Aviv to Cape Town two years previously. Wearing a trench coat and big sunglasses, *a la* Audrey Hepburn in *'Breakfast at Tiffany's'*, a present from Simone, I sit next to two American businessmen who keep telling jokes, which takes my mind off my fear of flying.

"How do you order an extra dry martini?" asks one.

"You tell the barman to pour the gin and whisper over it 'vermouth'," replies the other, and both roar with laughter.

I don't understand the joke as I've never heard of martinis but I laugh too and, trying my best to appear sophisticated, drink the three martinis the guys offer me one after another. When dinner is served just one whiff of the food makes me lunge forward and throw up into the airsickness bag, after which I remain bent over with my head between my knees throughout the meal.

I expect the excitement of New York to start straight away, from the moment I land at Idlewild airport in my Audrey Hepburn disguise. I watch the other relatives and friends meet up and go off in little groups until all that remains is my Aunt Dora and her husband, Hersh. She, a little woman with tearful blue eyes and an air of woe, hugs me. He, a bulky man with a face like a frog, eyes set far apart, lips curling upwards at the corners, and glasses sitting on the end of his turned up nose, shakes hands with me, turning his shoulders sideways and looking at me askance. Dora says: "Don't worry about him, he's a bit shy, he'll get used to you."

On the way to their flat there are none of the skyscrapers I expected to see in New York; we drive through dull suburban streets that could be anywhere in the world. When we finally arrive in Brooklyn, Dora tells me that they both work in a sock factory, and points out the high-rise block of flats for factory workers, where they live. My elated heart sinks all the way down into my Audrey Hepburn pumps.

In their one-bedroom flat my aunt shows me the sofa in the living room where I'm going to sleep. As my Aunt promised, it doesn't take long before Hersh 'gets used to me'; on my first morning I wake up and find him on his knees next to my bed, stroking me over the covers. I scream. He jumps up: "If you don't like it you must tell me. I'm an amateur photographer, I thought you might like to pose for me in the nude, I have contacts with magazines." My aunt is in the shower and doesn't hear me scream, those American showers are very strong and noisy. Husband Hersh remains as weird as my first impression of him, but he never tries anything like that again.

While they are at work, I stay at home, watch *'I love Lucy'* and dream of being discovered. My clothes are popping at the seams from all the double thick chocolate malts from the ice cream machine outside the compound, but I still insist that I am size twelve.

Then I meet my mother's family; her brother Nathan, who left Russia with his young wife after the Revolution and now lives with her and their son and daughter in the Bronx. Next door to them lives my mother's sister Sonya, with her four adult children living nearby. The story goes that after the war ended, her husband, the boorish ex-mill owner, dug up the gold he had hidden, and managed to get to America with his family, driven by dreams of the land of opportunity where the streets are paved with gold. "*Nu*, the poor *schlimazel* realised his Great American Dream; he opened a coin laundromat in the Bronx and died of cancer a year later," is how my mother described it. So for the first few months I travel between Brooklyn and the Bronx, still not seeing any skyscrapers. I also don't see any prostitutes in dark doorways or unemployment queues and beggars littering the streets.

There is an air of *shidakh,* matchmaking, around; my relatives are determined to marry me off so that I can settle down ... like dust. Uncle Nathan tries to set me up with Shlomo, an orthodox Jewish lingerie manufacturer. He wears a *yarmulke,* has a big belly, takes me only to kosher restaurants and won't press the elevator button on a Saturday, but if I press it, it's ok ... and I find him sexually irresistible. My burst of sexual freedom can only be attributed to having an ocean between me and my mother for the first time in my life. But my euphoria soon vanishes when late one afternoon we drive over Brooklyn Bridge in Shlomo's brand new Cadillac. It's an early spring evening, just after sunset; the light is disappearing between the buildings of the Manhattan skyline and, as if that's not enough to press all my romantic buttons, Frank Sinatra's voice is on the car radio, singing, *'I'm a fool to love you'*. I look at Shlomo, wanting to share the magic of the moment. He looks straight ahead and announces importantly: "Next year I'm exchanging my Cadillac for a new model; they depreciate rapidly."

Things look up when my cousin Selma introduces me to her friend, Masha, whose father owns a toy factory and who lives in a house overlooking Manhattan Beach. She has been educated at Vassar, has her own Corvette convertible, a present from her father for her twenty-fifth birthday; her clothes come from Bergdorf Goodman and she's just as lost as I am. Masha's parents invite me to stay with them for a while and offer me a room in their luxurious house. To swim first thing in the morning, sit on the terrace with the view of the sea having a leisurely breakfast with Masha, is sheer bliss.

Masha never remembers wanting anything and I never remember not wanting everything. She envies me my capacity to want: "As soon as a new toy appeared at my father's factory it was delivered to my playroom, which was already full of toys," she says with sadness in her voice. When I tell her how we starved when I was a little girl she says: "Do you mean you didn't even have any tinned food in the larder?"

"What's a larder?"

It reminds me of the joke about an American, a Russian, a Chinese and an Israeli meeting at a World Food Supplies Conference. A reporter comes up and asks:

> *"Excuse me, what's your opinion on the shortage of meat?"*
> *The American: "What's shortage?"*
> *The Chinese: "What's opinion?"*
> *The Israeli: "What's 'excuse me'?"*
> *The Russian: "What's meat?"*

When I see Masha watching me with tender curiosity, enjoying everything in New York and finding it new and exciting, even a supermarket filled with so many varieties of food, she looks like an adult watching a deprived child in a toy shop. She says my enjoyment lifts her out of inertia and *ennui*, reviving her enthusiasm, so she invites me to spend a holiday with her at Lake George in the Adirondacks.

I'm not familiar with anything resembling lasting happiness but I'm sure capable of bursts of joy; it fills me with delight to speed in Masha's convertible with the top down, through breathtaking scenery, on this beautiful autumn day. We arrive at the hotel overlooking the lake at sunset and check into our room, which has the most glorious view of the lake. Masha suggests that we don't go downstairs for dinner, but stay in our room and order room service – another luxury I've never heard of.

We spend the days walking and rowing and the evenings having dinner in our room and talking, talking, talking late into the night. One evening we decide to dress up, Masha in her Chanel and me in my Audrey Hepburn, and venture downstairs to the dining hall where there's a live band playing. No sooner do we sit down than we're invited to dance.

After whirling me round and round the dance floor to a foxtrot, which he says was invented by the vaudeville comedian Harry Fox, my partner declares: "I'm a photographer. You're so beautiful I'd like to take pictures of you and send them to Hollywood. Shall we go to my room? I'll show you my camera, it's very professional."

Wow, everything's coming my way! I came to New York to get discovered! I didn't yet know that if things are coming your way you might be in the wrong lane, just like the Russian lunatic driving on the motorway: his mother calls telling him to be careful as she heard on the news that there is some lunatic driving the wrong way. The son replies, 'yes, and not one, there are lots of them!'

Before long, *this* Russian lunatic is sitting in the nude, with a kerchief tied under her chin, looking seductively at the camera. The camera clicks and clicks and I turn this way and that. Suddenly, before I can say '*Vanka, vstanka*', he's in the nude too with his dark hairy chest and a gigantic erection. The camera clicks, his erection bobs, and I keep on turning this way and that, looking at the camera upon his request.

All of a sudden he puts the camera back in its case and approaches me with his bobbing erection: "Shall we take a rest?" he says in a husky Marlon Brando voice. I stretch my arms in front of me in self-defence: "Oh no!", and am relieved when he doesn't insist. I watch in disbelief as he runs to the basin, turns the tap on and sprinkles cold water on his penis, then runs back to me doing high knee bends, like a soldier in the army doing his training exercises. He does this a few times, sprinting to the tap and back to me, looking at me quizzically, in case it turns me on, and, not finding any encouragement, gives up. We get dressed and go downstairs where Masha is sitting at our table all alone wondering what happened to me.

Later in our room, we nearly wet our pants laughing when I impersonate him running to and from the cold water tap, and tell Masha '*Vanka, vstanka*' means *Vanka*, stand up!

At the Village Gate, in Greenwich Village, where we often go to listen to jazz, I meet a tall, skinny writer, dressed all in black, except for his white sneakers. He looks like Anthony Perkins, straight out of *Psycho.* The next day, at his invitation, pretending I'm super-cool in moss green corduroy trousers and a matching ribbed jumper, I take the subway to his beatnik pad in Greenwich Village. That's where I first hear about the ancient Chinese philosophy of The Tao. He tells me to read the Tao Te Ching in order to realise the unity of life – a way of being which is based on not forcing, not obstructing, not getting in one's own way – going with the flow. It sounds totally new, yet strangely familiar, as if that knowledge is already somewhere deep within me and it's a matter of reconnecting with it.

But I still have many lessons to learn in the school of life and the Anthony Perkins look-alike soon gives me the opportunity when he suggests I give him a blowjob. I'm so disconnected from myself that I think I'm being cool to go with the flow and not resist; he ejaculates straight into my right eye. Later, sitting in the jazz club, wearing my Audrey Hepburn dark glasses to cover my bloodshot eye, he tells me that he is gay. My eye remains bloodshot for a week. Now, at the age of sixty-*few*, I can't help wondering whether that 'shot in the eye' has anything to do with the cataract in my right eye.

Then there is the guy who takes me out for a drink. On the way back his dilapidated old Chevy breaks down in the snow, so I invite him in, knowing that my Aunt and Uncle will be out. We have sex and, after he leaves at midnight, I am shocked to discover that he has left the condom inside me. I run round and round my Aunt's condominium trying to shake his sperm out of me.

I naively believed that America would greet me with open arms after my life in Stalinist Russia, but when I try to renew my visa I am refused. I even write to a member of Congress, telling him about my life of suffering and deprivation, but get no reply.

So I get engaged to Bernie Reitkoff, a salesman at Masha's father's toy factory. I don't think love or even fancy enters the equation; all I want is not to have to go back and live with my mother and stepfather and to prove to my mother that somebody will marry me and not throw me out a week later. The signs that our union is not exactly a match made in heaven are clear right from the start. Often when we arrange a date, he calls at the last moment to say that his mother has cooked a chicken and insists that he stay and eat dinner with her. She is suspicious of me as a candidate for her daughter-in-law and 'interrogates' me about my life in Russia: "What kind of friends could you have had in Russia? All *Goim*?" She is trying to say that I am not a proper Jewish girl for her *Boinie*, as she calls him.

I have to hand it to him and his instinct for self-preservation; it takes a little longer than the week my mother predicted but a few days before the wedding Bernie breaks off our engagement. I cry for three days and three nights, and it isn't for Bernie. In those tears is *all* the grief, *all* the pain, *all* the loss, *all* the hurt, *all* the humiliation from my past, plus exasperation about *all* the things in the present that are going wrong, and I don't understand why. I also cry for my glamorous Saks 5th Avenue black coat that was stolen from Bernie's car.

When my mother and stepfather arrive from South

Africa for the wedding, victorious that at last I have managed to find a husband, 'thanks be to God and in America *nokh*', instead of the wedding they attend an autopsy of the broken engagement, held by the gathered relatives.

Then my visa expires and I have to leave America. Trying to postpone my return to South Africa for as long as possible, I exchange my air ticket for a sea passage on the *Transvaal Castle* to Cape Town via Southampton, hoping, by some miracle, to be saved *en route* from having to go and live with my mother and stepfather again. I am still convinced that only a miracle can save someone as 'hopeless' as me. So I scheme: 'I'll have four days on the ship from New York to Southampton, then two days in London and, if nothing happens there, I'll still have two weeks on the ship to Cape Town. There'll be swimming, sunbathing, dressing up for dinner, dancing, star-studded nights on deck, I might even get invited to the captain's table.' Nothing happens during the four day crossing from New York, but hope is still in the air when I take the train to London and book myself into the Cumberland Hotel in Marble Arch.

On my way to dinner that evening I spot an attractive young man sitting on a loveseat sofa in the lounge. Feeling confident in my Bergdorf Goodman suit and high heels, a present from Masha, I sit down next to him; the sofa is S shaped, so the two seats face the opposite way from each other; my right shoulder is next to his right shoulder. He turns to look at me, smiles and says: "I'm Michele Kindinis, what is your name?"

"My name is Mina."

"Mina, would you like to join me for a drink?"

After the first sip of vodka I'm sure that God has at last sent me my soul mate, so I waste no time and ask if he's read *The Little Prince* by Saint Exupery, quoting the lines: "It is only with the heart that one can see rightly; what is essential is invisible to the eye". He says he hasn't.

"I'm from Paris, here on business," he says, "Would you like to have dinner with me?" Oh well, soul mate or no soul mate, he is full of that notorious French *charme* and, after a romantic dinner, I end up in bed with him in my habitually cut-off way.

In the morning he comes with me on the train to Southampton to see me off on my journey to Cape Town. The Bergdorf Goodman suit and high heels, which made me feel impeccably groomed and confident the night before, have lost their allure, and as we say goodbye before the embarkation, I have that familiar, hollow dishevelled feeling of 'the morning after the night before'.

Once the ship is out at sea my hope awakens again: surely anything can happen on this six thousand mile journey. On deck I have my eye on a young English photographer, but he has his eye on a very slim, young girl in a white bikini, who swims and dives beautifully. I can't swim, let alone dive and, after all the double thick chocolate malts in Brooklyn, I'm bursting out of my one piece swim suit. I have a picture of me at the fancy dress party on ship, standing by the bar, togged up as Carmen Miranda, with a basket of fruit on my head, an off the shoulder blouse, a red gypsy scarf on my hips and a rose in my teeth; in the background the photographer is snogging the slim girl on the dance floor, while I'm flirting with the barman, pretending I don't care.

But I've often found that, when I hit an all-time low, something comes to my rescue to sustain me; nothing I would call miraculous, but something that lifts my spirit just enough not to sink below sanity level. Maybe *that's* the miracle. This time, out of the blue, the steward brings me a telegram. It's from Michele Kindinis and it says: *'Les possibilite illimite'*. It's not that I'm dying to see him again; it's the fact that someone out there thinks of *me* in terms of unlimited possibilities that perks up my wilting spirit.

The next morning I sit on the sun deck after a dip in the pool, taking stock of my year in New York, and my thoughts go to the two major events that have happened during that year of 1962: the Cuban missile crisis, and the death of Marilyn Monroe.

Preoccupied as I was with my dreams of love, glamour and stardom, and more or less oblivious of anything else, surprisingly, I was aware that there was a Cuban missile crisis about to affect the world. I didn't know, or want to know, what the crisis was about, but when something as big as that is happening in the world and it's all over the newspapers, the radio and TV, it's impossible not to have some of it get through to you, no matter how a-political you feel, and how stuffed to the brim with wars and Soviet propaganda you are and how concerned you are with finding a safe place in the world and some personal satisfaction and recognition.

So in spite of my total lack of interest in politics, I knew that the main characters involved in the drama were Kennedy, Castro and Khrushchev. I heard that it was incumbent, (I was proud that I knew what 'incumbent' meant), upon John F. Kennedy and Premier Khrushchev to reach a compromise, because the Russians had installed nuclear missiles in Cuba and told Castro to use them if the U S invaded. Khrushchev then proposed removing the missiles if the U S would guarantee not to invade Cuba.

Was that 'cold' war? I hadn't recovered from the 'hot' one yet. I heard people saying that the world was on the brink of a third world war, but to me nothing could be worse than the second one. I was already shocked to the core by 'political events'. I just wanted a break from wars, I wanted to start living, for God's sake and I didn't even know how to do that. I didn't know how to relate to people and that's a big part of living. I was crap at it. Being totally absorbed with myself and my emotional survival didn't go hand in hand with making friends.

The Cuban crisis, *shmaisis*; in essence it is all about whose missiles could reach further, like schoolboys comparing whose penis is longer. Why don't we rather spend our time and energy on finding ways to live peacefully and in harmony?

But what did concern me, and still makes me sad and angry, were all the artists, writers, musicians, poets, composers and many other innocent people who'd been banished to *gulag* labour camps in Siberia by orders coming from our 'leader and protector', Yosif Vissarionovich Stalin. At first, after the revolution, the Soviets welcomed the most avant-garde forms of art; they had wanted to bring in the new and throw out the old with the execution of the Tsar. But that hadn't lasted long. Stalin's regime clamped down on nearly every means of self-expression. Committees were set up to judge artworks according to Soviet values. Anything that didn't glorify the socialist worker and the accomplishments of the Soviet state was considered 'decadent' and 'anti-democratic'. Everything personal was ruthlessly repressed. The artists, whose art expressed their efforts to keep body and soul together under the torture of Stalinist oppression, were either shot or sent to the *gulag*. The Great Russian poet, Anna Akhmatova described the terror of living and writing in the shadow of Stalin, 'They are arresting people for nothing.'

So I think I can be forgiven for hating history lessons and not giving a shit about having to remember what power-crazed megalomaniac won what from whom and on what date, because he shouldn't have been doing it in the first place.

Then, sitting on the sun deck, I remember being in a taxi, hearing on the news that Marilyn Monroe had died at the age of thirty-six and how deeply touched I felt, as if she was my close friend. The taxi driver said: "Good thing she died young, her audience can't imagine her growing old." I loved Marilyn Monroe and felt an affinity with her innate intelligence and vulnerability. I read an interview with her where she said how disappointed she'd be if, after a hard week's work, she saw a film where the acting was sloppy, and then had to wait for another week before she could see another film. This made her want to work hard to be really good in her films, because she wanted other people, who also worked hard the whole week, to have something to inspire them. She said, 'love and work are the most important things, one without the other not so good; work is a kind of love, I'm happiest when I portray a scene perfectly, I take pride in doing it as well as I can; I don't generally feel happy, I feel moments of happiness, mostly when I feel satisfied with my work ... if I feel anything generally, it is miserable.'

How misunderstood this vulnerable, highly sensitive, deeply intelligent woman must have felt if her iconic, seductive beauty was all that some people, like my taxi driver, thought her life was for.

The Jewish millionaire

After seven days at sea the *Transvaal Castle* glides into Cape Town harbour. I stand on deck wishing I could stay here forever and never have to disembark. I spot the little figures of my mother and stepfather waiting for me on shore and instantly feel trapped. If I'd been in touch with myself I could have imagined other possibilities than having to go and live with them again, but I couldn't, torn as I was between the desire to be free and my need to be protected, even if it was suffocating.

Walking towards them, savouring the last few moments of freedom before 'internment', I still get a kick out of my elegant new suit and my high heels click-clicking against the cobblestones. Beni is polite and cut-off in his usual manner, my mother has that distant dejected look especially reserved for me – a cocktail of pity mixed with exasperation, leaving no room for anything new. She kisses me on the mouth, then looks me up and down and says: "*Nu*, they don't have hairdressers in New York?"

And so I go on living with Beni and my mother in Vredehoek. And at dinner Beni spits fish bones into his plate just as before and tells the same two unmemorable jokes.

I get a job modelling coats in a factory owned by the notorious Robbi Brothers, the magnates of the Cape Town fashion world, and one day get invited to a party to meet a divorced, Jewish millionaire – the most eligible bachelor in Cape Town. As soon as he hears my Russian accent he tells me how fascinated he is by everything Russian. I milk my fascinating Russian accent for all its worth and at the end of the party he offers to drive me home in his red E type Jaguar and asks for my phone number.

I go to sleep elated and wake up in the morning with lightness in my heart. Wait till I tell my mother that I met a millionaire! After I blurt it out she looks at me in disbelief and starts wringing her hands and beseeching God: *"Alevai, Alevai* – it should only happen, may it come to pass." She becomes extra tender towards me and makes me pancakes for breakfast.

Sure enough, a few days later, when I come home from work, my mother greets me with respect, as if I've been awarded the Nobel Prize and tells me, reverently: *"He* called,"

I call back. He says: "Would you like to come for dinner at my place?"

Would I ever!

I feel like I'm 'a somebody' when he picks me up in his E-type Jag and takes me to his flat, sparsely decorated in Japanese style, with figures of geishas and samurais here and there. The black maid serves our meal and discreetly disappears into her quarters. After dinner we retire to his living room overlooking the Atlantic Ocean. Twinkling lights in the far distance are from Robben Island, where Nelson Mandela is in jail for life. In thirty years he will be released and tell the world that all the time he was in jail he refused to think negative thoughts: 'It is not how many times you fall but how often you get up'. But these lofty ideals haven't reached my consciousness yet; for the moment, the twinkling lights in the distance look ever so romantic.

We drink coffee and liqueurs and talk. He is indeed fascinated by my Russian stories and asks me more and more questions. When we hear the sound of seagulls greeting the dawn he says: "I'm going to take you home," which startles me because I was expecting him to at least try and kiss me.

In the morning my mother comes into my room with freshly squeezed orange juice, looking at me expectantly; her whole face a question mark: "*Nuuu*?"

"Nothing," I mumble under my breath.

"Never mind, it's the first date," she says optimistically.

He invites me to dine at his flat on a few more occasions and each time we eat dinner, sit till the early hours talking and laughing, with not a whiff of romance in the air.

And suddenly he stops calling. I feel drained of any vestige of confidence. It's the same story again; I am not in love with him, nor do I find him particularly attractive, it's just that the only way I feel real is being wanted by a man. My mother doesn't say a word, mainly because I don't let her; I erect an iron wall around myself.

A few months later he calls out of the blue: "Mina, I have wonderful news for you. I'm so happy. I'm in love!"

Wonderful news for *me*?

"Congratulations," I hear myself say, feeling confused, unworthy and unlovable; wishing I had a father to turn to.

He carries on: "She's still at school; she is sixteen." And then adds, as if apologising to his mother: "She's not Jewish."

I am *shtum,* don't know what to say.

"And you know her, her name is Gail; you modelled bathing suits together. You must come and have lunch with us, how about tomorrow?"

"Thank you, I'd love to." Anything! Just to get out of the house.

Next day we pick Gail up from school and go to his Japanese flat for lunch. After lunch she takes off all her clothes, just like that, and starts dancing in the nude, a vision of long blonde hair and the soft rounded body of a woman-child. He gets up, leads her to the couch, falls on top of her and fucks her. I sit on the sofa as if I'm totally accustomed to this kind of thing. I'm cool. He gets off her, fumbles with his fly and says to me: "Sorry, I couldn't help it," in a 'you can understand' sort of way.

"It's all right," I say, feeling, at the age of twenty-five like his elderly confidante.

'Maybe I'm not this millionaire's type,' I try to console myself, 'maybe being Jewish, I remind him of his mother.' But one night, when they've invited me to stay and his *Lolita* gets into my bed, her body exuding heat abundantly, that is the final straw. I never go there again. Much later, I hear they got married and had a child.

I'd been living in London with my husband and our baby daughter for two years, when a thick package arrived from my mother with cuttings from a newspaper; big headlines: 'Millionaire kills wife with Japanese statue'.

I phone my mother.

"Thank God," she says.

"What do you mean 'thank God'?"

"Niet huda bez dobra: there is no evil without good. I told you, don't cry; everything is for the best, thank God he didn't marry *you*."

But she does continue sending me cuttings from the Cape Argos about another millionaire I've met and 'could have married, if I hadn't been so obstinate'.

Oy, what my mother only had to put up with; I lose my virginity to a *goy* in Warsaw, meet a Jewish boy in Israel and he's a *shwartze,* and when I finally meet a millionaire, he turns out to be a psychopath.

Interflora – 'From Portugal with love'

Ever since I was a little girl I always felt that I was destined for the better things in life. I don't know where that belief came from. Often, in the midst of despair, the hope would surface out of nowhere that, as compensation for all my childhood misery, life would raise me into the limelight, revealing all my best qualities and my childhood hurt would be fully vindicated.

I saw myself becoming a cabaret star, dancing the tango, singing Russian romances and gypsy songs, telling stories and making people laugh. Nothing wrong with that; the trouble was that the demons of sabotage would move in and before I knew it I was complaining, like a woman possessed, 'What's the point, it's too late, I've got what it takes, but nobody can see it.'

Now I'm supposed to be a fashion model, but every morning, after having cried myself to sleep the night before, I wake up with swollen eyes and a sore heart, not the best shape to be in for the catwalk.

I have a notebook for collecting jokes; I always memorise a few before going out to a party, anxious that otherwise I'll have nothing to say. The only subject I feel totally at ease with is my Russian childhood. There is at least one man at every party who, initially mesmerised by the attractive Russian girl with the exotic accent, telling strangely fascinating and amusing stories of childhood disappointments, ends up looking dazed and fumbling for an excuse to get away: "I think I'll go and get another drink." Next I see him talking animatedly to an attractive woman. I can't bear the humiliation, so I learn to feign aloofness.

The modelling agency sends me to Johannesburg to take part in a fashion show. There, at a party, I meet a young Portuguese businessman who takes a fancy to me and invites me to his flat. I still flirt with men in the same disengaged way that led to losing my virginity in Warsaw. I come on as if I'm free and easy and when they assume that this is an invitation to have sex, I get coy and play hard to get. They persist, as men do; I give in, partly out of a belief that men can't deal with their erections and that it is cruel to arouse a man and then not follow it through. They certainly seem to behave as if their lives are in danger. As Barbara Streisand says in *'Funny Girl'*, when Omar Sharif is trying to charm his way into her knickers: "He's trying to take a Jewish girl ... if I stop him now, can he sue me?"

While keeping my dreams of true love safe in my secret heart, I sleep with the Portuguese businessman, not knowing why exactly, except, I suppose, to have a chance to try out my charms and to prove that they work. When I get back to Cape Town, flowers arrive with a note: 'From Portugal with love'.

"How on earth can flowers get from Portugal to Cape Town?" I ask a friend.

"Haven't you heard of Interflora?" she answers in disbelief.

"Interflora? What's that?"

When she explains how Interflora works, a curtain lifts and suddenly all sorts of impossible things become possible: 'Aha, if there are things like *Interflora* that I've never heard about, what other amazing and wonderful things are there still waiting to be discovered?' The song from the first musical I ever saw – Rogers and Hammerstein's *'No Strings'* – comes to mind:

The sweetest sounds I've ever heard are still
inside my head
The kindest words I'll ever know are waiting to
be said
The most entrancing sight of all is yet for me
to see
And the dearest love in all the world is waiting
somewhere for me
Is waiting somewhere, somewhere for me

Naïve though it may seem, like a chick coming out of an egg, discovering Interflora cracks open my limited view of the world and jolts my imagination, enabling me to run away from home – at the age of twenty-six. I don't really run away, but the inner effort of finding the courage to leave my mother makes it feel like it.

And at last I'm on my way, off to live in Johannesburg. My mother doesn't object: "Johannesburg is a big city with goldmines; more chances to find a rich husband." I notice that she's reduced her ambition from a millionaire to a rich husband. She comes with me to the station and keeps repeating: "Don't forget to eat." I get a seat by the window and she stands on the platform looking up at me, casting her spells: "*Oy*, may you find a good man, from my lips straight into God's ear."

As the train gathers speed, leaving my mother standing there, her lips moving in prayer, I start to cry the same old familiar, endless, uncontrollable tears. In the meantime the train cheerfully chug-chugs along, leaving my mother further and further behind, giving me space to try and figure out, for the survival of my soul, what on earth she means when she keeps on asking me, 'Who will marry you?' and answers, 'Whoever will be so stupid will throw you out a week later. Without a husband, you're nothing. You are helpless and useless. You have to marry a millionaire, so then you won't *have* to do anything for yourself.'

Suddenly, for no particular reason, I cheer up. The words of Heinrich Heine, the German poet and satirist come to mind, 'Whatever tears one might shed, in the end one always blows one's nose.' So I do precisely that, blow my nose, look in the mirror and, in spite of my tear stained face, like what I see; I don't look half as bad as reflected in my mother's worried eyes.

The mirror figured as greatly in my life as it did in my mother's. I also looked in the mirror constantly, mainly to reassure myself that I was really there. I even looked at my reflection in shiny soup spoons, in restaurants.

My cousin Mendel, who has changed his name to Martin, comes to the station to pick me up and take me to his family home in a dismal part of Johannesburg where poor whites live. He lives with his parents, two sisters and a younger brother. My Uncle Zalman is my mother's eldest brother, the one whom she pitied; the star brother was Isaac from Cape Town. Zalman came to South Africa from Russia in the 1920's, worked hard, scraped together enough money to buy a truck and started a coal delivery business. The business is small. He does all the deliveries himself, his hands trembling from Parkinson's disease. In the evenings, when he tries to talk about the old days, when sons took over the father's business, his insinuations fall on deaf ears. At dinner his wife Sonya, trying to make up for my years of starvation in Russia, beseeches: "Have another piece of meat."

Nekhamke, the older daughter of the family, whose age, twenty-six, has become an unmentionable subject, is considered irrevocably on the shelf. The younger daughter, Gitke, informs me that girls never go out alone in Johannesburg: "It's strictly for the birds not to have a date for Saturday night." The younger brother, Meishke, with his mischievous face, is the most spirited of the lot. He commits suicide by shooting himself fifteen years later.

Poor as they are, they have two middle-aged black servants whom they call 'the boy' and 'the girl'. The servants call my uncle and aunt 'master' and 'madam', and the children, 'master' and 'miss'. The atmosphere in the house is dangerously dull and I don't yet know how to be kind and merciful, and have respect and recognition for every human being, because I don't yet have it for myself.

Don't tell me you've read Tolstoy and Dostoyevsky in Russian!

As a child I loved the fairy tale *Kolobok,* the Russian *Gingerbread Man,* about the little bun with raisins for eyes baked by an old grandmother and left on the windowsill to cool, before being served for tea. But he has other ideas; he rolls off the window sill and runs away. The pluckiness of that little bun was instrumental in waking up a bit of daring in me. Even though, because of his vanity, he gets gobbled up by a fox, he is fearless in his last moments of freedom, strolling through the woods singing his gutsy song, managing to get away from the hare, the bear and the wolf, all threatening to eat him up:

I ran away from grandfather,
I ran away from grandmother,
and from you, hare and from you, bear, and
from you, wolf,
I have no trouble running away.

But the fox is the smartest of them all; when the little bun sings his song:

I'm kolobok, kolobok!
I was scraped up in the flour-tin,
mixed with sour cream into a bun
baked in butter till I was done,

then left on the sill till I cooled some.
I ran away from grandfather,
I ran away from grandmother,
I ran away from the hare,
I ran away from the grey wolf,
I ran away from the big bear,
and from you, fox, I'll have no trouble running away.

The fox says: "It must be a beautiful song, but I'm rather hard of hearing, please sit on my nose and sing your song again, a little louder."

Kolobok, flattered, hops onto the fox's nose and sings the song again, a little louder ... and the rest is history. To cheer myself on, I sing my own version of *Kolobok's* song:

I ran away from my mother,
I ran away from my stepfather
And from you Uncle Solomon and Aunt Sonya
I have no problem running away.

And I do succeed in getting myself together enough to 'run away', before being swallowed up by the apathy all around me and by my own lack of oomph. I manage to find a room in a block of flats in Hillbrow, a suburb of Johannesburg, known in those days for its nightlife. In it there is a single bed, a small table and one chair. My cousin Martin takes me to a second hand furniture shop to hire a wardrobe. We carry it through the streets and up six flights of stairs into the very first room of my own, not counting the one in Russia, with the big gaps in the wooden partition and my stepfather peeping through. The wardrobe is brown and gloomy, smelling of mothballs, with a murky mirror in the front.

While waiting for a modelling job to turn up I work as a waitress in The Golden Spur, a fashionable steak house run by three handsome and eligible young bachelors. Clusters of giggly young girls hang around outside trying to catch their attention and every evening a long queue of customers stretches across the square. Being a waitress is not what I'm meant to be; I know I ought to be in movies. The sulky look on my face makes me unpopular in the most popular restaurant in town – the only waitress not to get any tips; except occasionally, when some guy takes pity on me: "*Ag* shame, cheer up man, it may never happen," and gives me a five rand tip. 'Shame' doesn't mean 'what a disgrace'; in the local idiom it means 'what a pity' or 'aren't you sweet'.

Arthur is one of the eligible young owners. One day he rings and I answer the phone. My '*khello*' with the emphasis on the Russian 'h', like in Khrushchev, obviously intrigues him, he asks: "What's your accent?"

"Russian", I answer, proudly rolling the 'R'. As a child I could never roll the 'R' and spent months learning how to do it because I was teased that Jews couldn't roll the 'R', and the boys would call out as I passed by,' say Ararat.'

"Don't tell me you've read Tolstoy and Dostoyevsky in Russian?" Arthur exclaims.

"Oh yes," I answer dreamily.

The truth is I read *War and Peace* when I was seventeen, skipping the Napoleonic War battles and looking for romantic love scenes. Although, come to think of it, I never found in Tolstoy the love and desire I was looking for; it was soulful and lofty but disembodied and without any spice.

But now, with the receiver in my hand, I am transported into the fairy-tale atmosphere of the ball in St.Petersburg, where the dashing, world-weary Prince Andrey Bolkonsky is wildly intoxicated by the spirited and charming Natasha Rostova with whom I am totally identified. I hear Arthur say: "Don't go away! I've got to see you; I'll be there in ten minutes." And my 'Prince Bolkonsky' arrives in his silver Lancia, crew cut, very good-looking and very shy.

We start going out together. On our first date we speak about suicide. I tell him about the cloud of hopelessness that hangs over me: will I ever be able to express what's inside me, buried under so much fear, frustration and insecurity? Arthur tells me how oppressed he feels by his Uncle George who actually grabbed the book Arthur was reading out of his hands, threw it on the floor and sarcastically called him 'Professor'. Uncle George brought the idea of the fast food business from America and opened a chain of steak houses. "We don't need professors in this family, we need good businessmen," he said, and put Arthur in charge of one of the steak houses.

Arthur's last girlfriend's parting words: "You're uncultured, you haven't even read any classics or listened to classical music," drove him to build a tiny hut in the garden where he starts listening to Tchaikovsky, Beethoven, Mozart and reading Tolstoy, Dostoyevsky, Henry Miller and Laurence Durrell, away from his disapproving Uncle. He falls in love with Justine from Lawrence Durrell's *Alexandria Quartet*, and dreams of marrying an exotic Jewess. And here she is, 'his Justine', living in a tiny room with a gloomy wardrobe on the sixth floor in Hillbrow, crying herself to sleep every night.

Arthur never stays overnight at my place; he says his traditional Greek family will forbid him to marry me if they find out that we sleep together; as it is they expect him to marry a Greek virgin. To bring some life into my cheerless room, Arthur buys me a second-hand record player with a Joan Baez record from his friend Warren.

Late at night, when he is ready to leave, he always puts on his favourite song, *'The Queen of Hearts'*

To the Queen of Hearts is the Ace of Sorrow
He's here today, he's gone tomorrow
Young men are plenty but sweethearts few
If my love leaves me what shall I do?

I love my father, I love my mother
I love my sister, I love my brother
I love my friends and relatives too
I'll forsake them all and go with you

At the sound of the lyrics and Joan Baez's wistful, melancholy voice I burst into tears. Arthur hesitates at the door and says awkwardly: "Bye, see you tomorrow" and I cry myself to sleep again. I hate Joan Baez.

Arthur's family house in Delarey Street reminds me of the Rostov's house in *War and Peace,* when all the cousins come together on summer vacation and the house is buzzing with activity. Arthur and his cousins play tennis on their own tennis court, swim in their own swimming pool, and I can't believe my eyes when I see them playing with oranges, throwing them to each other by the pool; it takes me back to Moscow and the first orange I'd ever seen, that my cousin brought for us to share, from Odessa.

Their African nanny, who has been with the family ever since the children were born, makes the most delicious Greek food, but won't sit down at the table with us, although she is invited to, over and over again. She says, bashfully hiding her face: "*Ag Baas* Arthur, leave me alone; I can't do it; I can't sit at the table with white people."

Arthur's sister Mel and her best friend Lolly, both fifteen-year-old schoolgirls, have a crush on me; they admire my silk turquoise trouser suit, and the way I eat like a 'normal' person while their cousins' girlfriends are on constant slimming diets and swim with their teased up hair-dos propped above the water. I can't swim yet but I don't mind getting my hair wet. Arthur doesn't hide the fact that he likes sun-tanned girls with flat tummies and since I have no hope of the latter, I try to make up for it by baking in the sun, totally ignorant of sun tan lotions, till I get second degree burns.

Besides not being a Greek virgin, there's another 'hitch' to Arthur's marrying me: his father walked out on the family when Arthur was eleven and his sister Mel, only two, and this young boy was made to promise his mother, a promise he still feels under pressure to keep, that he wouldn't get married until his sister finished school.

My mother's words are imprinted on my mind, 'Who do you think you are? Who will marry you? Whoever will be so stupid, will throw you out a week later.' I feel hopeless; my one prayer in those days is, 'Please, dear God, let me get married, just to prove that I can, even if I have to get divorced later on.'

The fact that Arthur is two years younger than me, he is *only* twenty-five and I am *already* twenty-seven – 'the older woman' – makes me worry that he won't marry me if he finds out, so I lie that I am also twenty-five and that my date of birth had to be changed for our repatriation documents from Russia. He believes it; anything to do with Russia is veiled in mystery and is unbelievably believable.

My prayer is answered; in spite of all the family oppositions and disapprovals, Arthur and I get married at the Johannesburg Registry Office. We have four witnesses, Arthur's three cousins, Georgie, Peter and Athos, and Arthur's friend Max Rifkind. They sit, side by side, on a bench in their dark suits and fedora hats, looking like

Greek gangsters except for Max, who wears a *kippah* for my benefit. I am wearing a light blue leather suit with a short skirt, high heeled shoes and a black crochet beret, playing at being a star playing at getting married.

The Registrar mispronounces my name and says in a heavy Afrikaans accent: "Do you, *Miner Fishel* take this man ..." and, I, unable to control my laughter, burst out, "I do."

My mother doesn't come to the Registry Office: "How can you do it to me, go and marry a '*goy*'? After all I've done for you? Why do you think I left Russia? Do you think I did it for me? Do you think my life means anything to me? And it's not even *me* I am worried about, how can you do it to your step-father? Beni is a respected man in the community and has done so much for you." What community?

Arthur's mother doesn't come either: "How could you? When your father left, you promised me you wouldn't get married till your sister graduated from school."

The only person clapping his hands jubilantly is the 'King of Fast Food', Uncle George: "Good for business! Most of our customers are Jewish."

Arthur moves in with me. To him it's Bohemian to live a life of voluntary poverty in one room in Hillbrow, with its jazz clubs and nightlife. To me the room with the gloomy wardrobe rakes up memories of soul-destroying poverty. But besides his Bohemian romanticism there's also the fact that he is riddled with guilt and fear of his family's disapproval and can't bring himself to rent a new flat, which he can more than afford. So I keep *nudzhing* (nagging) till eventually he has to choose to put up with my complaining or stand up to his family. He contacts an estate agent and we move to an upmarket suburb, Sandown, into a one bedroom flat with a swimming pool in communal gardens. It has servants' quarters in the yard. Whether you want to or not you have to have a servant; I find this most unsettling, having lived all my life until then under the proletariat regime, which frowned severely upon such bourgeois habits.

For our honeymoon, we fly in a small, bumpy airplane from Johannesburg to Paradise Island, off the east coast of what is then Mozambique; literally a paradise of yellow sands and coral reefs.

After a heavenly swim in the ocean we lie on the beach and Arthur reads Freud's theory of personality aloud to me, making three holes in the sand with his index finger, for the *Id*, the *Ego* and the *Super Ego*. He makes each hole deeper to emphasise the point: "The *Id* is what we have as very young children. When the *Id* wants something, nothing else matters, like when a baby wants his feed. The *Ego* develops after the age of three when the child understands that other people also have needs and desires. The *Superego* develops after the age of five, the moral ethical part of our personality. In a balanced person, the *Ego* is the strongest so it can satisfy the needs of the *Id* without being restrained by the *Superego* and still take into account the reality of the situation."

All these Freudian terms are new to me and it takes some effort to get my head around them, but it feels so cosy and safe to just lie there on the sand, like a child listening to a fairy tale. My whole being calms down to what feels like total happiness and I get a rest from obsessive feelings of inadequacy and guilt, and from my eternal mantra: 'I have nothing to wear.'

The first story I ever wrote was conceived on the day we came back from our honeymoon.

Arthur comes out of the bathroom of our new luxury flat and says: "Don't panic ... but..."

"A mouse," I say with total certainty.

"No, worse, a rat has just run over my foot," he says trying to hide a smile.

I put my head in my hands: "That's it. It's all over. Just as I'm beginning to live, this has to happen."

Even though Arthur has heard my stories about my life in Russia in mouse infested rooms, he still can't quite comprehend how traumatised I am by it all.

I carry on whimpering: "I can't sleep here ever again. How can I ever let you touch me again?"

Arthur looks bewildered and says softly: "Let's spend tonight in a hotel and tomorrow I'll call the pest control ..."

"Oh no, don't even say it!" I scream.

We go to a hotel where I lie on the edge of the bed the whole night so that no part of Arthur comes in contact with me.

The next day, after the pest control has been and gone, I lock myself in the bedroom and write my first story *'Mice on the day of Victory'*.

Mice on the Day of Victory

Outskirts of Moscow, November 1945

I am seven years old and it is 1945. I have such a sore throat, that each time I swallow it feels like I'm swallowing broken glass. I've had a chronic sore throat ever since the day my father was sent to the Siberian *gulag*, never to come back. My stepfather is at work. My mother has gone out to try and exchange the last pair of Polish silk stockings, which she's saved since before the war, for a piece of bread. She's left the radio on so I won't feel lonely.

The war has ended and there is non-stop talk on the radio about the men who died as heroes of the Soviet Union defending their Motherland. In solemn monotonous voices, sympathy to their parents, wives, children and sweethearts is expressed. Then music and laughter celebrates those who have survived and come back to their families. On June 24th, everybody goes to the Red Square to the Victory Parade to join in the celebrations honouring the twenty million Soviets who died in the war, but we stay at home; we never go anywhere. Zukov, the three times hero of the Soviet Union, is given the honour of riding on a white horse, inspecting the Parade. Stalin is jealous, wishing he was the one on that white horse, but he is afraid he'd fall off the horse; still later he accuses Zukov of taking too much honour for himself and has him demoted.

I know my father didn't die a hero's death; he sold his coat to send us a little money and died of pneumonia in the bitter cold of the Siberian *gulag*. I feel that the radio is not talking about him, or about my mother and me.

Mice scuttle all over the room. They even run up and down the curtains. I lie in bed watching and kicking my feet to stop them from climbing onto my bed. They come so close that I can smell their musty smell and feel their fleshy bodies. I am hungry and cold. Mama sternly told me to wait for her to return with the bread and not to go outside. But I can't bear to stay here. I can't stop thinking about starving people eating mice. Each time I swallow I imagine the meaty rodents slithering down my throat.

I get out of bed and stand by the frosted window, mesmerised by the softly falling snowflakes and the delicate fernlike patterns made by the frost on the window pane. I see a Snow Queen and a carriage, which makes me think of the fairy tale, where the Snow Queen turns the boy's heart into an icicle and he doesn't recognise his sister when she comes looking for him, until her tears melt his heart. I always felt, when my mother wouldn't talk to me for a whole day, that the Snow Queen froze her heart and if I cried long enough it would melt again.

On the hill outside I see children playing, sliding down on sledges, laughing as they climb back up again. The squeaking of the mice brings me back into the room. I panic and despite my mother telling me not to go out, put on my old torn coat with the hem undone and the pockets hanging loose and go outside.

The air smells of snow and everything is still. A squirrel sends a chunk of snow tumbling down from the top of a tree. Snowflakes land softly on my skin and cool my face.

I don't have a sledge so I climb up the hill and slide down on my bottom, up and down, up and down.

Suddenly I see the children laughing and pointing at me. The holes in my coat have gotten bigger and chunks of dirty cotton wool from the lining are lying in the snow making it look even whiter.

The children are shouting: "Look, a beggar, a Jewish beggar! Yid, Yid, dirty Yid. Beat Yids and save Russia ... beat Yids and save Russia."

A snowball hits me; I start running; they run after me; I just manage to get inside and bolt the door.

On the radio a woman sings a war song: *'The train has disappeared into the distance, my beloved is gone, maybe forever ...'*

The children bang on the door and, unable to open it, run to the window. They press their noses against the frozen glass pulling faces and shouting:

"Coward ... *Zhid* ... *Zhid,* Yid ... Yid ... coward."

The song on the radio continues: *'and with such sadness did the black eyes with long eyelashes look at the train disappearing into the distance.'*

I always thought the song was about my father on the train and my mother's black eyes, rimmed with long eyelashes, watching him disappear forever.

My throat aches, tears stream down my face and the children at the window shout:

"Beat Yids ... save Russia."

I run to hide on the bed because it's out of sight of the window.

The bed is teeming with mice.

Writing that first story to recover from the rat's appearance in our new, luxury flat was my first inspiration for this book, in finding a way to forgive and heal from my past.

The struggle to find my identity

Johannesburg 1966

So now that I have a new husband I decide I need a new nose. I think it will solve all my problems: I don't want to look Jewish, in case there's another war and more anti-Semitism, and I truly believe it will be easier to age with a shorter nose. And besides, I want to get as far away as possible from looking like my mother. I don't even look like my mother; she always said, 'You are a copy of your father; *akh*, even the soles of your feet are exactly like your father's.' But it seems to me that a shorter nose will free me of my mother. There's also more than a touch of spiteful glee there, 'You controlled the length of my skirts, but you can't control the length of my nose!' And ... I want to look like a model, a film star, glamorous, aloof and unapproachable, so I won't have to deal with all those impossible intimacy issues. I am in fact terrified of intimacy; having spent my childhood determined not to make eye contact with anybody, I'm incapable of looking a lover in the eyes.

So I beg and nag poor Arthur for a new nose.

"Are you mad? Why?"

"If there's another war I won't look Jewish."

"You don't look Jewish anyway."

"Yes, I do."

"But you look beautiful as you are."

Of course I don't believe him. I go on nagging till he

agrees and drives me to the plastic surgeon. He waits in the car while I *run* in, let the surgeon measure my nose, propose another one by showing me pictures of noses disconnected from faces, like showing me a nose on a plate, and I am crazy enough to accept. It's as if I'm having a dress shortened. The operation is performed, I have plaster all over my nose for a week and then the new nose is unveiled. Everyone says I look cute, which is all very well at the age of twenty-seven, but do I really want to look cute at the age of seventy?

At least I don't go as far as the Jewish girl I saw in a BBC documentary, who had one plastic surgery operation after another to make her look Chinese. She wanted to wipe away every trace of her mother. After five operations she actually did look Chinese, but when the reporter asked: "Are you satisfied now?" she answered: "No, I will go on having operations until all family resemblances are removed."

My new nose didn't give me the confidence I'd hoped for, and it didn't remove the constant ache in my heart. Everyone said it hadn't improved my looks either because, they said, I had looked just as attractive before. Turns out my looks weren't my problem; it will take a hell of a lot more than changing my nose to shift my deeply ingrained lack of self-worth and mistrust of the world.

When I eventually came to my senses and started to enjoy being me I realised, to my regret, what a self-destructive thing I'd done – cutting off my nose to spite my face, and for what? Back then I had wanted to look like somebody else; Marlene Dietrich or Greta Garbo. Why didn't I want to look like Barbra Streisand, or even better, like Anna Magnani, who had quite a *schnozl* on her and even big bags under her eyes and was utterly sexy and beautiful. But I didn't believe yet in that kind of beauty.

In London I became ashamed of having had a 'nose job' and kept it from my new friends. I was upset when people told me that my daughter, Kira, didn't look at all like me, and that she looked more like Janet, her stepmother.

Like Woody Allen's character Zelig, all through my youth I wore different masks for different people. I swung between wanting to look either like a wild barefoot gypsy with long hair, gold hoop earrings, and a bright flowery skirt, singing gypsy songs in a deep husky voice, or an alluring, seductive *femme fatale* on high heels, ensnaring men with bonds of irresistible desire while singing *'I'm the laziest girl in town'*. But at times when my spirits wilted and I lost my *pizzazz*, I crawled for 'safety' to my mother, did a typing course and tried to look respectable and neat like a secretary.

In one of the flats in our fashionable block lives a divorced, sporty looking woman with her little boy. We see her beside the pool wearing the briefest bikini; she has a very firm, flat abdomen, just the kind Arthur keeps telling me he likes on a woman, and a boyish hairstyle. We nickname her 'Muscles' and Arthur doesn't miss a chance to tell me how much he admires her type of figure. I secretly want to look like her and, not so secretly, eat nearly all the time, so when I have my hair cut *'a la Muscles'*, the hairstyle is the only resemblance between us. To top it all, still feeling like the rejected little radish in the Polish kindergarten who doesn't know how to play, I'm jealous of Arthur's playfulness with Muscles' little boy.

Shortly after I acquire my new boyish haircut, we go to Spain to check out the possibilities of emigrating there. What a delight to discover Spain for the first time; the excitement of Madrid with its art galleries, tapas bars, guitar music and flamenco dancers. Except that now Arthur's admiration goes to the barefoot gypsy dancer with long dark thick hair, just like mine was before I had it cut. I start pleading with Arthur to let me buy a wig: "I'll make up for the money by not going to the hairdresser ever again," I buy the wig, put it on immediately and wear it every day. It looks just like my own hair before the cut and costs thirty dollars, which is quite a lot of money in 1967.

From Spain we fly to Israel to visit my cousin Bella. Not once, in the sweltering heat of Tel-Aviv, do I take my wig off. I wear it on the beach, in the bath, in bed, just in case someone comes in and catches me without it. Once, after several vodkas, my heart jumps when my uncle puts his arm around me rather vigorously and I feel the wig beginning to slide off my head. Occasionally I catch my cousin looking at me a bit too fixedly. As far as I know, my secret was never discovered, or maybe they were just being polite.

After we come back, I take the wig to the hairdresser to clean the Israeli sand out of it and absentmindedly hang it on a light fitting when I come home. Arthur doesn't notice and turns the lights on, so my wig, all thirty dollars of it, slowly smoulders away until nearly half of its linen scalp is burnt. I start growing my hair long.

Given the struggle to find my identity, separate from my mother, I'm pleased to say that I don't go as far in my survival strategies as the girl I saw on a postcard: dressed in black leather, with heavily kohl-lined eyes, studs piercing her tongue, nose, ears, lips, eye-brows and navel, her green hair sticking out in orange peaks, with the caption: 'I survived a Jewish mother'.

I only had a nose job.

Deciding to leave South Africa

Although Arthur, like me, was sidetracked from himself by the craziness in his childhood, he is the first safe shore I have ever reached. At last, I feel secure enough to feel how insecure I am. All the things I had no chance to do in my childhood and youth are now opening out before me. We read to each other from Proust's *Remembrance of Things Past,* look up words in the dictionary and at night in bed test each other on the meaning of the words. I learn how to swim and ride a horse. Arthur teaches me to play tennis and squash and drive his silver Lancia; and to operate the cash register at the steak house, where we both work a couple of evenings a week. And he buys me my first guitar!

Having grown up in sunny South Africa, Arthur is outwardly more secure and more at home in the world than me. He has many friends, from lawyers and doctors to magicians and gangsters and other dodgy colourful characters. He makes friends with some African artists but he is not allowed to invite them to his house for dinner, for God's sake. I'm impressed how Arthur treats everyone with equal respect. The Africans working in the steak houses all, without exception, adore him. He gets woken up in the middle of the night to go and bail out one of the guys, arrested for not having his pass on him, which Africans are obliged to carry on their person at all times.

But inside Arthur there is also the little boy who had five ear operations by the time he was two, and was left alone in the hospital because, in those days, they didn't yet realise the obvious – that a sick little two-year-old needs his mother to stay with him. A lot of hurt is hiding inside him and he has his dark phases, which he calls 'going punchy', but with all that, he is my lifeline, and I feel loved, cared for and accepted by him.

I started biting the inside of my lip in childhood out of intolerable anxiety and was still addicted to it when I met Arthur. I made a vow to God that I'd give it up if only he would marry me and broke the vow immediately after we were married.

Now we are on our way to Cape Town for a holiday, driving through the night, over a road stretching endlessly through the Karoo desert. Arthur, behind the wheel of his silver Lancia, is hell-bent on trying to beat his previous year's record – Jo'burg to Cape Town in twelve hours. The tension in the car is mounting. Our friend Allen is sitting at the back, nervously humming the Beatles's song: *'Yesterday, hmm, hmm, hmm, all my troubles seemed so far away, hmm, hmm, hmm, hmm'.* I am just about managing to control the urge to scream, by biting my lip, even though I know that I'm breaking my vow, when the headlights of the car illuminate a large rock on the right side of the road, seconds before crashing into it. Allen screams: "Arthur!" Startled and trying to avoid the collision, Arthur turns the wheel sharply to the left, sending the car spinning down the embankment. Thoughts race through my mind: 'this is what it's like to have an accident ... when we stop there's no knowing who will still be alive ... and it's all my fault, because I was biting my lip.'

When the car comes to a stop, I hear Allen's voice: "Are you alright?" Next I see the driver's door flung wide open and, oh my God, no Arthur! We climb out of the car, shouting: "Arthur, Arthur!" No sound, just the silence and stillness of the Karoo desert in the middle of the night, pitch dark, no moon, the stars small and far way and the car on its side, one headlight shining dimly. When we eventually find him lying alarmingly still on the ground, I sink down on my knees calling his name. He doesn't answer. I can hear his breathing, but he is unconscious. Allen instructs me to cover him up and stay with him while he goes back up to the road, hoping to stop a passing car. I speak to Arthur, but he doesn't reply. I notice myself thinking, 'Just like him to be unconscious, and just like me to be physically alright, but mentally in agony.' After we got married I became obsessed that Arthur would die on me, just like my father did; if the phone rang when he was out I'd think it was the police calling to tell me, 'I'm very sorry but ... your husband has had an accident.'

Suddenly he opens his eyes: "Where am I? What happened?"

"We had an accident."

"Accident ... what accident?" he mumbles and loses consciousness again.

In the stillness of the night the melody from *'Zorba the Greek'* starts to play on the tape recorder in the car. Later Arthur told me that, through a haze he heard Anthony Quinn's voice: *'Do you want to dance, my boy?'* and thought he'd died and gone to heaven. Zorba was his hero; he represented the ecstatic, spontaneous will to live and bring joy. *'Happiness is a simple heart'* was Arthur's motto.

Allen comes back, after what feels like forever, with no luck. We sit next to Arthur, watching him go in and out of consciousness, when a car suddenly appears. Two railway workers heard the crash and somehow managed to find us. They take us to a doctor in the nearest town. We knock and knock on his door and after what feels like an interminable wait, the doctor finally appears in his dressing gown. Allen and I manage to help Arthur to the sofa, where the doctor examines him and says: "I don't think there is internal bleeding, but one can't tell. I'm going to call an ambulance. You are only about sixty miles from Cape Town."

In the ambulance I can't get the doctor's words 'internal bleeding' out of my mind. Every few minutes I want to ask the nun who, I don't know why, happens to be travelling with us: 'is he alive?' but I don't, because her face looks totally impenetrable.

At last we arrive at Groote Schuur Hospital where Arthur is x-rayed and the doctor's diagnosis: 'concussion and a fractured hip ... three weeks in bed and six weeks on crutches,' feels like being under house arrest.

Two male nurses in green overalls carry him on a stretcher, down seven levels of stairs, to our holiday flat on glorious Clifton beach. I'm so traumatised by Arthur's brush with death, which resurrects all the unresolved grief around my father's death that, during the whole time by the sea, not once do I go for a swim or a walk on the beach; I only dash out to get food and rush back. I'm afraid to leave Arthur in case he dies while I'm out. After three weeks inside that flat, with Arthur in a lot of pain and me in a lot of panic, we fly back to Johannesburg.

Our decision to leave South Africa is made on the plane, in that timeless zone flying above the clouds thousands of feet above the invisible earth. Arthur tells me that the accident and being immobile for six weeks has made him take stock of his life. He's always found the apartheid situation unacceptable, and done all he could for the Africans who work in his Uncle's steakhouses but now he's reached a point when he's either got to get actively involved in the cause of liberation or get out of the country. With my history I feel most certainly like getting out. Arthur doesn't need any more persuasion: "We'll go and live in Mallorca, open a café on a hill overlooking the Mediterranean, and study Existentialism."

After six months, by which time Arthur has fully recovered, we leave South Africa for good, off to live in Mallorca. Before our final departure we fly to Cape Town to say goodbye to my mother. Our goodbyes always have a tragic undertone, so I'm in my usual gut-tearing conflict; I can't wait to get away and, at the same time, I feel acute guilt. It is heartbreakingly sad, and the sadness is that we can't relate to each other except through the painful memories we share, which continue to keep both of us enslaved. There's always the fantasy that 'someday everything will be alright', but nothing ever is.

On the day of our departure, mother comes with us to a café just to be together a little longer, so we say our goodbyes in Market Street with her holding onto me, pleading: "Please write, don't forget to write, and listen to me, you must eat," making it sound as though I'm leaving a remote Polish *shtetl* for a faraway war-torn land.

We become existentialists in Mallorca

Arthur and I rent a flat in Illetas, overlooking the Mediterranean, and adopt the 'look' of European existentialists; we wear black all the time, grow our hair long and I line my eyes thickly with kohl. We sit in cafes furiously discussing existentialism: 'Is it existence preceding essence, or is it essence preceding existence?' It does my head in if I think about it, so I don't. But, I suppose, if Sartre didn't believe in God, there couldn't have been any essence before human existence, therefore 'existence precedes essence', and that's 'existentialism'; if God has created everything and given existence to the essence, then, to God, 'essence precedes existence'. Phew!

But one thing I do get from Sartre that begins to loosen my morbid obsession with my father's absence is that he says in his autobiography, *Words*: "The absence of my father saved me from inheriting values I would have had to shed in the end".

The film of the year is *'Un Homme et une Femme'*. Everybody says I look like Anouk Aimee and Arthur like Jean Louis Trintignant. We revel in being 'the beautiful people'; we study Spanish, drink *café con leche* on the beach and make friends with other existential wanderers like ourselves, one particularly, the famous American science fiction writer Robert Sheckley.

Our new life is exciting and stimulating until I start feeling caged in on the island. It seems to coincide with me falling down the stairs outside the obstetrician's after being told I'm pregnant. I feel totally incapable of even imagining having a baby, but having had a couple of abortions, this time I know I have to face reality. I hope not being fully conscious of what I was doing *('forgive them, for they know not what they do')* will serve as extenuation if and when I have to answer to God on the Day of Judgement for the abortions I've had. I certainly didn't take them lightly; I went through hell, one way or another. Winston Churchill said: 'If you are going through hell keep on going'. I kept on going, feeling terror at what I had done and at the same time unable to take responsibility for being a woman with all that it entails.

Although Arthur and I try to rationalise our doubts about having a baby by quoting D.H Lawrence: 'Stop bearing children, start bearing love and giving hope to those already there', we decide to have the baby. The pregnancy unleashes even more unresolved pain and grief from childhood. I feel an inexplicable pull towards London, a strong gut feeling that I'll find help there. Arthur, on the other hand, is in paradise just to be far away from his Uncle's oppressive authority, so he isn't ready to leave just yet. He is confused by my tears and tries to make me happy in all the ways he can think of and, having run out of ways, he even hits me once. But seeing that I just won't stop crying he eventually decides London isn't such a bad idea after all; he can go to the London Film School, become a film director and make me a film star; maybe that will stop me crying.

We drive from Mallorca to London in June 1968 when I'm five months pregnant and crying all the time; I only stop crying long enough to eat. Arthur says: "Do you realise, you've cried all the way through the Swiss Alps?" He also tells me that he's never seen anyone hate their mother as much as I do. I am thinking that anyone who doesn't is emotionally cut off. I can't allow myself to even imagine that a good relationship with a mother is possible.

On our way we decide to spend a week at the Cannes Film Festival. It is the year when the student uprising sweeps through France. I can sort of see, out of the corner of my eye, students running through the streets of Cannes, burning with revolutionary zeal, carrying slogans, 'Be realistic. Demand the impossible'. I have an aversion to revolutions; all I care about is for *my* impossible dreams to come true.

On our first day on the beach who should we bump into but Genevieve, a girl we know from Cape Town, who runs up to us in the tiniest bikini, her hair platinum blonde and very short, exclaiming: "Guess what? I've got a part in a film! Tonight I'm invited to a party and Orson Wells is going to be there. You can come as my guests. I've cut my pubic hair O-shaped for Orson," she giggles. Earlier in Cape Town, when she fell in love with our friend Alan, a medical student, she cut her pubic hair A-shaped!

Genevieve Waite actually landed a part in the film *'Joanna'* with Donald Sutherland and later married John Philips of the 'The Mamas and the Papas' and made an album *'Romance is on the Rise'* – all the things that are my absolute heart's desire and I am secretly eaten up with envy about. But our fates led us along different paths: Genevieve's into celebrity and drugs and mine to R. D. Laing and Yoga ... and some drugs on the way too.

But back there in Cannes it's because of Genevieve that we end up at the celebrity party. Here am I, in this posh hotel banqueting room, in the company of movie giants the likes of Orson Wells, Sharon Tate and Roman Polanski, who are looking for new talent, and I'm six months pregnant, feeling fat and ugly and craving pickles. With conflict raging inside me between the dead certainty that I'm a star too and frustration that the world may never know it, I polish off a whole baguette with pastrami and dill pickle, not taking my eyes off Arthur flirting with the young starlets and being his shy, but charismatic self.

Before we left South Africa, Arthur, desperate to get out of the clutches of the family business, sold his shares in Uncle George's steakhouse and ended up with a limited sum of money and no regular income, which intensified my insecurity, already rife with fears of starvation and poverty.

Through a friend's introduction, we move into a cosy duplex flat in St. John's Wood. Arthur, as planned, starts a course at the London Film School. We join every cinema club in London and spend so much of our time watching movies that I'm afraid I might end up giving birth in the cinema.

On October 4th, 1968, the day Arthur started at the London School of Film Technique, I gave birth to a baby girl. To say I 'gave birth' is a gross exaggeration; I felt no connection with the baby in my womb and had never heard of anyone who did. My two main impressions of birth were Anais Nin's description of a horrific life and death struggle ending in a stillbirth, and my mother's version of my birth: "The worst experience of my life; if I had my life over again I would never have children."

The Harley Street obstetrician said: "If you want me at the birth we better have you induced, dear, because I might be on the golf course when your baby decides to come." I agree; I can't even imagine that I could give birth naturally, even though women have done so since history began. I knew nothing about the courses in London to prepare women and their partners for natural birth. My baby was forced from my womb with forceps, before her time, while I was under heavy sedation. All I remember is coming round momentarily and not having the faintest idea what was going on.

When I come to from sedation, Arthur is next to me, saying: "It's a little girl." The first time I see her she is asleep in a hospital crib with a red mark on her forehead where the forceps have bruised her. Do I dare to admit that I had no natural desire to hold her? When I do hold her she is all wrapped up and I'm in a hospital gown; there is no skin-to-skin contact and no looking into each other's eyes. The nurse rolls her eyes, showing her impatience with me for not wanting to breastfeed. I feel guilty, I feel ashamed, I feel bad, but totally unable to let go.

I was reading a Russian book called *Kira* at the time, about an aristocratic family during the Russian Revolution, forced to give up their home when the Bolsheviks abolished private property. The family had to leave with only a few belongings – little girl, Kira, in haste, grabbed her most precious possession – her photo album. The story took me back to being six years old with my mother and stepfather, in a shop in Moscow. On a shelf is a small photo album. I pick it up, stroking its red velvet cover. My stepfather takes it out of my hands, reaches into his pocket for money and buys it. I jump with joy – it's for me! Grisha says to my mother, "I think my nephew Borechka will like it."

After three days in the hospital, on the way home in the car, holding the little bundle in my arms, hot tears streaming down my face, all I can think is, 'What have I done?'

We called our little girl Kira. I felt sad for a long time that her name came from associations with my gloomy past but then I discovered that the name Kira also derives from Latin for Light, Russian and Persian for Sun, and Slavonic for Strong Woman. Kira has certainly more than lived up to all the meanings of her name and grown into a beautiful, sensitive and strong woman.

My natural maternal instincts were veiled in fear and unresolved grief. I didn't even know that women can feel instinctual communication with their babies from the moment of conception and instinctively continue feeling it through implantation, gestation, birth and all stages of life. This awareness eluded me until I met R. D. Laing, who opened this previously hidden world to me and supported me in the painful process of feeling the disconnectedness and allowing love and tenderness to enter my heart.

But at the time I continued to cry. Arthur did his best to cheer me up. He played the Beatles a lot, their songs made me feel even more alienated. I couldn't understand what '*Lucy in the sky with diamonds*' was all about; and what was all this '*Let it be, let it be*'? Everyone else seemed 'with it', but I had no idea what this 'it' was, that other people seemed to be 'with'. I'd never heard of the Beatles in Russia. I discovered in London that in the Soviet Union the Beatles were considered 'capitalist pollution' and people were afraid of being arrested for listening to their music. The old boys of the Kremlin twigged that the Beatles popularity with the young could sweep over their stuffy repressive authority; '*All you need is love*' was not big on the agenda of their five year plans.

Before I paint my self-portrait as the mother from hell, I want to put in a good word for myself: at times when the mental fog lifted, I could feel tenderness, love and delight in playing with my little girl, and a deep desire to become a better person and a better mother for her sake. But often I was submerged in self-pity, traumatised by my past and by the power it had over me, without a clue how to move through it and beyond.

But, a new life was waiting for us and began to become

real a month after Kira's birth when Arthur's friend from film school handed me an article entitled: 'R. D. Laing – Scottish existentialist psychiatrist, the guru of the sixties.'

In the Tatra mountains with Lekh Kovarsky.

My mother (far right) sends me a postcard of herself with a group of women at the spa. She always told me about one girl in her village, who dared to leave and become an actress, and how in group photos she always looked in another direction. In this photo from the health spa, where they all look like prisoners, my mother is the one looking in another direction.

My photo on arrival in Cape Town, for my first passport.

What a welcome to Cape Town!

In Cape Town. From left:
My aunt, my uncle Isaac,
my mother and I.

Me (far right) in my
Audrey Hepburn trench
coat, with my mother next
to me. In New York for
my broken engagement.

At the fancy dress party on the ship, togged up as Carmen Miranda, with a basket of fruit on my head, an off the shoulder blouse, a red gypsy scarf on my hips and a rose in my teeth.

On the boat from New York to Southhampton, trying to look like Audrey Hepburn in *'Breakfast at Tiffany's'* and still hoping to meet somebody on the way. Behind me is the young photographer I kind of fancied, but who liked the girl standing next to him.

Working as a fashion model in South Africa.

'IRON CURTAIN' MODEL

ATTRACTIVE Russian mannequin **Minoichka Fischel**, who spent all her life behind the Iron Curtain until last year, successfully combines beauty with brains, as apart from modelling her hobby is studying foreign languages.

"When I lived in Russia I studied languages at Moscow University, and can speak Russian, Polish, English and a little French," said 22 - year - old Miss Fischel.

She hopes to perfect her English and French at the University of Cape Town here.

Raven-haired Miss Fischel was born in Lithuania at the outbreak of World War II—"my father was killed during the war, and two years ago my mother and I decided to leave our home in Poland and settle in South Africa, where we have relatives".

Like many visitors from far-off places, she imagined finding small villages teeming with lions. "I never dreamed that skyscrapers and elegant departmental stores existed here," she said.

● Miss Minoichka Fischel

From left: The Jewish millionaire, his young wife Gail, me, and a man who told me I was too philosophical to be marriage material.

Arthur Balaskas was the first safe shore I ever reached.

Arthur and I get married. My hair is cut *a la Muscles*, the very slim woman in our block, whom Arthur admired and I tried to emulate, my insecurities abound!

Arthur's nanny in South Africa who had lived with them all his life. As much as he tried to get her to sit with them at dinner at the same table, she wasn't able to let go of her status as a black servant.

In a photoshoot with Arthur on one of Johannesburg's many goldmines.

Wearing hoop earrings *a la* Monica Vitti (the Italian film star).

Wearing my expensive wig and clutching a hairbrush.

"Film star material"?

It's not how it looks. Here, I am five months pregnant and in deeply miserable, stuck in my Russian gloom.

PART THREE
The Dawn of Light

Even broken hearts can be mended if we have the heart to let them.

– R. D. Laing

I want to do something in life

It began to dawn on me that crying every day is not part of every human being's daily ritual, like brushing teeth or eating breakfast. I decided to have a look at the R. D. Laing article that Arthur's friend had given me. It spoke about Kingsley Hall, where R. D. Laing and his colleagues established a community in the sixties for people in different states of mental distress. It became home to one of the most radical experiments in the psychology of the time. The aim was to create a model for non-restraining, non-drug therapies for people diagnosed as schizophrenic or psychotic. It was based on Laing's ideas that psychosis was not an illness simply to be eliminated through drugs and electric shock therapy, but could be a way of unravelling "a special strategy that a person invents in order to live in an unlivable situation," from *The Politics of Experience*.

I was not psychotic or schizophrenic, but what Laing said about Kingsley Hall and the people in mental distress made me feel that here was someone who would understand how alienating and devastating my childhood was. The world suddenly felt a safer place with a man in it who believed that there was no unbridgeable abyss between us human beings; given enough compassion and patience, every human experience could be understood and the person who had withdrawn into him or herself, reached.

I went out and bought two of Dr Laing's books: *The Divided Self* and *The Politics of Experience*. In the opening paragraph of *The Divided Self*, Laing explains that the term schizoid, "refers to an individual the totality of whose experience is split in two main ways. In the first place there is a rent in his relations with the world, and in the second, there is a disruption of his relation with himself. Such a person is not able to experience himself together with others or feel 'at home in' the world, but, on the contrary, he experiences himself in despairing aloneness and isolation."

Laing's words spoke directly to me, describing my experience of not feeling at home in the world and having no clue about relationships with other people. I hated labels of any kind; being repeatedly called 'helpless and useless' by my mother got absorbed into my blood and made me feel trapped, separated from the truth of who I was. R. D. Laing didn't label anybody; he was genuinely interested and empathetic to the way people could feel totally trapped in their experience of the world without knowing how to get out of it, or, seeing no light at the end of the tunnel.

To discover that there were other people who felt the same as me and that the pain of alienation didn't only belong to the horrors of war, Stalin's oppressive regime and my emotionally unpredictable mother, immediately made me feel less alone. There were people, from well-to-do middle class families in democratic societies, brought up in houses with gardens and swings, who also felt alienated. I felt understood and validated and hopeful.

I looked in the telephone directory, not really expecting to find his name, since it said in the article, "R.D. Laing, the guru of the sixties, is harder to get hold of than Mick Jagger," and was thrilled to find: 'Laing Dr R.D. Psychiatrist, 21 Wimpole Street, W1.'

I knew nothing about gurus; I just knew this man was talking sense. I phoned for an appointment and was told that Dr Laing was not taking on any new patients. I phoned a couple of days later and was told the same thing. Not letting this put me off, I phoned again, saying that I had to see him. After a few more phone calls his secretary finally gave in, "Write to him and say why you feel you have to see him." I wrote him a letter and got an appointment.

Dressed and made up as though I'm going out on a date: mini skirt, high-heeled boots and Vidal Sassoon hair-do, I sit in the reception, waiting to be called in. I couldn't wait to bask in the rays of attention of an older, wiser man, and tell him all that's in my heart. Suddenly a head pops around the door: "Mrs. Balaskas?" It's him! I remember the article said, "to his patients he is Ronnie". 'Typical,' I thought, 'not crazy enough to be called by my first name and not sane enough not to be there in the first place'. The only way I knew of relating to men was to flirt, like a little girl with her Daddy, or rather, like an awkward little girl without a Daddy. But, as I approached him, I was struck by something in his presence that instantly stopped me in my flirting tracks; I experienced myself, in a lightening moment, stripped of all attitudes. A shock of recognition? His eyes seemed to see straight into my soul, disorientating and, at the same time, strangely safe. I followed him up the stairs, his walk kind of low at the knees, a more elegant version of Groucho Marx and the very opposite of up-tight.

His consulting room was warm and cosy, the walls lined with books, a colourful oriental rug on the floor and two big inviting armchairs. He gestured me toward one, and sat down in the other. Sitting opposite him, stunned by the stillness and depth of his dark eyes, so full of wisdom and intelligence. Silence.

After a while he asked: "Why did you come to see me?"

I felt instant disappointment. That he even had to ask! Surely he must know why I'm there, like a little girl wanting her Daddy to understand her better than she understands herself. And like a little girl trying to impress him, I kept looking at the books on the shelves, wanting to appear intelligent and well read.

Long silence.

Finally I had to force myself to say: "I come from Russia."

One eyebrow moved a little.

"My father died during the Second World War when I was four."

The other eyebrow moved a little.

"I want to *do* something in life."

"Then *do* something."

"I don't know what."

"Then do nothing."

"But I want to do something."

"Then do something."

"But I don't know what ..."

At that moment, when I was beginning to feel like a trapped little girl who couldn't hold her ground any longer and will either pee in her pants or start crying, or both, he smiled.

I said: "I made a deal with I don't know who that I would forfeit my gifts and talents so long as I never have to experience again the trauma and tragedy that befell me at a very early age; let nothing exceptionally good happen to me, so long as nothing exceptionally bad happens either." I wanted to say I had made that deal with God, but felt I wouldn't know who I was talking about and that it would be phoney.

"Do you realise that you'll have to give up the deal if you want to do something in life that is meaningful to you? Do you think you can?"

"No, I can't. I want to do things, I want to write my story, I want to sing and play the piano. I've dreamt of it all my life, but I'm afraid that if I start doing what I really want to do, I'll be punished, or the Third World War will break out and I'll lose everything again. My father was a violinist and if he had lived I would have studied music, but he was sent to a Siberian labour camp and died there. It was so cold that people's tears turned to ice. My mother and I heard that his body was thrown onto a heap of dead frozen bodies. As a child I felt ashamed that my father didn't die a hero's death, like the ones we heard spoken about on the radio or immortalised in songs, like the song White Cranes, '... *the soldiers who haven't returned from the battlefield are not lying now in the earth, but have turned into white cranes*'. My father wasn't one of those who turned into a white crane. He wrote to us from the labour camp that he found it impossible there; 'it was either escape or death.' He sold his coat to one of the guards for a few roubles, which he sent us, and then died of pneumonia."

"Selling his coat was an act of despair; your father was trying to commit suicide."

"No, he wasn't, he sacrificed himself for us."

"Your father committed suicide," said Dr Laing with such intimate directness that it made my father, whom I had no memory of whatsoever, real for the first time: his despair, his terror, his longing and his death. Somehow it felt like a relief to hear it, because it rang true.

Ronnie Laing had the knack of making you see into the core of your pain if you were prepared to look and move through it; and I was prepared, due of the sheer, unbearable mental agony of being in it.

"I feel incapable of doing anything creative and at the same time I feel I have a lot in me that is yearning to express itself, but I don't know what and I don't know how. My mother always told me to throw these *mishugaes* out of my head and do something sensible, like marry a rich man and have children. This discrepancy between the creativity I feel inside and my inability to express it makes me feel suicidal. When I read in your books about other people who also experienced their childhood as a time of emotional persecution, I felt validated for the first time in my life and didn't feel so alone. I've never heard anyone say such things before. That's why I feel I have to see *you* in therapy."

Dr Laing's response was to tell me that he had come to an impasse spiritually and needed to take time off. He was planning to go to India and Ceylon for a year to further explore Buddhist *Vipassana* meditation. He said that he wanted to look into the practice of the Four Foundations of Mindfulness, the Four Noble truths, the teachings of the Buddha. I'd never heard of these things; I'd never even heard of the Buddha, but what spoke loud and clear was that this wise man shared his feelings about his life with me and didn't think I was too stupid and ignorant to understand.

We sat silently for a bit and then he said: "I don't think I can take you on in therapy at the moment. In six months I'll be gone and, since you lost your father when you were so young, you'll be in deep emotional waters by then. You may find the separation hard to handle."

"I don't care about *then*," I said, which was a lie, "all I know is that I have to see you *now*," which was true.

He thought for a moment, then said: "Make another appointment and we'll see."

In those days I was so terrified of flying that although I never took any tablets, for flights I was prepared to take a sleeping pill. But after I left R. D. Laing's consulting room in Wimpole Street that day, I looked up defiantly at an aeroplane in the sky and felt no fear. Being accepted and treated as an equal by someone so wise instantly toughened my spirit and filled me with new confidence.

At the next appointment he agreed to take me on. To commence on the journey of coming to my senses with this glamorous wise man felt like nothing short of being given the lead in a Fellini film with Marcello Mastroianni as my screen lover.

Life lessons with R. D. Laing

> "Your task is not to seek for love, but merely to seek and find all the barriers within yourself that you have built against it."
>
> – Rumi

When I was six years old the man of my dreams was an imaginary doctor who comes to see me when I'm ill. At night in bed I used to take my pyjama pants off, put two empty wooden cotton spools under each buttock and pretend that the doctor comes to examine me and when he touches me, I feel flushed and sweetly ashamed. When I told this story to Laing, he said: "That was probably your first innocent orgasm."

As I grew older, every night before falling asleep I would conjure up a wise, older man who knew, understood and accepted me so deeply that even hurt from him was mixed with sweetness. 'He' was the captain who took me to exotic places on his ship, where I delighted everyone with my dancing – so wild and free that it elevated people beyond envy. I was already afraid to be good at anything out of fear of other's envy. As I grew older, different film stars took on the role of the captain in my fantasy: Ives Montand, Gregory Peck, Spencer Tracy, Jean Gabin ...

When I started seeing Dr Laing in therapy, I thought, 'here *is* the captain of the ship, who will heal all my wounds and make my dreams come true'. But he was quick to pick up on this projection: "I'm not Noah, and there isn't a Noah's Ark." I thought, 'Ok, if he says so there must be something better.'

And there was. There was a safe place where I could be myself, say how I felt and not be condemned for it. I could actually tell him the truth and know that he was not going to judge me, or mock me, so I confessed to him: "I truly believe that after my traumatic childhood I should be exempt from responsibility, like flat-footed men are exempt from Army service. Am I really expected to stand on my own two feet?"

He said matter-of-factly: "Yes."

I knew it was a daft thing to ask, but it felt reassuring to be able to voice it and get a straight answer.

When I showed him a list of all the things my mother called me: 'useless, helpless, you'll be lost without me, you can't even wash a glass or wipe your own arse ...' he asked: "Do you really believe her?"

"Yes."

"Your mother hypnotised you into believing her and now you are suffering from post-hypnotic suggestion. Ask yourself what her motivations could have been."

"I don't think she really knew what she was saying. She wasn't fortunate, like me, to find someone to talk to, who'd listen with his heart. She tried to keep me helpless and dependent on her out of fear of losing me. She claimed that she loved me 'with all my shit', as long as I didn't do anything adventurous, like be myself."

"Have you ever thought that maybe you are not all those things your mother called you?"

"No ... not really; if I dare do anything she wouldn't approve of I still feel as if I'm stepping out of line and expect to be punished. I feel like a wounded bird flapping its wings, unable to take off. My life feels like a nightmare."

"It's easier to wake up from a nightmare than a pleasant dream."

"Are you saying that there is a need to wake up, whether one is in a pleasant dream or in a nightmare, and that the advantage of a miserable childhood is that it gives you an incentive to wake up?"

"You have above average emotional intelligence." It didn't escape him how I immediately got puffed up with pride so he quickly took it back: "Well ... average." He was quick to give encouragement, but also quick to cool it when he saw that I wasn't ready to take it in the right spirit.

One day I smoked a joint of Thai grass 'to get in touch with my feelings', before going for a session. It worked, memories from the past flooded in so intensely that the only way I could cope was to lie down flat on the floor and be still. When the time came to go to the session Arthur had to drive me, while I was trying to hold onto the feelings that surfaced. But once I was in Laing's presence I was unable to say a word. That's when I had an insight, which I never forgot, "I don't have to hang on to the 'now' and try to carry it with me into the future; if I can be 'here now', I'll be able to be 'there then'."

But one insight is not enough. I was still arguing: "If I start living in the now I'll have to admit that I've wasted my life up till now."

"If you don't admit it, you'll waste what's left of it also ...don't lose your nerve."

"I haven't a nerve to lose."

"That's even better; you have nothing to lose."

"I'm so unhappy."

"Become happy."

"I've nothing to be happy about."

"You are certainly making the most of it."

"It's too late."

"Better later than never."

"It's already later."

"Take as long as it takes.'

"Mina, why do you wear black all the time?"

"I'm in mourning for my life, I'm unhappy," I said quoting Masha from Chekhov's *The Seagull.*

"The difference between you and me is that *you* identify with Chekhov's characters and *I* identify with Chekhov."

He was telling me to wake up and be the author of my own life and not a character in somebody else's play. This was 'love' the way I'd never experienced it before; as he said, in *The Politics of Experience*: "Love is letting the other be, but with concern and affection". I heard him say some years later, "Imagine you are in a cage and the door happens to be open, but you won't get out till you figure out how you got in. Knowing how you got in doesn't necessarily help you to get out; it might, but it's not necessary to know how you got in, in order to get out."

I was so used to being told what to do and what not to do that at first it felt like he didn't care. It took some time before I realised that to be given the space to be me and to trust my own experience was the best kind of love there is.

Sometimes I just sat in front of him crying throughout the whole session while he just there; the silence between us was not awkward or confusing and neither of us tried to fill it in.

"My husband says that I don't *want* to be happy."

"He's probably got a point. By the way, why do you keep saying 'my husband'?"

"What should I say?"

"His name of course."

"But you don't know him."

"That makes no difference."

"Yes it does," I argued.

Eventually Ronnie and Arthur met.

One evening, in our St. John's Wood duplex flat, Arthur, having bought some hashish for the first time, decided to eat a piece 'to get in touch with *his* feelings'. We sat around waiting for it to work but nothing seemed to be happening. Arthur ate another piece, still nothing. So we went to sleep.

Suddenly I'm woken out of that special sweetness of the first stage of deep sleep by the whole bed shaking. In the dark I see Arthur's pelvis moving up and down like a '*Dirty Dancing*' routine.

I panic: "What are you doing?"

"Shh ... don't interrupt."

"But you're scaring me."

"Please don't interrupt. Don't say anything."

The bed is shaking as if there's an earthquake. Now I really am panicking.

"Arthur, should I call a doctor?"

"Don't be stupid. Shut up."

"But what are you doing?"

"I'm fucking my mother."

Great! That's reassuring!

Arthur has been reading Wilhelm Reich's *The Function of the Orgasm*, where he talks about the streaming of energy during orgasm resulting in involuntary movements of the pelvis. So he started practising breathing techniques while we made love, to try and achieve that streaming. But I thought it was contrived and instead of turning me on, got on my nerves.

And now he's mixing Wilhelm Reich with Oedipus. I was furious. 'What an idiot, how unconscious ... stupid ... emotionally thick! Luckily I have a session with Ronnie tomorrow morning; I'm going to tell him all about it; he'll agree with me that I married an idiot.'

The next morning, bursting with righteous indignation, I told Ronnie the story of the previous night, fully expecting him to be on my side. Instead to my amazement, he smiled his enigmatic smile and, true to his dedication to understanding the complexities of the human experience said, "Can you ask Arthur to describe his experience in writing and give it to me."

Soon after that Ronnie invited Arthur, Kira and me to a meeting of friends, patients and colleagues to discuss alternatives to the existing nurseries for our children. I knew this kind of gathering was most unusual in the psycho-therapeutic world, but that's what made him a shamanic healer. The meeting was to take place at the home of Hugh Crawford, Ronnie's colleague and a member of the Philadelphia Association, a UK charity founded in 1965, which was concerned with the understanding and relief of mental suffering, without resorting to drugs and electric shock therapy. Philadelphia means 'brotherly and sisterly love'.

His invitation made me feel like Gelsomina, the half-witted girl from Fellini's film *La Strada*, who was sold for a few liras by her impoverished mother to a travelling circus performer Zampano, to be trained as his side kick. He was physically and emotionally cruel to her, and, when occasionally he was kind, she was so overwhelmed that she expressed her pleasure in a clowning, awkward, clumsy way. That was me; I was so unaccustomed to being included in something so meaningful, that I went all weird and said: "I'm afraid I'll have nothing worthwhile to contribute, I feel inadequate, I don't know how to express myself."

"Join the club," he said, "There are many more people

who feel they can't express themselves than those who feel they can."

The people around R.D. Laing were less conforming to social norms of behaviour, less into role playing, and if they had issues with all those things, they were becoming conscious of it and were developing skills of letting go and communicating it. The women were in beautiful long colourful Indian print dresses, and I'd never seen children being treated with such respect by adults. Ronnie, as everyone called him, was wearing an Indian print caftan and looked like a prince.

Leon Redler, a psychotherapist and also a member of PA, was playing with the children, crawling on all fours being a lion, with little pieces of coloured paper stuck on his eyelids and nose. All the children roared at the 'lion' except Kira, who started crying. I was frustrated with her for not being brave like the other children. I was so insecure and inadequate myself that I couldn't bear to see the same insecurity in Kira; I felt responsible for her and at the same time unable to comfort her and guide her socially.

Adam, Ronnie and Jutta's three-year-old son, was just about to hit Leon the Lion over the head with a big wooden pole when Ronnie, at the very last moment, quite calmly and without fuss, diverted the pole. Later, as it got dark and candles were lit, I was again impressed by Ronnie, as he took Adam's hand away from a candle flame, without startling him, just seconds before he was about to touch it. I had never before seen an adult give a child that kind of space for his or her curiosity. I remember my mother's anxiety overriding all my spontaneity, trying to prevent me from hurting myself, or worse, getting mortally injured.

In *The Divided Self*, R.D. Laing says: "The psychotherapeutic relationship is a research; a search for what we have all lost and which some can perhaps endure a little more easily than others, like some people can stand lack of oxygen more easily than others. We must continue to struggle through our confusion to insist on being human."

It was new to me that when you enter into therapy you enter into a mutual relationship, and are not going to see some specialist, who is supposed to be an expert on what's the matter with you, and who's going to sort you out, whether you like it or not.

I read in Martin Buber's philosophy that there were epochs when disciples lived with their master as apprentices in the trade called 'life'. The network around Ronnie became my spiritual family. The people I met were united by the need to discover a way of being free of dogma and conditioning by society and parents, and finding a caring, authentic way of relating to each other. We met often, at seminars and social gatherings. So many suppressed emotions surfaced in all of us, that it was often impossible to cope with the intensity *and* be sociable at the same time; the most we could manage then would be to sit still with our eyes closed. Sometimes Ronnie would come up and put a candle in front of someone so they could focus their attention on the light of the flame to calm their mind and bring it into the present. To be given space to gather ourselves without feeling under any pressure filled us with gratitude. The atmosphere would transform as if by magic and Ronnie would play the piano, with some of us singing, others dancing; and everyone would stop trying so hard and become more relaxed ... simpler.

One evening, when a group of us is sitting by a log fire in a Norfolk house, where we are spending the weekend together, Ronnie starts reading the 'Parable of the Prodigal Son'.

After my childhood in the Soviet Union, the Bible had become a book filled with threatening images and superstition, dark and punishing. When I saw a Bible for the first time in the drawer of a bedside table in a London hotel, I hastily closed the drawer, as if I'd seen a ghost. I grew up with the notion that religion was the opium of the masses. I could never figure out whether that was meant to be a good or a bad thing, and I still can't.

But I really listen when Ronnie reads, in a deep and profound voice, the parable from the Bible about the son who squandered his inheritance in a life of debauchery, getting into debt with creditors after him and having to work his arse off to pay them back. Finally, exhausted and at the end of his tether, he appealed to his father, asking for help. The father was so overjoyed that he ordered a big feast to celebrate the return of his Prodigal son. The other son, who had spent all his time tilling the ground and working hard, felt jealous: "Why do you order a feast for my brother who hasn't worked and for me, who's been working so hard, nothing?" And the father replied: "One sheep that is lost and found is more of a cause for celebration than all the other sheep that have never been lost."

In the silence of the room I can hear my heart beat at an alarming rate, as it always does when I feel moved to say something and block it out of fear of appearing stupid. Ronnie asks us: "What do you make of this?" My mind is teeming with all these new ideas; the idea of not appreciating my good fortune and squandering what I have been given brings up fear. But in my heart I'm encouraged to hear that there is hope; it is possible to acknowledge your mistakes and 'go back to your Heavenly Father' ... or, in non-religious terms, return to authentic being. You don't have to be condemned for your mistakes forever. Forgiveness is possible. Starting anew is possible. These are all the things I'm bursting to say and don't.

Nobody else said anything either; people were often

drawn into an awe-filled silence in Ronnie's presence. I appreciated years later how Ronnie offered no explanation, no analysis; the subject was left for us to ponder and mature, each in our own individual way and in our own time. Deep gratitude to Ronnie arises in my heart over and over again for the things he said, and for the things he didn't say.

Once I asked him: "When you pray, who is it you pray to?"

He answered: "Who indeed?"

Years later I heard him say: "Prayer is listening to the silence of one's own heart, a waiting or attentiveness that doesn't specifically ask for anything. You can't do better than that."

Someone once asked Mother Teresa: "What do you say to God when you pray?"

She answered: "I don't say anything. I listen."

"And what does God say to you?"

"He doesn't say anything. He listens."

When I started listening to the silence in my heart I began to hear the voice of my own conscience. The hardest thing is to continue listening, when we don't like what we are hearing, but continue we must.

Finding myself where I left off

Wimpole Street, London, 1970

> "In this particular type of journey, the direction we have to take is back and in, because it was way back that we started to go down and out. We have a long way to go back to contact the reality we have all long lost contact with."
>
> R. D. Laing, *The Politics of Experience.*

At my next session Dr Laing asked me: "Have you heard of LSD?"

"I've heard of people who have taken it and had psychedelic experiences, but I have no idea what that means."

"It's probably better you don't have any ideas about it. Would you like to try it?"

He was the first person in my life to make me feel that such a thing as trust was at all possible, so it was a new experience to be able to say 'yes' wholeheartedly. The glimpse of myself that I had caught in R.D. Laing's eyes when I first met him inspired me to risk embarking on the journey back to myself.

He said he had access to pure LSD and a legal licence to use it in therapy. We arranged a date and time. It would take six hours and I must have Arthur pick me up at the end of it.

I woke up nervous and excited at the prospect of spending six hours taking 'a trip' in the company of the amazing R.D. Laing. When we sat down he handed me a glass of water containing the substance, which I drank; then he put some more water in my glass, swished it around and drank it himself.

After what seemed like minutes I began to feel as if I was going down a well, deeper ... deeper ... deeper ... and then found myself in a damp, cold room in the Tatar republic curled up in a little ball on the floor.

I'm four years old. My father is dead. My mother is lying in our narrow iron bed with the blanket over her head, crying. The Tatar landlady, whose son has just been killed in the war, lies behind the Russian oven, wailing. I'm sitting on the floor in semi-darkness. I feel utterly and devastatingly alone. My shoulders are hunched, my dress stiff with constant wear and cold. I am very hungry. There are no toys. I'm the most unlovable little girl in the whole world, abandoned and beaten down by life – a nobody.

I don't know how long I was there, in that grief stricken state of my four-year-old self, on the floor in the Tatar republic, but all of a sudden, as if it were time travel, I'm thirty-one years old again and back in the room with 'the good doctor'. He is so present that I feel as if that scene in the Tatar republic has just been projected onto a screen and we've watched it together. Tears are streaming down my face. By feeling and re-experiencing the full extent of my deprivation, by going to the rock-bottom of it, I feel myself whole for the first time.

"Could it have been as bad as that?" I ask.

He answers in his Scottish brogue: "Probably worse."

"I found love inside me by feeling the full pain of the absence of it. If I can stop resenting what I didn't get, I'll be in a state of love. I experienced a moment of forgiving my mother for not letting me be. She didn't know how to let herself be. If I don't forgive I'll continue the same old tradition of blaming and complaining; it's not that 'it runs in the family'; it only runs because we let it."

Insights keep pouring out of me: "My heart has melted; now I feel free to give love – not just expect to be loved."

"That kind of love comes by the grace of God," he says very gently. There is a moment of deep, peaceful silence between us.

"I feel as if I've been out of focus all my life and have just come back into focus. Now I understand that the pain and humiliation of loss, starvation, cold, fear, neglect, is what made me go out of focus. The only way to cope was to pretend I wasn't there, to disconnect. It feels as if all the disconnected parts of me have clicked into one, I feel whole. Did you notice when I came into focus?"

"Yes I did. I even felt a little tingle when it happened. The experience you've just described is called *catharsis*. Do you know what that means?"

"No."

"It's a Greek word meaning clarification and cleansing, renewal, by being purged of excessive suppressed pent-up emotions. The healing comes from the Healthy Spirit, the grace of God. And it is by the grace of God you have the native intelligence to be able to understand any of it."

There were no psychedelic colours. But Ronnie transformed in front of my eyes a few times, from an ancient sage back to Ronnie and back again to the sage.

When the effect of LSD gradually started to wear off, the feeling of wholeness began to fade. From one minute to the next doubts crept in, as my disturbed and restless mind flooded back. I no longer felt the love I had experienced only minutes before. It became a memory. I desperately needed to hear that the experience I'd had was real: "Did it really happen? Did I really feel love? Was I really so sure of being able to love others? Now I don't feel it anymore."

He said: "Mina, *you* told me that you felt you came into focus by experiencing the full trauma of the deprivation in your childhood; *you* realised that the love you felt you were deprived of has always been within you. You just couldn't experience it."

After he had pointed out that the ball was firmly in my court, he suddenly seemed distant and separate and not at all at one with me, as I'd experienced him during those six hours of the session. I wanted him to reassure me, tell me again what he saw, what he witnessed. But Ronnie, in his love and wisdom, wasn't going to; I had to learn to trust my own experience and keep connecting to love again and again. It felt terrifying. I had no experience of trusting my own experience. Grasping for straws I said: "You understand me ... but how can I be *sure* you understand me? *Do* you understand me?"

"You want *me* to tell you if I understand you or not. How will you know, even if I tell you I do?"

"You mean I have to trust my own experience? But how can I?"

Leaving the magic of oneness and feeling my separateness felt harsh; it reverberated with the sense of leaving the womb and finding a disconnected mother on the other side. But in this case Ronnie was very much present, reminding me of the truth of my own being and my direct connection to life, without any intermediaries.

As if tuning into my thoughts, Ronnie said: "We may have a memory of the experience of coming out of the womb and not having a real connection with the mother. It *is* terrifying, even more terrifying than when we re-experience it, as you have just done."

Suddenly I heard him say: "Arthur is coming to pick you up in half an hour."

"Oh no." I felt like newborn baby who was expected to be an adult. "Would you like a cup of tea?"

"Tea ... what do you mean ... tea?" I was furious. "You offer me tea when I've just found myself and lost myself again?"

The relaxed, casual way he got up and put the kettle on *was* reassuring; it brought me into the present where there was no need for panic. But when I saw him standing with a mug of tea, looking suddenly a lot younger and not at all like the wise, older man who earlier seemed like a father and a wise sage at the same time, I came out with the worst insult I could think of: "You ... you look just like any guy in a pub." He grinned and his face gleefully turned into that of a Glaswegian hooligan.

When Arthur came to pick me up my everyday reality walked in with him and in the car on the way home, I felt gut-tearing longing to be back with Ronnie, where I'd found myself.

The LSD trip combined with Ronnie's extraordinary ability to connect with others' deepest thoughts and feelings, illuminated the abyss that separated me from myself, allowing me a glimpse of the memory of wholeness that was mine before I became so drastically fragmented as a child. This experience gave me the courage to continue the day-to-day inner work of moving towards love and forgiveness with the added help of Meditation and Yoga, which came into my life shortly after.

Although the experience was stimulated by a drug, it had made me realise that only by fully feeling the depth of my childhood pain, and not cutting off from it, could I experience wholeness. It also awakened the realisation that forgiveness can only come about by admitting that all the things I blame other people for are also in me. By realising my own transgressions and how much forgiveness I need, I become forgiving towards others.

I didn't get hooked on LSD; I got hooked on being in the present.

Stealing a pair of knickers from Miss Selfridges and the gift of Yoga

> 'Yoga is controlling the activities of the mind'
>
> – *Patanjali's Yoga Sutras*

Ronnie Laing suggested I should write a book about dissociation after I told him in my therapy session that I got caught stealing a pair of knickers from Miss Selfridges in Regents Street.

"What is it you stole again ... a pair of knickers? Couldn't you have gone for something bigger, like a diamond?" He is obviously irritated by the whole thing.

"Why did you steal a pair of knickers?"

"I don't know ... I had a fifty pound note in my hand-bag ... I think getting something for nothing gives me a feeling of independence and achievement."

"Can't you think of another way to independence and achievement?"

Dying of shame I ask if he will come to court to testify. I don't know what I want him to testify – that I am nuts, I suppose.

He says yes without a moment's hesitation and I appreciate that he doesn't keep me waiting for an answer while I'm holding my breath and choking with embarrassment.

After a short pause he says: "I'm going to plead that you are suffering from dissociation."

I take my first deep breath since I arrived and give him a conspiratorial smile, relieved that he is devising ways to dupe the judge.

"I am not going to lie," he says, noticing my smile, "I'm serious. You have used dissociation as a defence against overwhelming pain in the past. You re-experienced it on LSD when you got in touch with being totally knocked out by hurt and invalidation in childhood. The same thing happened when the rat ran over Arthur's foot in your luxury flat in Johannesburg and you lost all sense of reality, as if you were still the deprived little girl living in a mouse-infested room in war-torn Russia. Your habit of dissociating and acting in a disconnected manner goes on and on, even though you are now living in a time of peace and prosperity. Instead of stealing knickers you should write a book about dissociation; it hasn't been done convincingly enough and you know about it first hand."

"If I'm honest I can't say that I didn't know what I was doing."

"At Miss Selfridges you were disconnecting from knowing what you were doing."

"But I can't write like real writers."

"If you write about your experience honestly it will say more than many books that are on the shelves in the bookshops at the moment."

That wipes the smile from my face and gets me thinking a little deeper about what I had done.

Ronnie continues: "Scientists have done experiments on amoebas. They prodded the organisms with a needle and found that after contracting, they returned to their original size. When they were prodded again, they became a little smaller and with each prod became more and more contracted. This is what happens to us when we don't become conscious of and release our original pain; we remain contracted versions of ourselves, cut off from our full potential."

Ronnie does come to court. As I stand there, enveloped in a thick fog of shame and panic, I don't even hear the judge recommending to have me examined by the prison psychiatrist and Ronnie talking him out of it, till I find myself outside the courtroom with Ronnie saying into my ear: "You are lucky, the Holloway Prison psychiatrist might not have been a nice chap like me." I've been let off the hook and cured – if not of dissociation, certainly of shoplifting – forever.

All this happened the day before Arthur, Kira and I were flying to Italy with the Laing family. Going on holiday with your shrink? Unheard of! Unethical! Irresponsible! Unprofessional! Ronnie had no problem with being clear and honest about his boundaries at any time, any place. As for me, my whole life was a problem, so it did me no harm to be confronted with myself in Ronnie's mirror-like presence in a social situation.

We hire a Palazzo by the sea, set in a beautiful garden of palm and fig trees. With the Palazzo comes a cook and a cleaner. Mel, Arthur's sister, and her school friend Lolly, arrive from South Africa to be with us and to help with the children. We swim in the sea and sunbathe on our private beach, eat ripe figs from the trees in the garden, have meals together prepared by the Italian cook and in the evenings Ronnie plays Bach on the clavichord he has brought with him from London wrapped in a green velvet cloth ... and I am constantly anxious and tired.

In the morning at breakfast I ask Ronnie: "Why am I tired all the time?"

"Have you heard of Yoga?" he asks.

"I heard about it from a friend of Arthur's from film school who said it made her grow taller and she started talking to trees."

He says with a chuckle: "Let's all meet in the garden tomorrow morning to practice some Yoga postures."

Eager for my first Yoga lesson, I get up at the crack of dawn and go for a swim and a run on the beach in order to be in good shape for my first lesson. When I come tearing into the kitchen I find Ronnie standing there, eating yesterday's ratatouille and talking to Arthur about the Buddha's Four Noble Truths and about *Vipassana* meditation which, he says, in Sanskrit means 'insight', insight into the true nature of reality and going beyond all our suffering. He says: "The Buddha's Four Foundations of Mindfulness should be the foundation discipline for all therapists."

As I listen to him speak, I feel hope stirring in my heart that it is possible and there is a way to stop all the spinning that goes on in my mind, taking me on journeys I don't want to go on any more.

So, after breakfast we gather in the gardens of the Palazzo. I find some postures Ronnie shows us easy and feel inordinately proud of myself, and I find other postures harder and feel dejected, swinging as usual, from 'I'm the best,' to 'I'm the worst'. Arthur, who has played a lot of sports from childhood onwards: tennis, squash, golf, swimming and boxing, and considers himself fit, is shocked when he tries to bend forward and the stiffness in his shoulders and legs doesn't allow him to move very far. When Ronnie asks us to sit on the ground and become aware of our breathing, I can only whimper with frustration, my ribs and chest are so tight I can hardly breathe. No wonder I'm constantly tired and anxious.

That day in the gardens of the Palazzo is a very

memorable day for me, one of the luckiest days of my life. I had my first experience of being totally absorbed in a moment of stillness. I had a strong sense that Yoga was going to save me from the torments of my mind, which constantly cast their shadows onto the present.

The long corridor of the Palazzo is lined with marble statues. One day I come out of our room to go to the beach and see Ronnie sitting next to one of the statues at the other end of the corridor, in a meditative posture, looking like Rodin's *The Thinker.* I'm in turmoil; how am I going to get past him without making a fool of myself? I especially went on a fast for a week before the holiday, so I would look slim in my tightly clinging purple Biba dress, but now, walking towards him, I feel so agonisingly self-conscious that my body has a life of its own doing involuntary twists. I see Ronnie watching me undulating awkwardly the full length of the corridor and, as I get closer, he falls about laughing. I feel so embarrassed I wish I could disappear, but all the same, I don't think that his laughter is meant to humiliate me; he can see through my posturing and is mirroring my self-consciousness, inviting me to have a good laugh at myself, which at this point I'm not quite capable of doing.

Back in London, sitting with Arthur and Kira in a taxi at Heathrow airport, I feel like Cinderella at midnight, the carriage has turned into a pumpkin, the horses into mice and my newly found hope into ashes. The first taste of freedom from my habitual anxiety, evoked by being introduced to Yoga, now seems entirely dependent on Ronnie. I'm just about to knuckle under the familiar hopelessness: 'what's the use, nothing ever lasts', when Ronnie comes up to the taxi and says: "How would you like it if a few of us meet early every morning and practise Yoga together before work?" Wow! Practicing Yoga with Ronnie every day and being part of a group doing something meaningful feels like nothing short of a miracle; as if my father had come back to life.

We meet every day at seven in the morning, to practice Yoga, using BKS Iyengar's book, *Light on Yoga* and take turns being the teacher by consulting the book. Every week we choose one new posture to learn. We discover health-food shops, I make my own yoghurt and we breakfast on yoghurt and muesli after Yoga.

I still have fears that my new life is just a mirage and will one day disappear. I have recurring dreams of my stepfather, Grisha, coming to the Yoga class and telling my new friends how useless I was when he asked me to make him the last omelette of his life.

One morning, while we are practicing Yoga in Ronnie and Jutta's exquisitely decorated living-room, overlooking the garden, I suddenly see a little mouse on top of one of the bright woven Indian cushions and start throwing a fit. Ronnie, who had always empathised with me on my trauma of living in mice-infested poverty, gives it no weight and makes it apparent to me that this little mouse and I are now living in more enlightened times, and that I don't need to hang on to my suffering, as part of my identity.

We find a Yoga teacher and start learning headstands and handstands; everybody has fun trying it, except me. I'm frightened and sad and don't understand why. Our Yoga teacher, Donna Hollerman, is not inclined to dwell on the psychological implications of my resistance to inverted postures; she stands over me, repeating, 'don't think, just do it!' till eventually, after a year of her encouragement and support, I can do handstands and headstands by myself.

Eventually I began to be able to live in the present more and more, experiencing every moment as new, but initially it was crucial for me to understand the connection between my early experiences and my present behaviour.

I wasn't the only one with painful associations with the past. When Arthur was eventually able to release the tightness in his shoulders, he realised what a heavy burden had been dumped on him at the age of ten when his father left and he was told: 'now you are the man of the family'. At every lesson someone in the Yoga class burst out sobbing, as our muscular armour began to give way and emotional pain started to surface. I had to release a lot of anger and frustration at not being allowed to grow in a natural way, having been manipulated according to my mother's fears, superstitions and prejudices which went back many generations. And all of us in the Soviet Union were manipulated by the craziness of the totalitarian regime. Forgive? Yes ... but not too soon! First I had to release my rage and fury at all the forces, personal and political, which blocked the creativity and joy in my life. I succeeded with Ronnie's encouragement, "If you allow yourself to remember what happened, rather than letting it haunt you all your life, you can be free of it."

My experience of therapy with Ronnie was that he put mental health into the context of spiritual health, which is why he introduced us to Yoga and Buddhist meditation: "Talking about your pain is not enough. In Buddhist terms being identified with one's mind is being deluded. We describe our situation and then suffer from the description." He spoke about the need for inner silence, the lack of which makes us unbalanced. He reminisced about the days when parents and children spent time sitting by the fire together, not doing or saying anything, just gazing into the fire.

Sometimes he'd play Bach on the piano and weep. Once I asked him, "Why are you crying?"

"Because I don't love enough," he said.

No one has ever made me feel more loved.

Ronnie didn't make me feel that I was suffering from a mental condition called dissociation which required treatment; he said that we are all dissociated to the degree that we are not fully present, not living in the sanctity of the present moment.

The crack in the armour

"Ring the bell that still can ring, forget
your perfect offering,
There is a crack in everything, that's how
the light gets in."

– from *'Anthem'* by
Leonard Cohen

As Ronnie warned me at my first session, the time did come for him to go off to India and Ceylon, to practice *Vipassana*, the ancient Indian form of insight meditation.

At my last session before his departure I surprised myself by not feeling the famous separation anxiety spoken of in psychiatric jargon; I've always been naturally averse to psychobabble. So to say it in *Mama Loshn* – mother tongue, in other words, plainly, as a human being, I didn't feel any anxiety at all. But still, as if nudged by the devils of the past, I came out with: "I'll never trust anyone again; everyone always goes away and never comes back."

Ronnie let fly without a moment's hesitation: "I'm not your father. I'm not going to sell my coat and die in Siberia. I'll be back in a year."

I regretted that my compulsion to look for reassurance from him had overridden my gratitude for all the gems of good sense he'd already given me. At the end of the session Ronnie gave me a gift. *The Yoga Sutras of Patanjali*, which he had copied out by hand himself some years ago, with each chapter underlined in a different colour. What a heart-warming, uplifting way to keep in touch!

I memorised the first three sutras,

> *Yoga is controlling the activities of the mind.*
> *When mind is controlled self stays in his native condition.*
> *Otherwise he conforms to the nature of mind's activities.*

Given my feelings of inadequacy and inferiority, I thought I'd found a treasure: the 'native condition' is in all of us and does not depend on how much money you have, or how much education or how many designer clothes, or what kind of car you are driving, or whether people like you or not. Yoga could help calm disturbing emotions and thoughts by restoring balance and equanimity and change your life. Wow!

The year Ronnie was away Arthur and I, in the first burst of Yogic enthusiasm, sold our collection of Proust's *Remembrance of Things Past,* intending to 'transcend our past and merge our individual transitory reality with the timeless Universal Consciousness'. I actually bought those books back some years later, realising that I do have to let go of the past, but not by brushing it away or selling my books.

Ronnie went to India to practice *Vipassana* for a year, and I went to the *Vipassana* meditation centre in Sussex for a week. Someone remarked: "Ronnie plays the piano – everyone wants to play the piano. Ronnie practices mindfulness – everyone wants to practice mindfulness." I couldn't see for the life of me what was wrong with that; for the first time in my life there was something sensible to emulate.

At the *Vipassana* centre the daily practice of Mindfulness starts at four am, when we are woken up by the sound of a gong. The instruction is to dress mindfully, wash our faces mindfully, brush our teeth mindfully and walk mindfully behind the monk in his long saffron-coloured hooded robe, down a little path to the meditation hall. We sit for two hours, observing our breath, repeating mentally three times, 'breathing, breathing, breathing' and when thoughts arise (which is all the time), 'thinking, thinking, thinking' and then back to 'breathing, breathing, breathing'. Irritation arises and you say, 'unpleasant feeling is present in me' and back to 'breathing, breathing, breathing,' and so on.

After the meditation we have breakfast in silence. If you need something on the table you say in a low whisper: "Pass the Marmite, please." You eat mindfully, observing the eating process; you acknowledge the intention to pick up the knife, 'intending, intending, intending'; you mindfully hold the knife, mindfully spread the butter, mindfully carry the bread to the mouth, 'chewing, chewing, chewing' ...

At first I am irritated by everything. The man next to me is breathing heavily, I feel hostile towards him. I hate him.

The instruction is to practise 'bare attention': *in the seen there should be only the seen, in the heard only the heard. Listen to the silence between the thoughts.*

After one week of following instructions to watch my mind and connect to my breathing, my irritation with my heavy breathing neighbour has decreased. I even like him a little.

Once a day, for twenty minutes, we see the meditation master. It is reassuring to be able to ask questions and find that my experiences are quite common.

I've always had a sense that my father must be somewhere in the recesses of my memory and now, in this extraordinary situation, I have a powerful feeling that in the stillness and clarity, his image will surface, but it doesn't. I have no memory of him.

Back home we become vegetarian, listen only to Indian music, cut the legs off our dining table, sell our chairs and sit on the floor trying to free our hip joints and keep our spines straight. When my mother comes to visit we have to borrow a chair for her. She sits on that lone chair looking down on us from above, totally perplexed and sighing from time to time: "*Aaagh.*"

Finally, a year has passed and Ronnie, as promised, is back from India. He has spent two months in silent meditation and three weeks living in a cave in the Himalayan Mountains with Gangotri Baba, a Hindu ascetic who has initiated him into the cult of Kali, the Hindu Goddess of creation and destruction.

I can't wait to see him and to continue therapy, but wonder if he'll take me on again, or am I supposed to deal with my emotional states without his support, now that I've practiced Yoga and meditation for one year? I phone and hesitantly ask if I can come to see him again. To my relief he says, 'Yes' without any hesitation.

When we meet, he immediately notices the change in me: "You've certainly broken through the first layer of your muscular defences."

It makes me think of the Leonard Cohen's song. After living inside my shell for so long it's reassuring to know that there is a crack where the light can get in.

I find a similar encouraging theme in this Chinese 'cracked pot' story:

> An elderly Chinese woman had two large pots, hung on each end of a pole which she carried across her neck. One of the pots had a crack in it while the other pot was perfect and always delivered a

> full portion of water. At the end of the long walks from the well to the house, the cracked pot arrived only half full. For a full two years this went on daily, with the woman bringing home only one and a half pots of water. Of course, the perfect pot was proud of its accomplishments. But the poor cracked pot was ashamed of its own imperfection, and miserable that it could only do half of what it had been made to do.
>
> After two years of feeling a bitter failure, it spoke to the woman one day by the stream: "I am ashamed of myself, because this crack in my side causes water to leak out all the way back to your house." The old woman smiled: "Did you notice that there are flowers on your side of the path, but not on the other pot's side? That's because I have always known about your flaw, so I have planted flower seeds on your side of the path; every day while we walk back home, you water them. For two years I have been able to pick these beautiful flowers to decorate the table. Without you being just the way you are, there would not be this beauty to grace the house. Each of us has our own unique flaw. It's the cracks and flaws we have that make our lives together so very interesting and rewarding. You've just got to take each person for what they are and look for the good in them."

Going to Ronnie's talk on *The Intrauterine Experience* at the Institute of Contemporary Arts, was another eye-opener. Ronnie told us that fairy tales come from the visceral memory of the intrauterine experience and listening to him talk about life inside the womb conjured up an enchanted world of fairies, monsters and witches.

This was the first time I heard anyone speak about conception, implantation, gestation and birth and that our different experiences of these stages can reverberate through our lives. For instance: while some people can conceive of an idea or project, but can't take it any further, others might conceive of a project, move it on a few steps, but be unable to finish it; others may always feel unwelcome when they come into a crowded room, or feel stuck in their life, unable to move forward, and experience panic, as if there is no light at the end of the tunnel. The memory of all those intrauterine stages is imprinted in our bodies. Connecting our experiences in the present to the intrauterine experience can help us to understand ourselves and become free of our conditioned limitations.

"Maybe the mother didn't want the pregnancy. Maybe her womb was not a welcoming place. The fertilised ovum and egg form the embryonic cell, which, like an omnipotent queen in its shimmering membrane, travels down the fallopian tubes to implant in the womb, but it might get rejected a few times before it finds a place, or it could be rejected altogether, resulting in termination of pregnancy."

"When you are born in a hospital your first experiences are bright lights, instruments, masks, and being slapped on the bottom. What a welcome into the world! Compare it to being born under the stars, your mother receiving you with tenderness and love; you meet her eyes and feel safe and welcome."

"Or, imagine the opposite," Ronnie continues, "the umbilical chord gets cut abruptly and the baby is shocked out of its being, so the first breath becomes a gasp. All this influences our breathing patterns later in life."

I had never heard anyone speak like this before. Apparently for centuries people believed that newborn babies didn't have feelings and could not feel pain and that crying was not a genuine communication but a reflex of an immature organism. Ronnie spoke about the exquisite sensitivity of a newborn baby, and that never again are we quite as sentient and open. He talked about the difference it makes when the umbilical cord is cut only after it has stopped pulsating and the baby has taken its first natural breath, so that there is no interruption in the continuity of the flow between mother and baby and between life in and outside the womb.

I became aware of how disconnected my mother and I had been and how I was swaddled at birth as I came out. Babies in those days looked like little cocoons; swaddling was the traditional thing to do, supposedly so that the arms and legs grew straight. Once again I had to come to terms with the fury and frustration of being held back from my most natural earliest movements, feeling like a tree being prevented from swaying in the breeze.

It amazed me to think that we all have these experiences and memories in us, of the magical world inside the womb, and of being born, whether we are aware of it or not. When I left the ICA I felt such a deep connection to myself that I walked alone through St. James Park late at night; it didn't even occur to me to feel unsafe.

You don't need to catch up with what you've missed! Start living now!

At my next session I told Ronnie what a revelation his talk was for me, connecting me to the deepest levels of what being alive really means and at the same time accentuating just how disconnected I was:

"When I think about how much I've missed in life my solar plexus gets into a knot and I want to die."

Ronnie lights a cigarette. The elegant way he does this instantly lights up my appetite for life and for my own potential for gracious living. His style isn't only in the clothes he wears or how he wears them, it's in his fundamental commitment to living life graciously, in all its aspects.

Ronnie casually leans back in his chair: "I've heard you repeat this sort of thing *ad nauseam*. You don't seem to express even the slightest wish to get out of this state of mind. I can only say I'm glad *I'm* not in that state of mind. Amongst the things I have to deal with, I'm glad this is not one of them."

"I feel there's nothing inside me. I just feel it's too late. I can never catch up with everything I've missed."

"You don't need to catch up with what you've missed. Start living now. If you take only two minutes generating the effort to make somebody else happy, it's repaid immediately, but if you are miserable and put it onto other people, it makes you even more miserable. Having to generate effort is an unavoidable stage of the struggle, before we realise that there is no need to struggle."

He goes on: "This feeling, 'there is nothing inside me', arises out of the memory of deprivation. It could be a mixture of deprivation and anger, wishing to destroy any memory of fullness out of revenge, for example: when a relationship goes bad there is great difficulty remembering the good things, they are sort of blotted out, out of hatred and anger."

"What difference does knowing that make?"

"If you realise it, then it opens up the possibility to stop doing it. You have glutted yourself on feeling empty and without resources."

"No I haven't."

Ronnie laughs: "You haven't? Oh well, maybe you need to go on like this till you feel you *have* glutted yourself. If you don't have sufficient desire to stop it then I don't suppose you will."

"So you think I won't?"

"There are two ways of thinking about it. Either you won't, or you can't. I can't say which it is. I can't even say whether it's good for you to stop; maybe you need to keep on going through all this misery, for some obscure reason. I'm very glad I don't have to, whatever other things I do have to go through.

"People live under the terrible illusion that acquiring all sorts of information makes up their lack of inner resources. Inner resources come from within. We are facing the unknown ... total darkness. Light comes out of this darkness, if only we can get our ego out of the way. Jesus said: '*Blessed are the poor in spirit.*' In the original it reads '*blessed are the spiritual beggars*', those who are spiritually empty-handed; this means being without ego, so that you can receive.

"If you don't believe in yourself beyond the ego, then you'll keep repeating the same old scenario. If we *drop* our expectations, we don't know how we are going to feel in an hour's time, or in the next moment."

"How come *I* know?" I ask.

"If you hypnotise yourself, tell yourself what you are going to feel in the future, with adamantine obstinacy and conviction, then it *is* quite possible that your future will be a perpetual self-fulfilling fantasy which prevents you from finding any true self-expression. I am suggesting that there's an error going on in the way you work it out."

Ronnie carries on: "This issue of 'no resources' will get taken care of if you get yourself out of your own way. When you are in the state of mind of feeling you have no inner resources, it is still possible not to want to be in that state of mind.

"The attitude to adopt when we are feeling helpless is ... I don't know, what would you take the word 'prayer' to mean, the attitude in prayer? What we do when we are praying is acknowledging that 'of my own self, I can do nothing'."

"My mother was always asking God for help and yet she was in constant misery and kept repeating that her heart was as heavy as stone."

"That's another matter. She didn't pray for inner resources, her expectations stopped her from receiving, even if it was given. But she didn't do so badly, did she? In making a prayer I suppose you need to consider the indications that have been given. The Lord's prayer, do you know it?"

"No."

"Ah. 'Thy will be done on Earth as it is Heaven' seems to indicate the state of affairs when His will is not being done on Earth, otherwise we wouldn't have to pray for it.

"'Give us this day our daily bread' – resources if you like, super essential bread; not only the bread we eat, but the bread of life that keeps us going.

"'Forgive us our trespasses as we forgive those who trespass against us.' It doesn't necessarily mean that if we forgive, we are automatically forgiven; we have to ask for forgiveness.

"'Lead us not into temptation.' Temptation has not so much to do with being drawn into all sorts of bad thoughts as it does with being intimidated by the worst sort of terrors and demons that one can be presented with. In the Buddha's last meditation, before he attained enlightenment, he was beset by demons and his only response was to touch the Earth – his final realisation that the demons and terrors were all manifestations of his own mind. This state of fearlessness is the final release from anything and everything that can be thrown at us. It goes beyond the need to be courageous.

"The grace of God is infinite, but we can't expect it if we are not making an effort ourselves. God enters into equal partnership. Knock and it shall be opened. Ask and you will receive."

"Receive what?"

"By being empty, you receive a sense of inner joy or any of the other graces. There is an indication here that we are expected to make some initial effort to reach out and ask, and even the asking is by the grace."

Hearing him talk about the possibility of getting out of my self-created 'prison', about prayer in a tone devoid of false piety and solemnity, resonated with me and brought tears from a spiritual depth I hadn't yet plumbed. I felt in my heart that he was speaking the truth, and that it went far beyond the boundaries of any religion.

Moaning, complaining and criticising

> 'Show yourself more human than critical,
> and increase your delight'
>
> – Hector Berlioz

There's a story about Noel Coward who apparently said to an actor friend, "if anyone ever tells you that I've been rude about you behind your back – believe them.' In my childhood there was always something going on behind someone's back; in fact the moment the person's back was turned people would start slagging him or her off. I thought it was normal until I heard Ronnie Laing speak about lies, deceptions and mystifications between people creating mental confusion and disorientation.

With startling candour he'd make public the gossipy rumours doing the rounds about someone in our crowd. There was something roguish, almost gleeful, about his candour, but also profoundly sane and refreshing. Although the effect was rather startling and embarrassing at the time, in the long run it cleared the air.

Then it was my turn to hear some plain, unvarnished truths: "Do you know that the women on the scene are talking about you, saying that you neglect Kira, while you practise Yoga?"

I was furious: "How dare they? Don't they realise that my aim in practising Yoga *includes* being there for Kira? How can I be there for her if I'm in pieces myself? It's not selfish to want to heal myself; only then will I be able to truly love. What's really driving me to practice Yoga is that I wish to give Kira the mother I would have wished for myself."

"You are extraordinarily naïve, which is not the same as innocent, and extraordinarily complex, which is not the same as experienced. Do you really believe that everyone can appreciate your intention to practice yoga in order to become the mother Kira deserves? Not many people make it their priority to become whole, or feel happy when others become whole, or feel that the wish to become whole is an expression of love. The definition of love in Buddhism is wishing others to be happy, feeling joy in the fundamental well-being of ourselves and others."

"How come everyone seems at ease with each other, except me?"

"Often what seem like friendships are temporary alliances, mutual congratulation societies."

My fear of relationships and of rejection was phenomenal. Shortly after meeting Dodo, who has since become a friend for life, she invited me to the Zoo with Adam and Kira. When we got back she told me, in no uncertain terms, that I had been 'insufferable' at the Zoo. The word – often used by Ronnie – was a good one to describe somebody who was being a pain in the arse. I felt panic; here I go again, spoiling everything. I always had an intense feeling of guilt, which probably originated from a childish irrational belief that I was responsible for my father's death. I felt responsible for bad things happening.

A few days later Dodo rang and invited me for a walk on Hampstead Heath. She told me about her fear of confronting me with how she felt, that she too was afraid of rejection, but felt she had to tell me the truth. This level of communication was new to me. It made me feel safe enough to admit that I had, in fact, been irritable and impatient with the children. And that I didn't have to be stuck with feeling guilty about it, if I could change my behaviour. The most valuable lesson I learned from this experience was that a true friendship can not only survive an honest outburst but be deepened by it.

But I still complained to Ronnie: "People like me at first but then seem to lose interest."

"It's not that they lose interest. They just can't be sure what you're going to spring on them next. They get a bit wary. Do you realise that when you approach, you carry the gloom of the Russian steppes with you? Get the book, *How to Win Friends and Influence People* by Dale Carnegie."

I was surprised: 'He can't be serious; surely he knows I have more depth than that?' I was prejudiced against 'self-help books' thinking they were shallow and filled with 'by changing the way you think you can get anything you want' platitudes. What did 'they' know about a Russian childhood of poverty and the tyranny of oppression? But since Ronnie recommended it, I bought the book, hoping secretly that maybe it would help me make friends after all. Feeling superior, I paid for the book, still pretending that I was buying it for somebody else with less discerning tastes.

I got knocked off my superior perch after actually reading *How to Win Friends and Influence People.* Dale Carnegie talked about being interested in other people, remembering their names, making them feel appreciated, or "do unto others as you would have them do unto you". And above all else, "If you want to gather honey, don't kick over the beehive".

I realised that I was only interested in having other people interested in me; I was actually stuck in a pattern of envying, moaning, complaining and criticising. Co-dependent relationships, characterised by a defensive system of dealing with the lack of self esteem, was all I was capable of. Colluding in mediocrity, rather than open to possibility, complaining about others and feeling superior, makes us more miserable than we already are. Not a healthy situation.

I thought I had better come out of the closet and tell Ronnie, the one person I could trust with this sort of information without being judged: "I'm envious of everyone. Even reading about the survivors of Dunkirk getting together to commemorate their escape from Hitler's armed forces makes me envious; at least they had something in common. I have nothing in common with anybody. I've never had anything. All I ever had were hungry mice scuttling all over our only room searching for non-existent crumbs, and lice crawling all over my forehead after my mother put kerosene in my hair to chase them out."

"Give it up, give up your envy and resentment, let bygones be bygones ..." said Ronnie, thoughtfully at first, and then added with a chuckle: "If you can't make it fake it; force yourself, it might become genuine in the end. Or if it doesn't, oh well, form a 'Mice and Lice' club."

I couldn't help grinning in spite of myself. It was fascinating to watch him shift so gracefully from a pensive mood to a quick-witted humorous one with flair and ease. It was an inspiring invitation to give up envy, or at least have the intention of giving it up; and every time envy came up, to become aware of it, let go and connect with my breath.

The best cure for envy is to become the best possible you. I decided to go on a mental fast from envying, moaning, complaining and criticising; apply the mindfulness practice – noticing the emotions arising and zap them with awareness of breathing. For the first two days it felt like a punishment to keep all my grudges and disappointments to myself; the noise in my head and the emotional turmoil became even more turbulent. But on the third day I started to experience something I never had before: moments of freedom from my obsessive feelings of lack and deficiency, and the need to tell everyone about it. It felt like a miracle. I discovered that I could choose to contain my feelings and not just moan out of control to anyone who'd listen. It gave me a break from my constant guilt and my anxiety about putting people off, and I got a sneak preview of what it felt like to have self-respect and integrity.

The habit of complaining had formed itself in my childhood as the only way of relating to my mother; she complained to me and I complained to her. There's a joke about five Jewish mothers out having lunch. The waiter comes up to the table and asks: "Is *anything* all right?"

When I go to visit my mother in Cape Town, I get another chance to see where my disposition to envy and criticism comes from. Every morning I notice her neighbour, a woman of eighty-five in a smart navy blue suit with an elegant hair-do, passing briskly by our window.

My mother says mockingly: "*Zi leift shein*, she runs already."

"Why, what's wrong with her running? Anyway, where is she running?"

"To the old age home," says my mother in an off-hand manner.

"What does she do there?"

"She goes and sits with the old people and reads them stories." My mother's tone is getting more sarcastic by the minute.

"What's wrong with that?"

"Who says wrong? Let her run, she has somewhere to run, she has her hair done twice a week, lipstick first thing in the morning, and she runs. She can run, her son comes and picks her up once a week and takes her to the theatre, so let her run."

My poor mother! That is her way of telling me that she is envious of the woman because her son comes and takes her out regularly, whereas *her* daughter, me, living in London, visits only once a year. Still, I feel furious at this familiar voice constantly slagging someone off, without realising that I am stuck in the same habit.

Back in London I still complain to Ronnie: "Arthur says I'm critical and judgmental of people."

"And you think you're not? That's all you do all the time when you talk about people. It's something for you to ponder about. Meditate on gratitude."

Gratitude – the opposite of complaining and being dissatisfied – wasn't big as a topic of conversation at our table in the suburb of Moscow. True, there wasn't much to be grateful for in the ordinary sense and the concept of gratitude, as a spiritual quality coming from a heart, which is ready to show appreciation in spite of what you have or don't have, hadn't reached our world yet.

The Hebrew term for gratitude is *hakarat hatov*, which literally means 'recognising the good'. Practicing gratitude is recognising the good that is already yours. As Rumi wrote:

'Who then is rich?'
'The one who rejoices in his portion is rich.'
Someone asked: 'What is the cause of ingratitude
and what is it that prevents gratitude?'
And the master answered: 'The preventor of gratitude
is inordinate greed.'

One morning Arthur woke up exclaiming: "I've got it! I've got it! I've figured it out! What you're doing most of the time is complain, and I've been thinking that your dissatisfactions were *my* fault. I'm off the hook! I'm free!" He got on the phone and called one friend after another, telling them about his liberating insight.

I finally figured out something too: certain situations provoke an intense reaction in me, but the intensity of my reaction has nothing to do with the situation. Once I stopped blaming outside circumstances for my emotions, I started to feel more joy and live more in the present. In the present moment there's no room for discontent.

But who, besides the Buddha, can always be content? So I reserve the right to have an occasional *kvetch*. Anyway, I can't stand people who *never* complain!

A civilised divorce is not a contradiction in terms

> 'If your life is a balloon that's hanging ten thousand feet up in the air there is no use stepping out of it, even if you don't agree with everything that's going on.'
>
> – Robert Musil

My life did feel like it was hanging ten thousand feet up in the air and I decided to step out of it, even though I had no idea how I was going to survive. I just couldn't get away from my inner voice constantly repeating: 'if you are to be true to yourself, you have to separate from Arthur'. If I was honest with myself and remembered my prayer: 'Please dear God, let me get married just to prove that I can, even if I have to get divorced later on,' then everything was going according to plan. Be careful what you ask for.

When I talk about it with Ronnie, he goes straight for the bull's eye: "When you took the marriage vows did you know what you were doing?"

"I don't think so."

"Then you don't need to agonise over breaking them."

I had to admit it was true; I did not take my marriage vows in full consciousness of what I was doing. And now that I was beginning to touch on being true to myself, I felt I needed to be on my own. But getting divorced? That was such a seriously grown up thing to do, taking responsibility for myself and my child? I was terrified.

To try and clear my mind I went on a fast for a week, grapes for ten days and brown rice for a month. I lost some weight and felt light and clear, which made the inner voice even stronger. I asked the I Ching what to do, hoping to be told that I was being self-destructive wanting a divorce. But the feeling, that in order to be true to myself I must separate from Arthur, kept being re-affirmed.

Arthur and I decided on a trial separation for a month and he and Kira went off to South Africa to stay with his mother, Lulu.

For the first time in my life I was on my own, in a comfortable flat, with a car and sufficient money. I was euphoric; just to be at home and know that nobody was going to interrupt, that I didn't have to answer the phone or the door if I didn't want to, that I could follow my own rhythm, do what I want, when I want, I could do nothing, I could read all day, go out for a whole day, I could sleep all day and stay up all night. This was freedom, new and intoxicating. Ronnie warned me: "It's all very well feeling free and euphoric when nothing has really changed; it's a different matter after the decision to separate has been made."

The day Arthur and Kira arrived back from South Africa, he said, as he came through the door: "I've decided to give it another go."

And I said: "I've decided we have to separate."

He said: "OK." A bit too quickly. He wasn't big on showing his feelings.

I noticed he was wearing rainbow-coloured platform shoes, which made him appear taller; he'd always had a complex about being a bit shorter than me. I never saw him wear shoes like this before, or ever again, but somehow to me, those shoes seemed to be the affirmation of our incompatibility.

I don't know where I got the nerve, all I knew was I had to separate from Arthur if I was to be true to myself and that if wasn't true to myself I'd regret it. It felt to me that his charismatic enthusiasm was like a bulldozer crushing the first delicate shoots of my awakening autonomy.

We tried to talk to Ronnie together. When I attempted to say why I wanted to separate, what came out was: "He gives Kira chocolates all the time, lets her stay up till 'Late night line-up', he takes ages, much longer than me, to get ready to go out, and he puts Bob Dylan on from the moment he wakes up."

Arthur said emphatically: "To ask me to change those things is like asking me to become six foot four."

Ronnie said: "Mina, the ball is in your court."

On the tip of my tongue was: 'In that case we must separate,' but instead I said: "Maybe I haven't tried hard enough."

"Good luck," said Ronnie, not even trying to disguise his irritation. It was clear that I was just postponing the inevitable.

Every time I came home, I found Arthur with his mates sitting cross-legged on the floor, smoking dope and listening to Bob Dylan. I felt as if I'd come to the wrong address. I couldn't stand the sound of Bob Dylan's voice and couldn't make out what he was saying. I'm more of a Leonard Cohen girl. Later, I used to joke that Arthur and I got divorced because of Bob Dylan.

Arthur's enthusiasm for life was quite phenomenal; when he developed an interest in something it was one hundred percent, be it watching the night sky through a telescope on his balcony with all the children in the neighbourhood and teaching them about planets and stars;

or studying the philosophers, Nietzsche and Kierkegaard or looking up words and underlining ideas that gripped him. It was the same with Yoga; when he realised that Yoga would free him from his unnatural posture and restricted movements and help him to discover freedom and balance, he immediately wrote a book on Yoga, called *Body Life.*

I was jealous of Arthur's friendship with Ronnie, feeling unable to break through my status as patient. I also wanted to write a book about my experience of how Yoga was helping me to free myself and was envious that Arthur went and wrote a book after only two years of practicing and Ronnie validated it with a very inspiring foreword. I was in quite a state about it all. So when Arthur was telling me about the insights he gained from the practice of Yoga, I felt he was saying that I couldn't possibly have any insights of my own and all my anger at invalidation in childhood would erupt like a volcano. He'd observe me calmly and say with a smile: "Have a look in the mirror; you are foaming at the mouth."

His second wife Janet tells how she once tried to talk to Arthur, when he was glued to the television, watching Wimbledon and totally ignoring her. She unplugged the TV, picked it up and threw it on the floor. Arthur calmly plugged it back in, found the tennis channel and said, with a marketing smile: "Always buy a Sony."

It didn't help matters that the Indian Yogi, Mr. B. K. S Iyengar, with whom we were having lessons while he was in London, kept praising Arthur during class: 'Good, Arthur', 'good, Arthur, good', and never once said 'good' to me. I complained to Ronnie: "It makes me feel as if I don't exist." Ronnie offered: "Would you like me to make you a one hour tape of: 'Good, Mina, good ... very good ... good ... goooooood', so you can listen to it while you are practising Yoga?"

"Yes ... but still ... why doesn't Mr. Iyengar ever say 'good' to me?"

These days I can laugh at myself and honestly say, 'Who knows and who cares?' But it mattered back then. Thankfully Ronnie's humour helped to unhinge this chronic craving for approval and recognition.

Arthur and I ended up having an amicable divorce. He came over and summed up our assets: "We have four Persian carpets, two red ones and two beige ones. How about you have a red one and a beige one and I have a red one and a beige one?"

I said: "Ok."

"I'll have the I Ching and you have the coins?"

"Ok."

"How about if Kira lives with you and feels free to move between us as her heart desires?"

"Ok."

It worked.

Arthur left. His charm and charisma brought him an offer by a friend of a dream house in the Vale of Health for a year, rent-free. He moved in and established his own scene there: Yoga, drugs and Bob Dylan.

The first thing four-year-old Kira did after Arthur left was memorise his phone number. She spent a lot of time with her father; it was more fun there. Arthur had a zest for life, which was contagious. Everyone loved his company.

Since I was the one who initiated the separation, I was surprised how painful it felt when Arthur brought me the divorce papers to sign.

Ronnie never tried to influence me one way or another, but he did lay his cards on the table when he said: "Statistics show that most couples who choose to separate never regret it." I never did either. My heart was breaking, but

I was now in touch with something that brought me the trust to keep going.

After Arthur and I got divorced and he married Janet, we eventually all became friends and went on holidays together. It wasn't always smooth and easy but we went through our difficulties and remain friends to this day.

Janet and I call ourselves 'wives-in-law' and feel that between us we make one good mother to Kira, and to Kim and Ias, Janet and Arthur's two children, who call me their second Mum. All the things I wasn't good at Kira learnt from Janet and, seeing how Kira has turned out, I too must have done *something* good. Arthur's sister Mel and her friend Lolly played a big part in Kira's early life, looking after her and helping her to deal with my ups and downs.

Being alone with Kira I found myself at regular intervals sinking into memories of dismal loneliness, like the one of being alone with my mother. Every day required a gigantic effort to let go of the old misery which sometimes still held me in its power, and do something creative with Kira instead.

I bought a book, *One Hundred Amazing Magic Tricks*, and we chose the one called 'Sink or Swim Eggs'. By following the instructions we managed to produce a salt liquid the same density as an egg, which we poured into a round glass vase. Then we carefully placed the egg in the solution and it floated, suspended in the middle. Kira and I gave it a place of honour on the mantelpiece, where it stayed for a couple of years doing its encouraging 'sink or swim' magic – a powerful reminder that life is, indeed, a 'sink or swim' affair and that I'd better get my act together and start swimming.

My last therapy session

> "Complain only that you are still complaining"
>
> – Meister Eckhardt

I delved into the pain of my past for six years and got more than my share of understanding and validation.

Yes, the way I got treated in my childhood could be considered emotional persecution.

Yes, that's why my confidence keeps wilting unless it gets constantly propped up.

Yes, that's why there is such a disparity between my talents and my ability to express them.

Yes, that's why I don't have a sense of continuity.

Yes, that's why I feel so worthless and find it agonising being with people who don't see the real me, when I don't know how to be me.

Yes, that's why I am incapable of cultivating and maintaining relationships.

But enough is enough already! If I was honest, to keep asking for more felt indecent.

At my next therapy session, after I sat down and started on yet another tale of woe, Ronnie said, as if tuning into my new thoughts: "Why don't you think of something else?" That startled me; he'd never said anything like that before.

I was getting tired myself of seeing life through the drama of my past, an addiction that had to be fed by looking for endless excuses for why I couldn't just drop it and enjoy the present moment. Still trying to make my last stand I said: "Even the Great Russian filmmaker, Sergey Eisenstein said how easily he could fall back into his deep-seated insecurity, 'a button falls off – I feel a pauper.'"

"But it didn't stop him from making the masterpiece '*Battleship Potiomkin*.'"

'Go and argue with that', as my mother would say.

In another session as I fall into the comfort of the familiar chair I say:

"Phew, the traffic was impossible."

Ronnie says: "Congratulations," and seeing my puzzled look adds, "This is progress. You never talk about such ordinary things."

I thought it would be best to stop therapy before he said I should, (although I don't know if he would have). I'd thrown enough tantrums about how miserable my life had been; maybe it was time to stop tantrumming and start counting my blessings.

I imagined my last therapy session to be like the scene in the film of my life: I arrive with a huge bunch of chrysanthemums to celebrate the end of an era; we sit recalling scenes from therapy, having a good laugh at what a neurotic, obsessive, lovable fool I've been and thanking God it's all over. Ronnie opens a bottle of champagne, we click glasses to celebrate new beginnings and he invites me to sing '*Ochi Chornya*', accompanying me on the piano; I sing from the heart and with ease, like never before.

Needless to say, I did not bring flowers; I was afraid I wouldn't be able to carry it off, in a way I had imagined, with an air of nonchalance and pizzazz, and instead, would end up looking like a nervous fool with flowers. I walk in and blurt out at the door, not leaving any room for hesitation: "I've decided this is my last session." Only now does it occur to me that, strictly speaking, I should have given him some notice, but he doesn't even bat an eyelid. "Ah! Congratulations!" he says simply.

Congratulations? I suddenly feel all alone, left out in the cold and terrified. But there is no going back.

I sit down for the last time in the 'confessional chair' and say: "I feel I have to tell you the one thing I've been too ashamed to speak about," wishing I could disappear through the floor with embarrassment. "I've been lying about my age; I thought my therapy wouldn't be complete if I didn't tell you."

His eyes instantly fill with mischievous glee: "How old *are* you then?"

"Thirty-six but everyone thinks I'm thirty-four."

"At least you haven't spread out like some women your age."

Your age ... what does he mean – 'your age'?

"Did you know that there are tribes in New Zealand who use older women for pin ups? Maybe you should go and live there."

Older women ...?

I've said it is my last therapy session and he has taken me at my word; he isn't going to give me a hand to get out of the emotional hole I have dug for myself; this time he isn't going to change my nappy and prop me up. I have to stand my own ground. Good thing I've done some reading, and "Sit up or be propped up", words from *Meditations* by Marcus Aurelius, the Roman stoic philosopher, come to my rescue. Here is a good opportunity to show my mettle; connect to my breathing and my centre without Ronnie's help.

Yes, in spite of all my doubts and fears, I had to find my own voice, trust my own experience and stay firm in my decision to face life without therapy. It didn't even seem so impossible, since therapy, in its original meaning – attending to the soul – was central to the relationships of the people around Ronnie who had become my friends. Listening and attending to each other wasn't something that stopped with formal therapy.

As at any other session, cool as ever, he says: "Time to stop."

I say good-bye to Ronnie and go out into the world: a divorced woman who has owned up to being thirty-six, with no lies in her body and with a trembling sense of her own autonomy, like a young green seedling pushing through the darkness towards the light.

After I give up therapy, I buy myself a second-hand piano.

With my lovely baby Kira, but not finding it easy to be a mother.

A delightful moment with Arthur and baby Kira!

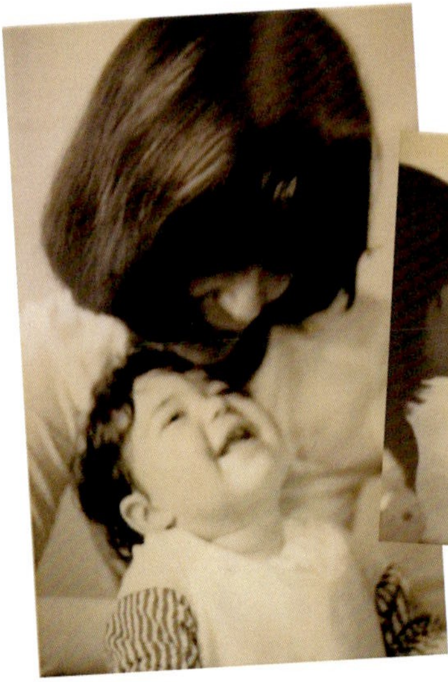

More of sweet baby Kira.

So lovely!

Kira with Daddy in Mallorca.

My mother did grow fond of Arthur, eventually.

Photo by Dorothee Von Grieff (Dodo).

Dodo, the photographer and a very dear, lifelong friend.

More happy moments, captured by Dodo.

Happy moments with Kira on Hampstead Heath.

In the sea with Kira on holiday in Corfu.

Still dreaming of stardom ...

PART FOUR

There is Life After Therapy

Student: "Ronnie what is your advice to someone studying philosophy?"

Ronnie: "Hang loose."

Starting to teach Yoga

A year after Arthur's book *Body Life* comes out, he is invited by BBC1 to make a Yoga film series called 'Every Body Knows'. With great enthusiasm he engages all his friends and family in the project, including the children. The camera films him teaching the class on the main screen, with me demonstrating the postures as a little unrecognisable figure in the corner of the screen, and feeling like I'm the star of the show.

When I next see Ronnie, he casually throws in: "Hugh Crawford thought you looked divine on screen."

"Did he really?" I ask, swelling with pride. It's just what I want to hear, at last I'm being recognised, I'm a *divine* star! Then a thought occurs that being divine and being proud of it don't go together like a horse and carriage, so I try to look humble. Ronnie calmly observes me for a while and then says: "But *I* don't think so, not yet." I know that his remark is not intended to put me down, but still, the brute honesty of it throws me off balance – I sprain my ankle when I leave, and it takes six months to heal.

When I finally began to stop wasting energy on clinging to my old fantasies and started practicing awareness of breathing instead, I found that, after a lifetime of feeling constantly tired, I was suddenly not tired any more. Well, it seemed like 'suddenly' but a lot of practice preceded it. Just like the guy who when asked, "How did you go bankrupt?" replied, "At first slowly, then suddenly."

In the early days of teaching I only had two Yoga students.

I asked Ronnie: "Why am I only earning £17.50 a week?"

"It's because you don't have an undeterred mind. It all depends on whether you can put in a good word for yourself."

Could I put in a good word for myself? What did I really feel and think? For one thing I didn't really want to teach Yoga. I felt split. One side of me wanted to be independent and earn my own living, while the other still dreamed of a man to take care of me. While one side felt there was profound meaning in Yoga and mindfulness, the other wanted to be glamorous, sing and dance, tell stories and risqué jokes. Eventually I realised that there was no need to choose one or the other; I could accept my contradictory self and let different aspects of my being come into harmony with each other, like themes in a musical composition.

At first it was hard work to stay on course. Every day I made a list of things to do, like the toad in the *Frog and Toad* story:

1. Wake up
2. Practice Yoga
3. Go swimming
4. Tidy the flat
5. Do the shopping
6. Go for a long walk
7. Sit in meditation for an hour
8. Cook a meal for Kira and me
9. and remember to thank God.

Before I started teaching Yoga, Ronnie suggested I go and see John Heaton to check if I was a good candidate for joining the psychotherapy training course at the

Philadelphia Association. I passed the test but didn't want to become a psychotherapist. The picture Ronnie painted for me of what the training would entail, 'you'll become a Freudian for one year, then a Jungian for another year, a Kleinian for another *...etcetera...* before you hopefully come to yourself', filled me with dread. He said: "Then you'd better teach Yoga, you'll be dealing with healthier people." And that's how I was initiated into teaching.

The first Yoga class I ever taught was at a retreat at Samiye Ling Tibetan monastery in Scotland.

The resident Yoga teacher, a skinny Frenchman called Didier, invited me for a walk in the woods. As usual, my susceptibility to romance transported me to the snow-covered Russian steppes: I am Lara, walking arm-in-arm with Dr Zhivago, both of us filled with intense passion. In reality, what should have been a friendly walk in the woods turned out to be thoroughly unremarkable shag in the grass, after which Didier informed me: "You're going to teach my class this afternoon." And he wouldn't take no for an answer when I protested that I'd never taught a class before.

"The best way to start is to be thrown into the deep end," he replied, in his boudoir French accent.

Having had such an unconventional start, it's not surprising that my teaching has continued to develop in my own way. Even though I didn't want to teach Yoga, I learned my most valuable lessons from it – patience, compassion and love for others.

I remained uneasy in the role of 'Yoga Teacher' until I realised that I didn't need to be in a role. Yoga teacher, relax! I didn't want to feel 'on duty', or to follow any fixed structure, but to find a way of doing nothing, in the sense of getting out of my own way and not interfering. Eventually the teaching became a spontaneous response to what needed attending to in the class. And it didn't stop me telling stories and jokes, which seemed to enhance rather than detract from the atmosphere.

I will forever be grateful to all my Yoga teachers, Donna Hollerman, Mary Stewart, Vanda Scaravelli, Sandra Sabatini, for their persistent encouragement to keep letting go of my fears and to find balance, guiding me through so much resistance towards releasing my body to its innate alignment. But, in the end, I needed to be free from the authority of even the best of teachers in order to find my own connection to the life force.

It took years of practice before the Yoga postures became an expression of stability and openness to the Divine, and not a matter of pride in how well I was 'doing' the postures. On one occasion, at a party at Ronnie and Jutta's place, I sat on the floor showing off how I could put my legs into full lotus position without using my hands. Ronnie came close to me and said: "Any whore in Paris can do that," which elicited an indignant gasp in the room: "Oh Ronnie!" But I knew what he meant – Yoga is not about being able to twist your body into all sorts of positions, and the fact that you can doesn't necessarily mean that you have let go of trying to grasp the ungraspable and have become capable of love. Yes, I was physically supple, bending and moving with effortless ease, but I also knew that it's easier to open your legs than to open your heart. And I'm sure Ronnie didn't mean that 'a whore in Paris' couldn't do both.

What did eventually develop is a way of teaching that feels fresh every time at every moment. In a class, we always start by connecting to our thoughts and feelings whatever the current inner weather, accepting what is without creating any conflict, bringing awareness to the breath and to the contact with the ground. It's important not to push away thoughts and feelings when they are unpleasant. The Hasidic teacher, Baal Shem Tov said, "Wanting to forget makes the exile longer, the secret of redemption is in remembering."

Or Franz Kafka:

"We are as forlorn as children lost in the woods. When you stand in front of me and look at me, what do you know of the griefs that are in me and what do I know of yours. And if I were to cast myself down before you and weep and tell you, what more would you know about me than you know about Hell when someone tells you it is hot and dreadful? For that reason alone we human beings ought to stand before one another as reverently, as reflectively, as lovingly, as we would before the entrance to Hell."

Before each class I always say a prayer: 'When two, three or more gather together in the name of the truth, the way and the light, may the Healthy Spirit be in their midst.' I use Ronnie's definition of the 'Holy Spirit', as the 'Healthy Spirit'. It is a sensible thing to pray for, because we suffer when we are disconnected from the healthy spirit and become isolated inside our private cocoons. Teaching Yoga has helped me to clarify my intention: for all of us to get our 'I' and 'me' out of the way, so that our hearts can open and allow the 'healthy spirit' to be in our midst. Then what happens between us in a Yoga class can be something genuine and fresh.

What's a girl supposed to do?

"It's a helluva start being able to recognise what makes you happy."

– Lucille Ball

It took a lifetime for me to quit being a victim, give up my 'why does everything happen to me?' syndrome, and at least sometimes admit that if my life is not working it's because of me. I had a perverse reluctance to being honest about what makes me happy, which was singing, dancing the Tango, juggling, hula-hooping, telling stories and making people laugh; inspiring lightness of spirit rather than vexation. And why not; as the Great Russian poet Alexander Pushkin said, "You can be a serious person and still think about the beauty of your nails." But I still felt as if I had no right to do what I really wanted to do.

When I told Ronnie about my striptease fantasy he said: "Not many things will get me out of my study, but this is certainly one of them."

It's not that I thought I looked so sensational in the nude that I had to share it with the world; my fantasy was about the art of seduction – with the right balance of suggestiveness and restraint to have all the men in the audience in my power without taking any of my clothes off. It took six years of therapy, brown rice diets and many self-realisation workshops to figure out what was behind this *mishugene* seduction fantasy; hiding in a secret corner of my heart was a naïve belief that if I had been a sweet, charming and seductive little girl my father wouldn't have gone away and died.

Now that I was minus a husband and a shrink, as part of my emotional survival strategy I started having parties at my Little Venice garden flat, with singing and dancing and Ronnie playing the piano. I'd invite all my friends and their children, creating an occasion to dress up glamorously and fill my flat with song and dance and laughter. It was delightful for Kira to have all her friends over – Adam, Natasha, Nina, Hannah, Amy – teasing and playing pranks on everyone and joining in the adults' singing and dancing, dropping off to sleep wherever sleep found them.

One of my parties had a theme – 'pimps and whores', which proved that I wasn't the only one with fantasies of power and seduction as I didn't have to twist anyone's arm to arrive with bottles of champagne, dressed up as a whore or a pimp. Everyone has their story!

I had to defrost my fridge the night before to free the iced-in bottle of vodka and, to buoy me up a bit, totally out of character, drank a pitcher of vodka and orange juice before everyone arrived, followed by champagne brought by the guests. And off I went, dressed in a tight skirt with a long slit and a slinky top, with a pink Sobranie in a long cigarette holder, dancing provocatively to the number from the film '*Gypsy*':

You can uh ...You can uh ...
You can uh ...uh ... uh ....
That's how Burlesque was born
So I uh ... and I uh ...
But I do it with a horn
Once I was Shleppa
Now I'm Miss Mazzeppa

With my revolution in dance
You gotta have a gimmick
If you wanna have a chance!'

I didn't have a chance. I could barely stand up, and ended up the rest of the night in my bedroom with the walls and ceiling spinning, hearing Ronnie at the piano with my friends singing '*They can't take that away from me*', and thinking 'this is what it's like when you die, life just goes on without you.'

Theo

Having no plans for the day ahead used to make me feel like an ostracised orphan, especially on a bright sunny day. It brought up memories from the war time in Kyrgyzstan after my father died, and my mother had to put me to bed while it was still sunny outside and I could hear all the other children playing, leaving me alone night after night to do while she worked night shifts. So on this particular day in Little Venice, trying to clear out these old memories and lift my spirit, I decide to put on my favourite gypsy dress with embroidery on the cuffs and the collar and go to the hairdresser.

When I come back with my hair slick and shiny I put on Louis Armstrong's *'It's a wonderful world',* and try not to think like my mother: 'all dressed up and for whom and for what?' but instead to think positive thoughts, like 'love comes when you least expect it'.

While I'm sitting there breathing deeply and trying not to expect anything, the phone rings and it's my friend Sally, telling me that someone has given her a billiard table, and would I like to come and play billiards with two Dutchmen from Amsterdam? "They are friends of a friend and are making a film in London." Well, I sure didn't expect that! But, mention film and I'm there!

After the introductions, one of the Dutchmen ignores me, but the other, Theo, passes me the cue and I can tell he is hooked when I flick my freshly blow-dried hair to one side and say my most seductive Russian accent: "I've never played billiards before, but I like games of aiming and hitting."

Sally makes ravioli and we all sit around her massive wooden table in the kitchen eating, drinking wine and talking. Theo sits next to me and asks endless questions about my life in Russia. One story after another from childhood begins to flow with such passion that once I get going there's no stopping me, so I try to conclude by telling him that I'm writing my memoir. He says he is a successful publisher in Holland, and is now trying to get into film. That's it! I can see my book published and made into a film with me playing myself.

As I get up to leave he asks if he can walk me home and read my manuscript. The minute we sit down he starts reading and only stops for moments to look at me admiringly and tell me that it's gripping. At dawn he asks me: "How old are you?"

I'm just about to launch into such clichés as: 'guess'; 'you don't ask ladies such questions', 'how old do you want me to be?' ... when he says, matter-of-factly: "I can work it out from your writing ... you must be about forty."

The tone of total acceptance in his voice makes me feel instantly loved.

I say: "I'm going to be thirty-nine next month. How old are you?"

"I'm thirty-four."

After that Theo starts coming over from Amsterdam, appearing at my door regularly with a Dutch Gouda and a bottle of Dom Perignon. It is like a fairy tale. I find it so alluring to sit with him in an elegant restaurant while he orders coffee and cognac after dinner, smokes Drum and tells me; I am star material, my writing is superb, my singing is special and I am the next Marlene Dietrich. But when the time comes to go home, the fairy tale facade starts to falter.

All the same, he means what he says about my writing and music and, what's more, he knows how to work and get things done. He sometimes locks me up in a room, like Colette's husband Willy, to encourage me to focus on streamlining a chapter.

Eventually Theo moves in. My flat is in poor shape, the carpet thin and worn, and paint peeling off the walls. He redecorates the whole flat, puts Kira into a private school in Harley Street, helps her with her homework, and tells me I can give up teaching Yoga and concentrate on writing and music.

I am confused as ever: 'What's a girl supposed to do?' Fate sends me such a nice man. Am I supposed to say no? Is it that I'm not strong and clear enough to say thanks but no thanks? ... or ... is it true that I am 'forever dissatisfied', as my mother always told me. And when he sends me a ticket to Amsterdam, surely it's a magical omen when I see a shooting star from the plane for the very first time?

Magical, *shmagical*, I still didn't long to sleep with him. Is it such a crime? It's not that he was unattractive, not at all. The thing was, for me, sex is the cherry on top of the cake. But Theo and I hadn't even baked the cake yet. We related to each other from our respective 'pain bodies', to quote the spiritual teacher Eckhart Tolle. Pain bodies are created by unresolved issues from the past, negative energy fields that occupy body and mind. We were each entrapped in our own stories. For my part, in Russia I had to wash myself in a basin of water in our one room and was constantly on edge because my stepfather would always be lurking somewhere; I had my very first bath in privacy in Warsaw when I was twenty-two and even then my mother didn't allow me to lock the door, don't ask me why.

Theo, although living in a luxurious apartment in Amsterdam, had a formerly respectable doctor for a father, who went suddenly mad and started to obsessively pick up rubbish in the streets and fill their bathtub with it. Theo, being the youngest of three children, got bathed by his mother last, in a plastic basin of water, which was cold by the time his turn came. He had a chip on his shoulder about it. So when I lay in the bath, savouring moments of privacy, he knocked on the door and, just like my mother, insisted that I open it. He would say in a sorrowful voice: "Having a bath?" which pressed the chip on *my* shoulder and made me see red. The chips on our shoulders communicated with each other so well!

Together Theo and I were not popular with my friends. We wanted to be, we tried to be; we even went to Heal's in Tottenham Court Road and bought a brown corduroy couch and two spacious armchairs to match so we could entertain and make our guests welcome. It made no difference. We colluded in the fantasy that he was going to make me into a cabaret star, while doing our best to hide the truth from ourselves and each other that our relationship wasn't really working.

My inner confidence was growing, but I still didn't have the guts to be honest. Once again, I'd returned to my familiar pattern of believing that I wouldn't survive without a man.

Every time I wash rice I think of Nod

> "No, not that way, you must wash rice so that not a single grain is lost."
>
> – Nod

Every time I'm about to wash rice before cooking, I remember Nod saying to me in a manner that didn't leave any room for argument:

"You have to wash rice in a pot, not through a sieve. You cover the rice with cold water, stir it and let it stand until all the husks rise to the surface, then pour the husks off and repeat the whole process again." He liked to teach. I still find myself doing it his way, fifteen years later, but I add my own touch – after I've washed it the way he told me to, I put it through a sieve.

I met Nod through Morris, and I met Morris the night Ronnie phoned to say that he had to entertain two ladies from Esalen, (the centre for humanistic alternative education in Big Sur, California). He asked if we could get a Chinese takeaway, invite Brian, the double bass player and have a musical evening at my place. Oh, *yes*!

That evening Ronnie arrived with the two ladies and Brian arrived with Jeanette, the double bass and a strange looking man called Morris, whom I had never met before.

I was still living with Theo, agonising over having to tell him that I wanted to separate and finding no courage to do so. This was my love life pattern – when I was alone, I wanted to be with a man; when I was with a man I wanted to be alone. Ronnie had told me a number of times that I could look ten years older or younger according to my mood; that evening I looked ten years older, wrinkling my brow over having to tell Theo the truth.

While Brian was setting up his double bass and the Esalen ladies were chatting with Theo, Jeanette and Morris, Ronnie came up to me and, out of the blue, whispered straight into my ear: "What are you waiting for?" I didn't know if he meant what I thought he meant, but it felt like an arrow had hit its mark. What *was* I waiting for?

I went into the bedroom, changed into something alluring, brushed my hair every which way, from underneath, from side to side, from back to front, to jazz it up; put on some make up and perfume and went off to pick up the food.

When I come back the music is in full swing. Ronnie on the piano and Brian on the double bass are playing and singing: "We will never ever meet again on the bumpy road to love ..." How I wish I could drop the food and join in, without missing a beat, "but I'll always, always keep the memory of..." That is my fantasy; the reality is that my voice feels stuck and I can't make a sound.

Morris, the strange guy who came with Brian, is sitting on the floor with my big wall mirror in front of him, lining up rivers of cocaine and offering them to everyone. I've never tried cocaine before. I have a line and find myself immediately at ease and curiously drawn to Morris, as though by a magnet. The music goes on till five in the morning, everyone leaving when the birds begin to sing. The next morning Theo goes to Amsterdam and I still haven't told him about my decision to separate.

That evening I'm blissfully alone at home when there's a knock on the door and it's Morris standing there, invincible like an Aikido warrior. Turns out he lives just the other side of the Little Venice canal. I invite him in, we sit down, start talking and the conversation starts to flow like the rivers he's again lining up on the mirror. There's something about him that I can't quite figure out. I'm not used to associating with darts playing pub blokes with beer bellies, but he is so naturally relaxed and there is a sensitivity and humour about him that I feel drawn to.

He casually starts asking me about Russia and my childhood – just up my street – and interrupts me at various stages in my story to tell me something about his own life when my stories remind him of it.

The phone rings, it's Theo. "I can't talk now," I say, "Morris is here."

"Who's Morris?"

"Brian's friend from last night, don't you remember?"

"Tell him to go, I'll wait."

"Why?"

"He's dangerous."

"No he's not."

The phone keeps ringing until I unplug it. Morris leaves at about five in the morning, 1959 in my story, when my mother and I had just arrived in Poland and I'd lost my virginity. At the door he says: "To be continued." At that moment I could have easily taken him by the hand and led him into my bedroom, if it wasn't for my rational mind asking, 'Are you crazy?'

While on duty as a truck driver, Morris had driven into a tree and lost an eye. He showed me pictures of himself before and after, and the contrast was remarkable. He said that the car accident and losing an eye had re-awakened his intuitive nature and his sense of humour. Taking the piss out of Sai Baba, the Indian Guru who was exposed for using conjuring trickery apparently to produce precious jewels out of thin air, Morris would sit there making movements with his hand, as if trying to catch something invisible. I asked: "What are you doing?" He laughed: "You've got to start somewhere."

To cut a long story short, unwittingly, or maybe wittingly, Morris gave me the confidence to take the plunge and separate from Theo. Then, we had a little fling. Well sort of; Morris's beer belly caused him to sweat a lot, which made it hard for sparks to fly between us.

One day Morris warned me: "I have a friend called Nod. He's a magical gardener. He designed the exotic gardens in the foyer of the Sheraton Sky Hotel. Don't you go falling in love with him; everyone else does." So I did.

I arrive at Morris's room and there is a young blonde man with blue eyes, just like Saint Exupery's Little Prince, sprawled out on the bed. He doesn't move a muscle when I come in, or when Morris introduces us. I think, 'what a rude young man', and at the same time feel intrigued. I am bowled over when, a couple of days later, Nod phones and asks me if I'd be his escort to a private party being hosted by Pink Floyd, nonetheless. My instant reaction, after the initial excitement, is the usual, 'what am I going to wear?'

Some people get panic attacks when flying on an airplane or going for a job interview. I get panic attacks when I have to decide what to wear, especially at the change of season, or when packing to go away, or when invited out. I know it's connected with never having had any clothes in my youth in Russia, but I sure wish I could become cool about clothes before I die.

Getting dressed for the party, I put on and take off all the clothes in my wardrobe a couple of times before I manage to recognise that one of the dresses is, as a matter of fact, a lovely strapless silk dress with colourful, small triangles on a white background, a straight, below-the-knee skirt with a slit at the back. I even have high-heeled sandals with blue, yellow and red straps to match it. I have to admit I look good.

Nod and I arrive when the party is in full swing. David Gilmour is playing the electric guitar solo, *'Shine on, You Crazy Diamond'* and we sit down and drink champagne with Nod's friends, John and Jean from Shropshire. Conversation sparkles, as does the champagne and, in the spirit of *joie de table,* John asks: "Why don't the two of you come and spend next weekend at our country cottage?" I say, "We are not together" to which he replies, "Come together separately."

So we go. After dinner by the fire in John and Gill's quaint cottage, when everybody is ready to retire, Nod suggests I follow him up the stairs to inspect the bedrooms. One bedroom is clearly uninviting with a single mattress on the bare floor and a dim bulb hanging from the ceiling; the other is luxuriously cosy, with thick wooden beams, a double bed covered with an exotic orange kelim and a warm, red light coming from a lamp on the bedside table. Nod says: "I know where I'm going to sleep; you can make up your own mind." I do, rather quickly.

But now, what am I going to wear in bed? Once again, I've managed to pack all the wrong things; I didn't even bring a night-gown. So, while Nod is in the bathroom, I hastily undress and get into bed in my T-shirt and knickers. Nod walks in leisurely, wearing a magnificent Chinese gown with dragons spitting fire, sits down on his side of the bed and starts rolling a joint. I feel mortified. Some High Priestess, lying there shivering in her knickers is hardly a match for this Emperor with dragons on his gown.

I'd always found men coming on too intimately, too soon, too fast. Not Nod. That's what I found most attractive about him, the way he gave you a chance to get those juices flowing. The leisurely ritual of smoking a joint, telling a joke, talking, laughing and playing, with no pressing innuendos in the air, is the best aphrodisiac. He probably had this game worked out to a fine art; it was hard to tell when he told me he loved me whether he really loved me or was just good at 'it'.

Although the end was in sight from the beginning, Nod and I ended up living together for two years. He had a rucksack packed with a full survival kit for any eventuality – a tent, an oil burner, packets of soup and a sleeping bag. It stood there in the bedroom: a symbol of his free spirit, of how he didn't need me and was equipped to take off at any moment. He really knew how to make a girl feel secure!

His wife had left him and gone to live in America with their two little girls and Nod visited them regularly, telling me that, frankly, he wasn't at all sure whether or not he'd go back to his wife, if she'd have him. But it looked like his wife wouldn't have him, when one time he came back from America with three cobs of red Mexican corn to hang above my front door as a symbol of commitment and harmony between him, Kira and I.

One week later a friend of his came to visit and when he was leaving I heard Nod rip one cob off and give it to him. I felt that rip in my heart and knew there and then, 'this is the end.'

I wished I was like Carmen in Bizet's opera – the fiery gypsy who didn't dilly dally once she stopped loving Don Jose. I admired her free spirit and always felt I had it in me but didn't yet have the guts to act on my more fiery instincts, so Nod and I went on living together for another year and a half.

Morris, who had put on an angry front after Nod moved in with me, let it go eventually and the three of us, in our version of Francois Truffaut's *'Jules et Jim'* – two friends and an impulsive, free-spirited woman, often spend time together at my place. Once, when Kira, then fifteen, came back from school, she found her mother sitting between Morris and Nod throwing knives at the living room door. I also spent evenings in the Warwick Castle pub, playing darts with the boys, doing my tomboy thing at the age of forty-five, in total contrast to the previous years of conferences and seminars on psychotherapy.

The phone rings, it's Morris: "I've shot myself, and I'm bleeding."

"Nod, Morris says he's shot himself and he's bleeding."

"He's bluffing."

"But what if it's true, don't you want to go and see?"

"No. You can, if you want."

I rush over the bridge. Morris has indeed shot himself in the arm with a pellet gun and the pellet is stuck under the skin; there is one drop of blood. I drive him to the hospital, where he is put in a cubicle behind a curtain, waiting for the doctor and asking the nurse if there's any chance of a blowjob.

Shortly after, I decided to throw a champagne party. On the night, Nod brought a large palm tree that reached up to the ceiling and some rocks from Sheraton Sky Hotel into my living room, trying to make us look like a real couple throwing a party together. After a few glasses of champagne, Ronnie put his arm around Nod's shoulders, and with the friendliest of smiles, said: "Do you realise that you're just a temporary prick around here?" Nod gave Ronnie a shove, which would have made him fall backwards onto the Sheraton Sky rocks if I hadn't stopped him. Nod was incensed that I took Ronnie's side. Of course I took Ronnie's side. Ronnie had a point, he always saw through appearances and conveyed it in his inimitable way which to be fair, wasn't to everyone's taste.

No doubt Nod was an interesting and colourful

character: he knew the basic principles of Martial Arts, how to stay balanced and cool and able to defend himself; he had studied acupuncture before being kicked out of the school with enough knowledge of the right points to press to get a woman into his power; he knew his trees and plants, was a good cook and could recognise the song of every bird. Having been born with a clubfoot, his feet were different sizes, making it a problem to buy shoes. He'd ask for two pairs of different sizes and then secretly swap them, taking one of each size. One day he came back from shoe shopping elated. He'd managed for once, to tell the truth and the shop assistant told him to take two shoes of different sizes, because many rejects got sent back to the factory anyway.

When his friends in Dorset offered him a lurcher puppy, a collie and greyhound cross-breed, we drove into the country to fetch it. Sitting in the garden talking, eating and drinking wine, we watched as twelve puppies suckled and played. Nod took off his shirt and put it on the ground. One of the puppies kept playing with it. When the time came to leave, Nod put his shirt back on and walked out of the door without even a backward glance, smugly confident that the puppy would follow him. And she did. Nod called her Frankie.

Frankie was the first dog I ever lived with and made friends with. Well, not counting *Dzhulbars*, (*zh* like in *Zhivago*), our Alsatian, who was tied up on a chain by the gate, summer and winter, in the suburb of Moscow. I had to listen to mother and Grisha's constant arguments about the atrocious smell of the mixture of meat and bones he cooked for hours for the dog. There is a photograph of me in the snow with *Dzhulbars* trying to jump towards me, dragging at his chain; I'm standing about a foot away with my hand stretched towards him, as if trying to touch him, but I'm actually frightened of him.

One evening I meet Morris at the pub. He says to me with an unconcealed smirk on his face: "Guess who's pregnant?"

"I don't know."

"Guess."

"Tell me."

"Celia."

"What has that got to do with me?"

He keeps fixing me with his one eye till I finally get it. Celia is Nod's ex-girlfriend and she is pregnant – with his child. I suddenly remember my dream from the night before, in which Nod had a new key on his key-ring. Morris winks at me and says, "Another of Nod's conquests."

Now Nod really had to go. And he did, but unfortunately not before he twisted my right hand so hard that I couldn't play guitar for a month. He was furious because he read in my diary, "my conch doesn't need your pecker", a phrase I picked up in *'One Thousand and One Nights'*, where Scheherazade, to save her life, tells the King an erotic tale every night and, to keep him captivated till the next instalment, "at the approach of morning she discreetly falls silent". I liked the translator, Powys Mathers' comment: 'The phrases, which could be considered vulgar in a European drawing room, do not give offence in what Kipling called, "the unblushing East".

It was disappointing that instead of appreciating the exotic eroticism in my diary, Nod chose to focus on the 'pecker' comment. And anyway, what was he doing reading my diary?

Singing with Ronnie

> "Every sickness is a musical problem. Its healing, therefore, is a musical resolution. The shorter the resolution, the greater the musical talent of the doctor"
>
> – Novalis – German philosopher and Prophet of Romanticism

One thing that was vital to the healing of my miserable past was the fact that my shrink was a musician and could hear the tune of my inner song. Another thing was that he didn't rigidly follow the traditional psychotherapeutic protocol of placing an iron wall between therapy and spontaneous human contact outside the consulting room, like some therapists who wouldn't so much as say hello to a patient if they met them in the supermarket buying a pint of goddamn milk. So there was always room for the unexpected, for the spontaneous dance between him and others in verbal and non-verbal dialogue: what is really going on between us human beings behind our social facades? How do we treat each other? Can we be truthful with each other? Can we hear each other without becoming defensive? Can we leave room for mistakes without condemning each other? Can we forgive and be a refuge for each other? Can we listen to our souls' inner songs together?

Sometime before I stopped therapy I said to Ronnie:

"I'm afraid that after I stop seeing you in therapy we'll have nothing to talk about."

He replied: "Only then can we begin to talk."

I had my doubts whether, after I finished therapy, I could meet with him and have a conversation that wasn't about me and my mother. I felt there was a grown up world out there that I wasn't part of.

I so longed to be able to relax, have my wits about me and, most of all, hold my ground when singing a song. But because I wanted it so intensely, the opposite would happen, I'd helplessly watch myself disconnect, lose my centre and get out of focus, like Woody Allen in *'Deconstructing Harry'*. If I picked up my guitar and sang a song in that unplugged state I could tell that no one was moved and there was no resonance between me and the audience. I'd end up feeling devastatingly embarrassed, wishing I could just disappear, or even die.

One day I plucked up the courage to phone Ronnie and ask with boldness covering up my embarrassment: "When can we have a conversation?"

"That's a good question; there aren't many people I can have a conversation with. One day we will."

But I wanted it *now*. So I telephoned again, trying to sound casual, as if I was ready for a conversation between equals, without needing to be propped up by him; in truth I still believed that he held the magical power to turn me into a cabaret star. Ronnie was not easily fooled, he said: "I don't have the inner space at the moment; I need to stew in my own juice." I gave it a few days and called again. This time he said: "Mina, as far as *you* are concerned, I am out of town."

Some people thought that was cruel. I didn't find it cruel. If I cared to be honest, I had to admit that I was trying to crawl back into the womb, while pretending it was just a friendly phone call, and his response was to give me a push – just like a wolf-mother shoves a cub out of her den if it's hanging on too long. His toughness, which matched the toughness of my childhood, is what actually helped to toughen me up. I knew it was intended as a Zen shock to cut through my pretences and whisk me out of my dependence.

Life without therapy took a bit of getting used to. The moment my mind got churned up by what somebody said to me or I became guilt-ridden about something I'd said, I wanted to run to Ronnie. Since that was not an option any more, I had to try and apply the skills at my disposal and deal with my rattled mind myself: slow down, become quiet, breathe out, stand on my head, do whatever it takes to align with my centre, take responsibility and let go of having to complain about life.

Then, when I least expected it, Ronnie called and invited Kira and me to go skating with him, Adam and Natasha. My immediate reaction was to jump for joy, followed by anxiety that, despite my best intentions, I would turn this potentially liberating experience into a therapy session on ice. So, by the time he arrived to pick us up in his white Jaguar with spoke wheels, I had worked myself up into a mixture of excitement and excruciating self-consciousness.

The kids got onto the ice, gliding freely from one foot to the other, laughing and frolicking and having fun. I wished I could also skate gracefully, to show off to Ronnie, but soon realised how tied up I must have looked when a handsome guy skating past me called out flirtatiously: "You can do better than that!" I wanted so much to just be normal around Ronnie and enjoy the skating, but instead I found myself complaining to him: "All my friends in Moscow skated at the skating rink in the park, surrounded by pine trees, in the light of the full moon. It was so romantic. But my mother wouldn't allow me to skate; she said I'd break my neck." Oops!

I'd blown it. I went all hollow inside, like the day I'd failed my driving test, only worse. But, at that moment something came to my rescue and I was able to reflect on what happened, rather than be helplessly sucked into it. I said to Ronnie: "Just as I'd anticipated, I fell into 'ground-hog day', I seem to be compulsively falling into the same hole over and over again."

Dear Ronnie. He said: "There's another way to look at the ground-hog day syndrome. Finish with it now and be done with it. Blunders creep in. Drop them as soon as you can. Now is a new moment. If you lift your spirit, you won't be encumbered with your old misery. Would you like to come back with us and sing some Russian songs?"

Would I? I sure would!

On the way, we pick up my Russian song book and when we arrive at Ronnie and Jutta's place the children go to play in the garden and I follow Ronnie into his study. He goes straight to the piano and starts playing my favourite song, *Ochy Chornya (Dark Eyes)* and explaining to me the key of D minor, satisfying my thirst for musical knowledge.

Yes, it was romantic, but not in a sexual way; it was romantic because *he* was truly romantic. He touched my heart and soul and mind with elegance and grace. In his company it felt that music, truth, love and life were one. The moment Ronnie played the first few bars of the song, the music of my heart began to flow and I felt totally myself.

As a child, if you draw a picture or sing a song or do a little dance, you need somebody to acknowledge and encourage you. I didn't have that experience; as far as creative expression went I was in a vacuum. But in spite of it I felt a strong connection to my innermost dreams – I just loved singing and entertaining. Ronnie told me when we talked about it: "I believe in you." Wow, that was big! I could live on that alone.

But if I wanted to get real, I had to become disciplined: swim every morning, go for long walks, eat moderately, practice Yoga, play guitar and sing every day, whatever my internal weather.

"Be like an athlete in training," he said to me, and he wasn't one to mince his words if he saw me neglecting my practice and getting out of shape:

"You'll have to pay the audience to listen to you."

"With your history, it's going to be difficult."

"You are on the wrong track if you think that being on the verge of tears while singing means expressing deep feelings. You'll have to become dry-eyed yourself, only then can you make *them* cry."

I knew what he meant. I could hear it in those Russian women singers and the gypsies, whose voices expressed the deepest human suffering without personalising it with overstated drama and sentimentality."

Finally he said: "You've got what it takes, but you're behaving as if you haven't. It's a dishonest position and confusing for other people. You are like a Rolls Royce without petrol. Whether you will come out of it and find your direct connection to life or not, I don't know. It's up for grabs."

Here I can put in a good word for myself. Despite all my ups and downs, I never gave up. Singing freely still eluded me, but I began to see that I had to practice like an athlete in training and be scrupulously honest with myself, getting to know my demons intimately and telling them to piss off, so that I could get out of my own way and let the voice that I felt inside, come through.

My singing teachers

I heard about Maestro George Cunelli from Jan Ward, who also saw Ronnie in therapy and was married to Justin De Villeneuve, Twiggy's boyfriend and manager, just to drop a few names, as they featured somehow in my life.

"You must go and see him," said Jan, "he's Russian, says he's ninety, but his old students say he's knocked off a few years. The walls of his waiting room are covered in signed portraits of celebrities. Vivien Leigh is one of his successes; he taught her to lower the tone of her voice to give the character Antigone more solemnity in the Jean Anouilh play. He also taught Rex Harrison to speak-sing the part of Professor Higgins in *'My Fair Lady'*. You should go and see him."

I didn't feel at all entitled to ask such a celebrated singing teacher for lessons and only dared to make an appointment because he was ninety and we were both from Russia.

I ring the bell. A little old man, quite bent forward, leaning on a walking stick, opens the door. He gives me a fiercely penetrating look and says: "You don't look like a Russian film star."

Don't I? Shit. I thought I did.

He sits down at his Steinway Grand and asks me to sing the scales he plays. I think I am doing what he asks me to do, but he smiles affectionately and says: "Ok, I'll give you ten lessons and, if I feel I can learn from you and you from me, we'll continue." We do.

Maestro was born in Russia and studied with the best teachers in Italy. He told the story of how, as a young man, he sang in front of Debussy and Debussy said, "*Bravo!*" But his beautiful baritone voice was not matched by his height – five foot four – so he became a singing teacher. He wrote a book, *Voice No Mystery,* with an introduction by the legendary bass Paul Robeson, with whom he also played ping-pong. In his book Maestro recollected how once, on a slanting stage at La Scala, he was wearing platform-heeled shoes to make him taller and to his horror began to slide down the stage. That was the beginning of the end of his opera career.

Although he never returned to Russia his patriotism never waned. He was particularly adamant about music in Russia being of higher calibre than anywhere else in the world: "The West has syphilis," he used to say.

"You are pregnant with voice ... I'll be a midwife for your voice ... don't be a rabbit, sing so they can hear you in Finchley Road ... don't make your mouth like a ravioli ... when you first came you sang like a seal, now you sing like a canary ... darling, in opera you will not sing, but those Russian Gypsy songs ... straight into the pants."

Maestro Cunelli had a twenty-year-old Danish *au pair* and told amusing stories about their life together: "One night I wake up ... someone's climbing through my window. Who is it? 'Maestro it's me, I forgot my key.' Next she'll climb into my bed."

Eventually almost everyone from the network of people around Ronnie started having lessons with Maestro. Sometimes he'd get exasperated with all of us amateurs and say to a new student in his short and sweet way: "Darling, it can only get better."

Maestro and I had arguments about his cast-iron certainty that 'after this life there is nothing.' Not that I was ever inclined to speculate about past lives or future lives, but I felt that everything we do in this life counts and creates a cycle of cause and effect. I tried to quote The Tibetan Lama, Chogyam Trungpa Rinpoche's: "Birth and death apply to everybody constantly at this very moment." Maestro was not moved.

When one of his old friends died, Maestro asked me if I'd come with him to the cremation. We sat side by side at the service, and as the coffin started to glide out of sight and the curtains closed, a deep sob burst from Maestro's chest. He looked up at me with eyes full of tears and said: "Darling, a rehearsal."

He died a year later, at ninety-three, having been ill for only three days. I went to visit him; Janet arrived a little later with baby Kim in her arms. Maestro had heard through the grapevine that Janet and I had fallen out: I didn't want to live with Arthur, but still craved his company and felt he was my family, so I hung around him a lot, often complaining of feeling lonely – which understandably got on Janet's nerves. Maestro looked at Janet and me with his piercing dark eyes: "Give each other a hug; there's no time for fussing and fighting." We did, but only to please him, still holding on to our grudges. I wonder if we would have dropped all our differences if we had known that he was going to die within the next hour.

After Janet and Kim left, Maestro asked me to sit next to him and massage his legs because they were aching so badly. He relaxed a little and, looking at the book *Leningrad* on his bedside table, said: "Used to be Petrograd, after Peter the Great. Truly great – six foot four!" Then he looked at me mischievously and his eyes shot towards his studio: "When I get up I'm going to teach you how to *really* sing '*Caro Mio Ben*'."

All of a sudden he made a move to get up. I asked if he

wanted me to bring him the bedpan. He said impatiently: "No, I want to go to the toilet." I brought him his slippers. He got up, moved two steps, held onto the table and started breathing heavily. "Open the window!" he yelled. I opened it slightly, afraid that he might catch cold. "Open the window!" he shouted. I opened it completely. Gusts of cold autumn air rushed into the room. He dropped into the chair and then slid onto the floor, lying face down. I turned him around and put a pillow under his head. But I knew he was dead.

The Danish *au pair* was away and Edie Irwin, who was taking her place, was out. I phoned and told her that Maestro had died and she came back immediately. We called the Royal Free Hospital and two men in overalls arrived in an ambulance, put Maestro Cunelli's body in a wheel chair, covered him with a blanket and wheeled him out of his house. It was all so quick and strange. I wondered what, if anything, was happening to Maestro's soul, the one which he didn't believe in.

That night I had a dream: I am with Maestro in his studio, and he is teaching me to sing *'Caro Mio Ben'* by Giordani, when suddenly Picasso's 'Dove of Peace' which had been hanging on the wall behind the piano, ruffles its feathers, flies out of the frame and starts doing circles over our heads.

After Maestro's death I continued singing lessons with his student, Mrs. Madeleine Findon. She was a soprano in her late sixties and a Christian scientist. Excellent at working with professional classical singers, she was not into being a 'midwife' for my voice.

To get to the studio at the back of Sadler's Wells where she teaches, I have to pass the reception. The switchboard operator, a little woman with a huge hump and so cross-eyed that all you can see is the whites of her eyes, greets me with overflowing *joie de vivre:* "Are you in London next Tuesday?" she bursts with enthusiasm, "I am going to sing at the Albert Hall in the Messiah and, did I tell you that I'm going to Egypt? Four hundred of us are going to sing in Zefferelli's film version of *'Aida'*."

I don't know what to say; her eagerness only accentuates how desperate I feel about my own lack of progress. What am I doing, *shlepping* my guitar in its heavy case up and down the backstairs of Sadler's Wells, wondering what will ever come of it?

When I walk into Mrs Findon's studio, she is sitting at the piano eating a Mars bar. With a mouth full of chocolate, she demonstrates in a clear tuneful voice, how the phrase I just sang should be sung. I have to go on a purifying brown rice diet for a week in order to sing in tune. I am mystified.

I tell her: "I notice that when I listen to my voice, I sing in tune."

"What? You don't *always* listen? You are the devil!" she shrieks.

After I recover myself I say: "Since I've realised that I have a problem with listening, I've been praying for help in being able to listen and to sustain notes."

"If that's what you pray for you are on the right track."

Maybe I am on the right track, but I still can't sing 'Happy Birthday' in the key everybody else is singing in.

Harold Miller and Irene, his wife, are both in their eighties. Harold gives singing lessons at Wigmore Hall and Irene has to come with him because she absentmindedly keeps leaving the prunes on the stove to burn. Harold teaches musical theatre performers the 'belting technique', pushing the voice to make it louder and bigger.

At my first lesson Harold, banging the piano keys, tries to make me force my voice out, which makes it even more tense and strained. Irene is sitting on the bench, dressed in a grey forties coat, a moss green hat with a feather in it and a half-open empty handbag over her arm, muttering to herself and occasionally bursting out: "No, Harold, stop banging the piano!"

"Irene, shut up."

Gradually Irene gets more and more loopy and Harold starts teaching at home.

During my lesson, Irene pops her head in and asks: "Darling, a cup of tea?"

"All right, Irene, bring us some tea."

A few minutes later she comes in, puts the tray with two cups of tea on top of the piano and leaves.

He tastes the tea, grimaces and shouts: "Irene!"

"Yes darling?"

"Irene, you put salt in the tea."

"Why would I do such a thing, darling?"

A while later a smell of burning comes from the kitchen.

"Irene, you've burnt the prunes again!"

"I don't burn prunes," says Irene, most offended.

A little later she pops her head in again and asks me: "Darling, did I show you my medal from the Royal Academy of Music?" And sure enough, she brings out the medal and proudly points out her name on it.

When Irene leaves, Harold tells me that she sang Bizet's '*Carmen*' at the Royal Opera House. Gossip had it that when they married Irene was a well-established singing teacher whereas Harold didn't have many pupils, so Irene gave up her successful career to appease his male ego which couldn't deal with his wife being more successful than him.

Sometimes, after another 'going nowhere' lesson with Harold, I sit down with Irene and listen to her stories.

"Darling, my parents came from Russia and settled in the East End of London. We had a very nice house and a grocery store in Brick Lane. Our house was always full of people, musical evenings every night; my sister played the piano and I sang. I had such a beautiful voice my parents pinched and scraped to send me to the Royal Academy of Music. Did I show you my medal? Harold and I never quarrel, but I know he is having an affair."

After Harold's death Irene was put into an old people's home until they sorted out Harold's will, which was to provide for Irene to be looked after in her own home. When I go to visit I find her standing in the middle of the entrance hall in her coat and hat with the same half-open, empty handbag over her arm. She looks at me and exclaims: "Oh darling, how long has it been? Yes, of course, you came to hear me in *'Carmen'* in 1945, I got wonderful reviews."

We sit down at a table in the visitor's lounge where the nurse brings us tea for two. I arrange the biscuits I brought on a plate. Irene tastes one and says: "What delicious biscuits, I wonder who brought them ... oh yes, Lucy."

Another resident of the old age home goes by in a wheelchair and says, in a friendly voice: "Hey, visiting your mother?"

Irene replies: "Don't be silly, she's too young to be my mother."

With the formalities of her husband's will completed, Irene is brought back to her home to be looked after by nurses. The nurses have the radio on popular music stations all the time and, with her exquisite musical sensibility, Irene finds it pure torture, exclaiming from time to time: "Stop this ear pollution!"

One day I come in while she is watching a Bette Davis film on TV. She looks up and, pointing at the screen, asks: "Do you recognise me? Darling where am I? Where is Harold? And where is my mother? I don't understand ... it's come to that, no mother, no father...darling, how old do you think I am?"

"I think you are about eighty?"

"Add eight, but don't tell anybody," she whispers.

She stands up: "I'll give you a lesson in elocution," suddenly the teacher she used to be. "Repeat after me: 'Tip of the tongue, teeth and lips' and 'We shall wander not unseen through the elms of hillocks green'." She pulls up her chest from under the bottom ribs and says jubilantly: "See, stretched without tightening!"

Loopy or not, she could still sing *'L'amour est un oiseau rebelle'* in a most melodious voice.

The last time we sat together before she died, she looked deep into my eyes and said: "You are blessed with a very nice face; nothing to be proud of, a lot to be grateful for."

The truth is I learned practically nothing from dear old Harold and quite a lot from Irene. She was the musician in the family and I felt the discordance in me harmonising, just by being near her and listening to her voice.

The Russian actor and guitar teacher, Alexey Chesnakov came next. When I arrived for my first guitar lesson he was standing outside his flat in Earl's Court waiting for me; a six foot tall Russian in his eighties, strong and sturdy like an oak tree, in a white shirt, a polka-dot bow tie and baggy brown corduroy trousers.

Before starting the lesson he showed me around his flat; it consisted of two rooms, the living room where he taught guitar, and the other where he slept. In the kitchen he pointed out two pots hanging on opposite sides of the only shelf and explained carefully that the pot on the left was for boiling water and the one on the right for boiling eggs. There were two cups and saucers and two plates neatly arranged on the shelf.

In the living room two chairs, with a foot-stool next to each one, stood facing each other, the precise height for playing classical guitar, and, hanging on the wall, four guitars he'd collected over the years. "Near the nail, near the fret," was his continuous instruction for finger exercises – as meticulous about his guitar teaching as he was about the pots in his kitchen. He put a card with my name on it in his file to keep a record of my progress and gave me a book with some simple guitar pieces.

I started coming for lessons once a week and soon began to develop technique, learning to play the pieces from the book. Sometimes he'd pick up his guitar; the moment he struck a chord and started to sing, the Russian folk tradition came alive in that spartan Earl's Court room, awakening deep, half-forgotten feelings inmy heart. Sometimes, after putting down the guitar, he'd settle back in his chair with a deep sigh and his hands would wander down to his nether parts and give them a little upward shove. I didn't know what to do, except pretend not to notice.

Alexey came from a small village in Kaluga oblast, situated on the *Oka* river; the youngest son of a *kulak* family.

"My father was the first *kulak* in our village, an independent farmer who owned a large farm and used hired labour, which meant he could afford to send me to boarding school. I remember being nine years old, sitting on my suitcase immediately before departure, which is, as you know, a Russian good luck custom, and then sitting on a sleigh drawn by a horse, my mother waving a handkerchief after a tearful goodbye. And that was it; after the age of nine I never lived at home again, except during summer holidays."

"When the Revolution started in 1917, I was at college studying to be a mechanical engineer and, suddenly out of the blue, I got arrested by the Bolsheviks for being on the wrong side. I didn't know there was a right side. I managed to run away from prison and cross the border into Finland, which had just declared independence from Bolshevik Russia and become a free country. As I crossed the border, I wept. I loved my country; I was being *forced* to leave it."

"Eventually I ended up in England and, having to earn a living, started to play guitar and sing Russian songs in small clubs. I formed a guitar society to which Segovia was invited to play. I also lectured on Russian history, as Russia was then on the agenda. I became an actor, playing secondary roles in some first class films; I played Brodsky, a Russian liaison officer, in the British film noir, '*The Third Man*', with Orson Wells; and I also acted with Clarke Gable. I kept bees during the war and supplied my neighbours with honey and wrote a practical guide to bee keeping."

"I never married; a few women proposed to me but I felt I had no means to support them in the proper style, so here I am, having lived alone all my life. I can't complain; it all feels biologically correct: everything is deteriorating at the correct rate and, if it wasn't for arthritis, I'd be quite comfortable and what's more important, my fingers still allow me to play guitar."

"How did you learn to play guitar?"

"Need, darling, need is the best teacher."

"And where did you learn to act?"

"I learned to act by watching my mother during my

summer vacations. Our village was by a lake, and quite a few people drowned in it. My mother would come back from washing the laundry and re-enact the whole scene: the turbulent lake, the drowned man, his wife on the shore lamenting, the children holding onto her skirt, crying ... the lake suddenly becoming still. She was a wonderful mimic, my mother, so that's how I learnt to act."

Alexey was a real star at my musical soirees in Little Venice. Wearing a white shirt with wide sleeves and a polka dot cravat he'd sing the old Russian romances, *'Do not scold me; life is hard enough as it is... My memories do not awaken...Seagulls are flying over the sea; their cries are full of sadness... 'I'll die to the soft rustle of the grass in the wind, my voice, full of longing, will tell you that I loved you with all my soul, so trustingly tender,'* accompanying himself on the guitar; his voice, a little cracked from age, but so tuneful and full of authenticity.

Ronnie loved listening to Alexey's singing, sometimes joining in on the piano. Alexey taught me more than guitar. One day he asked me: "Why so worried?"

"I worry about money," I replied dejectedly.

"Have you read Gurdjieff's *Material Question*? No? Read it. You've heard of his project 'The Institute for the Harmonious Development of Man'?"

"Yes, I have."

"Well, he was a major Western guru; he was at once the sage, the adventurer, the comedian and the trickster. Have you heard the story of how he raised funds for his Institute by catching sparrows, dying them yellow and selling them as 'American canaries'?"

"Yes, I read the story of how one day at the market everyone stood around watching as the rain washed the paint off his 'canaries' and Gurdjieff had to grab the cage, the birds dripping with paint, and run from the angry customers demanding their money back."

"Oh yes, I remember that. I'm not saying you should start painting sparrows yellow, but I suggest you get imbued with his spirit. Gurdjieff had an unshakeable belief that his knowledge, aspirations and efforts to sustain The Institute for the Harmonious Development of Man deserved financial support. What you are doing is of as much benefit to humanity; you are helping people become more harmonious by aligning their bodies, minds and breathing; if you'd only believe in the value of it, you'd also get enough money. You can learn from every situation, as Gurdjieff used to say to the new-comers at his Institute: "Remember, you come here having already understood the necessity for struggling with yourself—only with yourself. Therefore, thank everyone who gives you the opportunity."

When I arrived for my next lesson, he looked very frail, wearing a red nightshirt instead of his usual dapper white shirt and polka-dot bow tie: "I'm very ill, darling; the doctor will be here soon." He shuffled back to his bedroom and asked if I'd make him some breakfast: "When you come into the kitchen, do you remember I showed you the pans hanging on the wall; the one to the right of the centre is for boiling eggs; please boil one egg, four and a half minutes after the water boils. To the left of the centre you'll see another pan, this one is for boiling water, make us a cup of tea."

After he finished his breakfast an idea occurred to me: 'Ah what the hell; be a free spirit, lie down next to him and just hold him and soothe him,' but sadly my imagination was ahead of my ability to just go with it.

The next day he was taken to hospital. When I came to visit he was sitting in the chair next to his bed, leaning forward, looking as though he was about to fall over. He gestured to me to come closer and, in a barely audible voice, asked: "What do I look like to you?"

"You look very weak, you should be in bed."

"Thank you."

At this point the nurse arrived and asked, in a chirpy voice: "Mr Chesniakov, how are we doing? Oh, you'll be home in no time."

"Can't you see he's barely able to sit up?"

"It's good for him to sit for a while."

Alexey died the following day at the age of eighty-nine. He passed away a few months short of realising his dream: to live until the Russians had completed laying the gas pipe from Siberia to Europe.

Alexey left me with another valuable lesson, this one after his death. He told me: "After I die, go to my book shelf, take Dostoyevsky's *Crime and Punishment*, published in Moscow in 1956, and read the last chapter carefully." I did as he said; I took home the large illustrated hard cover volume in Russian. On the inside sleeve I found an inscription, written in a very shaky hand:

> *To my dear Russian friend Mina – unforgettable Mina – from an old Russian man, who remembers Russian life more than eighty years ago. – Alexey Chesnakov, November 1981.*

I read the last chapter, as if reading it for the first time. It was the chapter about redemption. In it Raskolnikov, who is serving a hard labour sentence in a Siberian jail for murder and is so unrepentant that even the other prisoners call him infidel, the most God-less of men, is touched by feelings of love for Sonya, the young woman who followed him to Siberia.

> How it happened he didn't know. But all at once

> something seemed to seize him and fling him at her feet. He wept and threw his arms around her knees. They wanted to speak but they couldn't, tears stood in their eyes. They were both pale and thin, but those sick pale faces were bright with the dawn of a new future, of a full resurrection into a new life. They were renewed by love. The heart of each held infinite sources of life for the heart of the other.
>
> Seven years, only seven years! At the beginning of their happiness at some moments they were both ready to look at those seven years as though they were seven days. He didn't know that the new life wouldn't be given him for nothing, that he would have to pay dearly for it, that it would cost him great striving, great suffering.
>
> But that is the beginning of a new story – the story of the gradual renewal of a man, the story of his gradual regeneration, of his passing from one world into another, of his initiation into a new unknown life. That might be the subject of a new story, but our story is ended.

Tears spring to my eyes. Redemption and love are possible, even for a murderer like Raskolnikov!

I'd been carrying the feeling of being condemned for my mistakes all my life. I was riddled with guilt; the hereditary Jewish guilt, like a man who suffers from Alzheimer's and forgets everything except his guilt. On a more serious note, I also felt guilt about things that I'd done irresponsibly, even if unconsciously. It seems that pleading unconsciousness doesn't exempt you from responsibility once you wake up and feel accountable for your actions. But there is a difference between guilt and remorse. Guilt means beating yourself up while still feeling sorry for yourself. Remorse is acknowledging that you've fallen short of being a self-respecting human being, forgiven yourself and begun to act more responsibly.

I felt guilt about the abortions I'd had; the way I'd spoken and behaved, how haughty I could be, acting superior while feeling inferior; how irritable I'd been with my mother; how disconnected I had been at Kira's birth and how self-preoccupied all through her childhood. There is a Raskolnikov in all of us. Just speaking and behaving unconsciously can be akin to killing – killing love. Guilt turned into remorse when I realised that, although I had not been exempt from the consequences of my actions, it did not mean I had to pay for my sins for eternity. I don't know; I pay as I go.

Ronnie Laing said: "True guilt is guilt at the obligation one owes to oneself to be oneself. False guilt is guilt felt at not being what other people feel one ought to be. Make up your mind which side of the footlights you want to be on."

Fran and Friends

When Fran Landesman, the famous songwriter, poet and cabaret artist, invites me to be part of her show, *'Fran and Friends'*, at the Old Red Lion in Islington, I am thrilled at the chance to be *at* the footlights. I could hardly believe it: Fran Landesman, whose song, *'Spring can really hang you up the most'*, was sung by the likes of Ella Fitzgerald, is asking *me* to be in her show; and not just for one night, but as part of the regular team, every night for two weeks!

While she was hanging out with jazz musicians in Greenwich Village, writing songs of bitter-sweet melancholy, living on the edge, loving and losing, depression and sadness, I was still living in a suburb of Moscow, in one room with my mother and stepfather, and I wasn't allowed my own key.

The day after the show opens I eagerly phone my mother in Cape Town, still trying, against all odds, to win her approval

"How are you?" she asks, with the usual anxiety in her voice, as if I'm on the brink of death.

"I'm really excited, I'm singing in a show! It will go on for two weeks, which means I'll have a chance to learn from my mistakes and keep improving."

Silence and a sigh: "*Akh, nu,* so long as you are healthy..."

I ought to be grateful; some of my friends say that the denial that went on in their families was much more subtle and more difficult to detect and unravel. One thing I can say for my mother; she didn't beat about the bush; her denial and insistence on her own version of me was always one hundred percent.

'Fran and Friends' was on for two weeks, with a different guest of honour every night. I was accompanied by Judy, a violinist with the Boston Philharmonic orchestra, and by the brilliant Spanish guitarist, Eduardo Niebla, with gorgeous Lolly, Mel and Janet as my backing singers for the chorus of *'Gari, gari – Burn, burn, love of the Gypsy'*.

Amongst the celebrities Fran invited were Ronnie Laing, the poet Michael Horowitz; the actor Phil Daniels; Lol Coxhill – the soprano sax player; and Heathcote Williams, the author of *Falling for a Dolphin*, a dramatic poetic tribute to the unity encompassing all life inspired by his sublime encounter with a hermit dolphin off the west coast of Ireland.

Ronnie suggested I ask Fran to write English lyrics for the Russian song *'The chrysanthemums faded'*. I give her a tape of myself singing the song in Russian with a translation of the Russian lyrics: *'The chrysanthemums have faded but love still lives on in my aching heart'*. She called the new song *'The chrysanthemums burn like yellow flames'*:

The chrysanthemums
Burn like yellow flames
They recall last fall
And our fireside games
But the seasons change
And the flowers fade
I suppose I'm not lucky in love

A French style *chaise longue*, a couple of quirky hats on an antique hat stand and a bronze cupid with colourful chiffon scarves hanging off his outstretched arm, straight out of Fran's boudoir, are all part of the stage set, a picture of decadent extravagance.

Fran asks me to start by reciting her poem 'Sparks'. I'm wearing a black pencil skirt, high heeled shoes, fishnet tights, a tight-fitting jacket and a grey beret, with a Russian *Sobranie* in a long cigarette holder, acting the *femme fatale* – speak-singing the poem, to the accompaniment of Eduardo's guitar and Judy's violin:

Sparks from too many cigarettes
Burnt holes in my favourite dress
Burnt holes in the blanket
But we had a good time
Now that you are gone old lover of mine
I spy all these unsightly burns
and how can I turn them into a rhyme
Now that my world is in holes
I am sick of my Russian soul
I feel like I am choking
And I wish I had the strength
to give up smoking.

The audience burst into laughter and enthusiastic applause, for which I took no credit whatsoever; I was sure it was all for Fran's witty lyrics. I knew I was holding back from really doing my thing with full razzle-dazzle. I could see myself opening the show by standing on my head with the Russian *Sobranie* hanging from the corner of my mouth and a glass of champagne beside me, then slowly standing up and slinking towards the microphone, champagne in one hand, *Sobranie* in the other. Putting the brakes on my wildness made me feel a bit flat. I got no kick from leaving the champagne in my imagination.

Part of my repertoire was Fran's English version of the

Russian war song *'Ogoniok (Little light)'* about a soldier going off to war and for as long as he could see he kept turning to look at the light in her window, which Fran transformed into *'On the head of a pin'*:

Love's a terrible teacher
I'm a desperate fool
I can't master its lessons
Still I run back to school
Everything that I've ever learnt
Of this mess that I'm in
Could be carved in large letters
On the head of a pin

I did receive many compliments after the show: Lol Coxhil said he would like me to sing some thirties songs with his trio; Heathcote Williams said I was the Russian Juliet Greco; Michael Horowitz said I was the Russian Marlene Dietrich. Obviously, I still had far to go to be me.

The review in 'Time Out' said: '... All through the two weeks at the Old Red Lion, Fran was supported by a sultry Russian singer ... but the star of the show was Fran herself. Fran Landesman is an American poet, songwriter. Her songs are full of humour, pathos and startling observations. Her famous jazz song, *'All the Sad Young Men'* became a standard in the repertoire of famous jazz singers, like Anita O'Day.'

My voice started to connect and find its place when I met Anthea Parashchak. Her teaching is based on the same principle as the Yoga I practice and teach: grounding in the centre of one's being and allowing the release to happen. This helped me understand how different it was to sing from within rather than trying to perform from without. But I didn't yet feel that I could really sing a song.

It's not my fault!

A Jewish mother sends a telegram: 'Start worrying ... details to follow.'

My mother is coming from Cape Town tomorrow. We haven't seen each other for two years. To my surprise I'm really looking forward to her visit. Now that my childhood wounds are healing, with the practice of Yoga bringing more balance and stability and singing lessons are freeing up my voice, I feel stronger and more confident that I'll be able to withstand her negative ways of seeing me.

I've spent years in therapy looking at my fear of her disapproval, her constant criticism and her habitual negativity, which always threatened to pull me back into the old misery in the blink of an eye. But now, feeling more centred and stable, I'm pleased to have a chance to experience the normal pleasure of a daughter looking forward to seeing her mother. I hope that she'll share my newly acquired positive feelings about life and be happy for me and with me. But I can also imagine how else it might go: she won't notice any changes in me and will continue treating me as a helpless, starving child; I'll get frustrated, lose my cool, revert to being rude and abrupt and then feel tormented by guilt.

Anyway, I'm picking her up from Heathrow at 8.15 am. In my mind I'm trying to prepare a report for her on what I have accomplished. To me it feels like a massive achievement; I'm managing to survive on my own in London; I teach Yoga, swim in the Ladies' Pond on Hampstead Heath every morning all through the year, enjoy good health, finally have a piano, take singing lessons, and drive a new acquired second-hand Vanden Plas with a wooden dashboard and leather seats. I feel ripples of excitement at being able to give my mother the pleasure of seeing me getting my life together – the *nakhes* she always wished for.

Childhood memories of mother's constant threats that she's about to die at any moment bring up anxiety while I wait for her to pass through customs. My fantasy creates an image of her clutching onto her handbag, sitting in a wheelchair pushed by an airport attendant in uniform. I feel surprised and relieved when she walks out all by herself. My heart beats faster as we approach each other. We hug. And straightaway she looks at me with those piercing, black, examining eyes and her first words shoot out like bullets: "You are too thin."

I notice a tightening in my solar plexus and say quickly, to change the subject: "Let's get your suitcase."

In the car I ask: "How is Beni?"

"Beni? As healthy as an ox, he is nearly eighty. *Nu,* I don't mind, may he be healthy and live a long life. As far as I am concerned, from my point of view, let him live. *Akh,* it's not pleasant for me to talk to him about what he is going to leave me in his will. So I ask him nicely, in a nice way, 'How much does one person need to live on for a month?' It's true, I don't know, he does all the shopping, I don't buy anything except skim milk and margarine, so I ask him nicely. I tell you, I am a good actress ..."

When we arrive at my place she throws a quick look around the living room and says: "Your flat is unrecognisable, thank God, it's very nice ... the only thing, is your health ... *akh* ... *oy, oy* my back ..."

The sense of equanimity I felt only an hour earlier, anticipating staying centred and calm in my mother's presence, is totally gone; this Yoga teacher is getting very irritable and has to use every trick in her book to calm down.

"I feel very well," I say, trying to sound super-calm.

"How are you managing?" my mother continues, her face scrunched into a worried expression.

"I'm teaching Yoga, how many times do I have to tell you?"

"Yes, teaching Yoga is all very well but how much do you need to live on?" she insists.

"This is new to me, having people come and pay me for showing them how to relax their bodies and free their breathing. It's only the beginning; my practice will grow."

"Ay, ay my back hurts something terrible ... you looked better when you came the last time to South Africa with Theo, it's because he looked after you," she says in a suffering voice.

"What? Then you kept telling me how unwell I looked. Remember, I was playing guitar and singing and you interrupted me and said, 'Tell me, you are on holiday; you are swimming in the sea, eating mangos and papayas, why do you look so bad?' And you turned to Theo and asked, 'and this is what you love?'"

She says: *"Akh,* I don't understand why you had to separate from him, such a good man ... *oy,* I am already hot. *Oy,* I put a vest on and it's already too much ... *oy* my stomach ... I don't know what to do with it ... *ay,* there is no life with Beni, with your father *was* life, people, concerts, but this one, eating and television, that's the only thing he knows."

That day I wrote in my diary: 'I've had indigestion today, which I don't remember having since I moved out of my mother and Beni's place. I'm constantly irritable. I try to stay centred and reasonable but I can't. I feel I'm being punished, tortured. I'm allergic to her; being with her feels like a prison sentence. What would be the right thing to do under the circumstances? The familiar feeling of futility, is emerging. I want to die.'

Obviously my mindfulness practice is not stable enough to withstand my mother. I try to remind myself that it's not all about my mother. I came into this world with my own karmic tendencies. I've read in Buddhist texts: 'We are the heirs of our own actions; our mental, moral, temperamental differences are for the most part due to our own actions and tendencies, both past and present.' I tell myself, 'whatever you do, don't blame, be kind, don't hurt.'

My mother has cooked dinner and we sit down to eat. "The food is delicious," I say.

"*Akh*, you haven't eaten the whole day," she sighs mournfully.

She drives me mad. I wish I could make her see that she has a habit of pouring a bucket of cold water over a beautiful moment.

I invite Morris for dinner. He's pretty unusual by many people's standards, with his glass eye and beer belly, teaching me how to throw knives at my living room door and he's obviously not Jewish. When she meets him she is so stunned, she's speechless.

I prepare sea bass in ginger and spring onion sauce, Chinese cabbage and compote of fruit with aniseed. She follows me into the kitchen and asks in a horrified whisper: "Who is he?" She can't believe her own eyes.

I have to confess to relishing this moment – getting back at her for all the times she's slapped me down just for saying something she didn't like to hear; now I'm doing a lot more than that and she is powerless to do anything about it! But then compassion stirs, 'Well, my poor mother wasn't fortunate enough to meet someone like Ronnie Laing, be introduced to Yoga and meditation and have her world opened up to her with new ways of being and thinking.' But no matter how much I try to share with her the possibility of letting go of attachment to the suffering we've been through and living in the present, even being happy sometimes, she still says, with unshakable conviction: "What do you know? You were too young to remember."

I take her with me to the Ladies Pond. I want her to see me swim in the cold water and be pleased with the robust health I'm enjoying now. When I was a child she always worried about my lungs, my tonsils, one breast being bigger than the other and how thin and pale I looked. While I'm swimming she stands with her back to the water, humming a nostalgic Russian song to herself. I know she thinks the cold water will make me ill, in spite of all the evidence to the contrary and is deliberately ignoring me; I'm still trying to get her approval, a little nod would do, when I emerge radiant from the cold water, but the first thing she says is: "*Ay, ay, ay*, my corns are aching something terrible..."

I quite deliberately don't rush to change out of my wet bathing suit because I know only too well that my mother expects me to; like a rebellious adolescent I stand there in my post-swim glow, willing her to recognise how fit and well I am. Suddenly her voice comes from another dimension: "Beni confesses his love for me in his letter, but when he got a parking ticket, which cost fifteen rand, I offered to pay eight rand and he took it off me."

"But you offered it?"

"Yes."

"Well, if you offer, he can accept."

"And if I offer to cut my head off will he also accept? *Akh*, what's there to talk about? Go and get dressed before you catch pneumonia." I can laugh now, but that was her kind of 'logic' that drove me berserk as a child.

On the way back in the car she tells me another story: "This woman I know, the doctor banned her from sleeping with her husband, it's dangerous for her health. 'It's bad for your heart,' he said, so she followed the doctor's orders ... now her husband wants a divorce."

Surprisingly my mother is enthusiastic about joining my Yoga class. She sits on the floor in the Yoga posture *Paschimotanasana*, with her legs stretched in front, holding her toes. I can see her surreptitiously throwing glances at the other people in the group, obviously proud that at her age she's suppler than some of the younger people.

On the last day of her stay she laments: "If only I could do Yoga every day, I wouldn't have this back pain."

"Why can't you?"

"I can't do it by myself."

"I'll give you the name and telephone number of a teacher in Cape Town."

She makes a despondent gesture with her hand: "*Akh*, you don't know."

"What don't I know?"

"You don't know that I am a prisoner."

"A prisoner? Why?"

"Beni wants me to serve him breakfast at 9 am, at 11 am, he wants his *milkhike lokshen*, at 1 pm, lunch; at 3.30, tea and cake, at 6 pm – dinner," she concludes, as if there is no way out for her, but to be a prisoner to Beni's eating habits.

"But surely you can go out once a week at least and do something for yourself?"

"I already do, I have my hair done once a week," she says

in her sarcastic tone, "and he is already waiting and asking me, why am I so late?"

"Can't you talk to him?"

"Talk to him? You don't know him," and again she makes the same despondent movement with her hand, "It's my bitter fate."

This is when I start to lose it; I feel the old guilt tearing through me, gripping my guts and my solar plexus tightening into the familiar knot of helpless fury and frustration. But now I have a weapon, I can breathe the knot away. Then I notice that I feel guilty about not feeling guilty, as if I'm betraying our misery pact. Ok, more breathing, more letting go. It might appear ruthless, but I have to let go. Is it better if both of us end up in knots? If she is not prepared or is not able to look at herself, what should I do? Drown with her?

I feel grateful for the spiritual teachings that are helping to transform my miserable view of the world, awakening me to the possibility of a freedom beyond Stalin and my mother. Now I have the choice to be free of the grip of the past by becoming aware of how I keep it alive with my habits of mind, body, speech and actions. I also feel deep compassion for my mother and I wish there was something I could do. Nothing seems to move her out of being stuck in the past. I don't know why.

One thing I finally do know: It's not my fault!

"Mum! Use your breathing, and drop it!"

It's not at all surprising that after her experience of my neurotic antics in childhood, it takes Kira some time to see me as a new woman and for us to be able to laugh at my emotional dramatics together.

We are in Chiang Mai, in a charming guesthouse, lying in the sun, enveloped in the stillness and timelessness of the moment, when out of the blue I suddenly ask Kira very intensely: "What's the date today?" as if I'm late for an urgent business appointment. We end up rolling on the grass with laughter at the comic aspect of the intensity, which has intimidated her all her life.

Kira feels at home in Thailand, having spent a few years in the north studying Traditional Thai Yoga massage, and speaks fluent Thai. She's excited to be able to introduce me to the Thailand that as a tourist I would never have access to.

"Mum, isn't it great, I'm going to meet my friend Sam and arrange our trek into the hills?"

"I'm experiencing dread," says a voice from the Siberian steppes.

"What are you dreading?"

"I'm dreading the whole day ahead."

"What do you mean?"

"It's this room. You are going to meet Sam and what am I going to do? I don't want to go anywhere alone."

"You can come with me."

Fortunately, just in time, before I turn into a replica of my mother, I say: "Don't worry, it's alright, of course there are many things I can do. For one, I can go and sit in one of those beautiful garden restaurants, write postcards and read, and you can meet me there when you are ready." And I really mean it; I'm not being the mother in the 'How many Jewish mothers does it take to change a light bulb?' joke, who replies: 'None, I'll read in the dark.'

I sit at a table in the garden restaurant. At the next table four young Thai guys are drinking whisky. My coffee arrives; I take out a cigarette but I have no matches. I wonder if one of the guys will offer me a light; now that I'm fifty-two, men don't jump to light my cigarette as they used to. In one way it's a relief not to be the object of men's desires, but I detect a hint of nostalgia for those days when men's heads turned. Soon I get a chance to find out that I'm not quite as over the hill as I think, when one of the Thai guys gets up to light my cigarette. He's the only Thai I've seen with rotten teeth; maybe that's why he's not too fussy.

Just then Kira arrives with Sam, our personal trekking guide from the Karen tribe, who is wearing a soft, colourfully embroidered hat that sits niftily just above his sparkly black eyes. He politely asks if we would like to visit a monastery, Wat Umong, outside Chiang Mai. We get into a *Tuk-Tuk,* a three wheeler vehicle so named because of the sound it makes, and, even though it totally defies all traffic rules, we arrive at the monastery in one piece. Kira asks the driver the price and when he tells her, she blasts him in fluent Thai slang: "It's a rip off." He shrieks with laughter at this unexpected response and asks her, pointing at me: "Is that your friend?" She answers in Thai: "*Mer*." He laughs again, and, repeats with surprise: "*Mer*?" Vanity of vanities, I love it.

He drives off and as the last sounds of *tuk-tuk-tuk-tuk* fade away, we are bathed in silence. We wander through the spacious gardens of the monastery, accompanied only by the distant sound of monks chanting, and enter the Golden Temple with its gigantic Buddha. The three of us sit cross-legged on the ground in front of the statue and meditate. 'I'm happy', in Thai, literally translates as 'I have good heart', and 'to breathe' is 'to give heart'.

When we arrive at Long Beach resort in Koh Chang, once again I have to adjust to change and the way I cope with it is to start complaining: "The beach is too narrow; we've booked a bungalow, we are told we have to sleep in a tent; and what is this American guy doing telling us to go and get a coke while we wait, what cheek – he thinks *I* drink *coke*!"

Although my mother's constant complaints and premonitions of disaster have nearly driven me crazy, my worst fear that I'll end up just like her, has materialised, and now Kira is the victim. But at this moment Kira is far too happy to get mad at me; instead, she observes me with good-natured humour and says delightedly: "Mum, use your breathing and drop it! Look where we are!" That cracks me up and opens my eyes to the tranquil golden, sandy beach right on the edge of the jungle with six primitive bamboo bungalows, a few tents and four tables covered with colourful plastic cloths under a green canvas canopy – our restaurant for the next two weeks. The only sound is the small motor boat for transporting people off the mainland ferry. And we *do* get our bungalow.

We have a swim, practice Yoga and then have lunch in the restaurant under the canopy, where Kira's friends, three smiling Thai girls, welcome us. They cook on the open fire and serve us the most delicious fresh fish with chilli and garlic, rice and stir fried vegetables. Pon, one of the girls, who is wearing an apricot T-shirt with the word 'Cherish' on it in multi-coloured letters, gives us the stir-fry recipe: Baby corn, roasted cashew nuts, mange tout, spring onions, thin carrot sticks, mushrooms, tofu and soy sauce.

Kira has been around Yoga from the age of two; she used to join in and do her version of headstands and backbends when Arthur and I were practising. As she got older she sometimes came to my classes, but she found it hard to accept all my profound pronouncements about balancing mind, body and breath, when she remembered from her childhood the depressed mother who could hide in the closet for a whole day. Fortunately, I understood her resistance and started guiding her towards my teachers; I wanted her to experience the benefits of Yoga and mindfulness which got me out of the closet, and to free herself from the mental, emotional and physical effects of her childhood. After a while she started coming to my classes and it made me really happy when I saw that she'd become more open with me and was able to receive my teaching.

On the balcony of our bungalow Kira and I practice Yoga postures, do sitting meditation morning and evening, give each other massages, enjoy the company of other people and laugh a lot. We have the most peaceful sleeps to the sound of gentle waves; the closest I have ever come to perfect peace. This is deeply healing for both of us.

Now we are ready for our trek in the jungle. We take a ferry to the main land, a bus to Chiang Mai and the following morning Kira, Sam and I set off walking through rice fields, and into the forests of evergreen trees and exotic wild orchids. We walk for hours to the rhythmic sound of insects and a chorus of birdsong without meeting a soul until a glimpse of orange appears through the foliage; a Buddhist monk bows to us with the gentlest of smiles and continues on his way. We watch his saffron robe and shaven head slowly disappear through the banana trees.

Walking up steep hills makes me anxious and tired, but when I remind myself to breathe, take one step at a time and let go of anticipating how far, or how high the next hill is, it becomes easy. It's great to have a chance to practice in the jungle all that I've learnt about staying in the present, in London. My breathing becomes calmer, the agitation settles down, and I don't feel tired any more.

We cross the river by a long, rickety rope bridge ten meters above the water; Kira, who has done it many times before, runs, bouncing, to the other side; when she sees me wobble my way across, her laughter rings out in the silence, accompanied by the sound of parrots chattering and cackling in the trees.

When we finally enter the hill tribe village of the Karen people it feels as if a gauze veil has lifted, revealing a new world; the natural beauty of the people living peacefully in their village in the hills; the children in colourful tribal dress playing till nightfall and then just dropping off to sleep, is enchanting. The women, having cooked, fed their families and cleaned up, sit outside with the men, smoking pipes filled with fresh tobacco from their fields, chatting and laughing.

Sam arranges for us to spend the night in one of the huts. They don't make a fuss about trying to make us welcome and yet we feel totally relaxed and at home. There is a guitar in the room and the one hundred-year-old aunt of the family squats on the ground and cackles with delight when Kira and I sing together the Polish tango, '*We will be strangers when we meet*'.

She says: "*Jen te te,*" and Kira translates: "I'm having a good time."

The next morning on our return trek, I share with Kira

the very strange dream I had had that night: somewhere, in an exotic market I meet an ancient man; he looks at the palm of my hand and says: "Long life."

I say: "Long life, but what else?"

He looks again: "A line of exasperation."

"But can it transform?"

"Yes, if you are willing."

Then he adds: "I am in contact with your father."

"You know him?"

He doesn't answer.

"How old are you?" I ask.

"At least a thousand-and-one", he says and vanishes into thin air.

In the late afternoon on our last day back on Long Island, Kira and I stand by the shore, mesmerised by the gentle rolling of the waves. Against the background of the setting sun – a huge bright orange sphere reflected in the ocean – a boat appears. In it are three men wearing conical Thai straw hats. One stands in the front, another in the back propelling the boat smoothly through the water with a long pole, the third lies flat on his back in the middle.

As we stand on the shore, both of us feeling sad to be leaving this paradise, I tell Kira a story: "Someone told a wise old sage about a man who travelled far and wide but whose travels did not improve him. The wise old man replied, 'I can easily believe it; knowing him, he brought himself and his past history along'. It's true; when I'm in my centre, breathing freely, and not dragging my own past baggage along, I can experience inner peace and happiness wherever I am."

"Yeah, inner freedom doesn't depend on where you are geographically," says Kira, "but I do like it better by the sea."

August 23, 1989 – Ronnie died

"The simplest things are the most difficult. The most difficult thing is getting through a day well. The most difficult thing in life is living – really living – not being in the past or the future, but partaking of the sacrament of the present moment. I endeavour to live in that way myself and to entice other people to live in that sort of way as best they can."

– R. D. Laing

The night before I heard that Ronnie died I had a dream: Ronnie and Francis Huxley are leisurely strolling back from one of Ronnie's lectures and talking about the 'innermost essence'.

I join in and say boldly: "Nothing can to stop me from staying in touch with *my* 'innermost essence' in spite of all hindrances."

Just then, a gigantic dog with a lion's mane walks by staring at each of us in turn. We stop in our tracks. Ronnie looks at me with a mischievous grin and says: "Unless it's a big dog with a lion's mane!" and we all have a hearty laugh.

I woke up feeling fearful, still full of the dream and suddenly remember something Ronnie said about fear, "I still get frightened myself. I cannot claim that I am not afraid of anything, but I am in the next best position, I am not afraid of being afraid."

I hadn't seen him for over a year. He was living in Going, a little village not far from Kitzbuhel, in Austria. I knew he was very ill. I'd heard that he'd stopped drinking and enjoyed a peaceful domestic life, collecting wood in the forest and 'keeping the home fires burning'. He was working on his latest manuscript, *The Lies of Love,* about how lies destroy love, and spent a lot of time playing the piano in his study with its spectacular view of Going's mountain. I felt happy for him that he'd found such peace and beauty in the last stage of his life.

I had resolved to be patient and not seek out his company until I could hold love in my heart without asking for his approval of my spiritual condition. But, like the guy who prays, 'God, send me patience, but please hurry', I telephoned soon after he moved to Going, eager to check out if I was ready to stand my ground and have a conversation with him like a *mensh.*

I asked: "How are you?"

"I'm very well."

"That doesn't sound like you, usually you say, 'plodding on', or something understated like that."

"One doesn't want to incur the jealousy of the Gods."

"But can't one say I am very well, thank God."

"That's what I'm saying."

I didn't have much more to say, but at least I wasn't asking for anything from him.

I'm not passionate about trying to find words to describe the emotion I felt when I heard that Ronnie had died. My passion is in my esteem for him as an authentic man of wisdom, who truly cared about what constitutes sanity and was deeply committed to unravelling and bringing to light how we drive each other crazy with lies and half truths and self deceptions; I honour him for his exceptional ability to empathise with mental suffering because he wasn't 'afraid of being afraid', of feeling suffering in himself and being confronted with it in others.

I don't know if J.D. Salinger knew, or read Ronnie Laing, but he is certainly describing someone just like him in *Franny and Zooey*.

Zooey is Franny's brother. Their mother is desperately worried about Franny's mental state, because she's been carrying around a copy of *The Pilgrim's Progress* and reciting the Lord's Prayer under her breath. The mother is thinking of calling a psychiatrist and asks Zooey's advice. Zooey says: "I don't know, it seems to me there must be a psychoanalyst holed up somewhere in town, who'd be good for Franny ... but I don't happen to know of any. For a psychoanalyst to be any good with Franny he'd have to be a pretty peculiar type ...he'd have to believe that it was through the grace of God that he'd been inspired to study psychoanalysis in the first place. He'd have to believe that it was through the grace of God that he wasn't run over by a goddam truck before he ever even got his licence to practice. He'd have to believe that it's through the grace of God that he has the native intelligence to be able to help his goddamn patients at all. I don't know any analysts who think along those lines. But that's the only kind of psychoanalyst who might be able to do Franny any good at all. If she got somebody Freudian, or terribly eclectic, or just terribly run-of-the-mill, somebody, who didn't even have any crazy, mysterious gratitude for his insight and intelligence – she'd come out of analysis in even worse shape than her brother.'

My memory of Ronnie is in poetic moments, like the forget-me-nots I planted in my window box a morning after Ronnie visited, years ago when we sat together and listened to Billie Holiday, the quality of his attention and respect enabling me, so fragmented, to feel whole in his company.

He never made me feel there was some mystery he was in touch with to which I had no access; or flaunted his authority, asserting his superiority and, therefore, my inferiority. He invited me to be 'full of myself' in the best possible sense. I'll never forget his chuckle when someone said to him: "You're full of yourself today," and he replied: "Who else should I be full of?"

He put out the relaxing message that we are all in the same boat, 'one foot in the grave – another on a banana skin', nothing to be smug about. He spoke about being able to tolerate the uncertainty and ambiguity of life without grasping for answers and envisioned the possibility of a truthful, authentic way of being: "Can't we relax and drop our masks and, instead of trying to outsmart each other, celebrate the healthy spirit in our midst; give each other heart, for God's sake. Come on – at this time of the night, sing me a song."

This sounds like a reconciled man to me.

His sense of humour and directness also come to mind, the way he called a spade a spade; like the time he reminded me that I hadn't paid my monthly bill and when I responded: "Here I am, regressed to a nine-month-old baby and you talk to me about money," and his response was: "Do you really think I'd be sitting here with you if I didn't need the money?"

On another occasion, at a sing-song, he poured me an elegant goblet of cognac out of a bottle that impressed me as very posh and expensive.

I said reverently: "But I won't be able to finish it all."

He leaned towards me and said softly: "Do you realise that you don't have to finish it?"

It was this level of care that can still bring tears to my eyes. He tried to teach me to be free and discerning and not fret unnecessarily about social proprieties and norms which had been drummed into our heads and remained there unquestioned for centuries.

I don't know how I ended up flying from a Psychiatric Conference in Amsterdam back to London with Ronnie, just the two of us; it was like a dream come true, the longed for opportunity to have a 'normal conversation'. But no matter how much I tried to be relaxed and cool, I came out with one more 'my mother' tale: "My mother always told me: 'all men want is one thing and then they leave you'."

"You should be so lucky," Ronnie grinned taking another sip of whisky.

I do get pissed off when people are only too eager to find excuses to diminish him: 'he was a drunkard; he could help other people but not his own family'. We see others through our own limitations; Albert Einstein said: "Great spirits have often encountered violent opposition from weak minds." Or maybe it's a case of 'When a pickpocket sees the Buddha, he only sees his pockets.'

I remember when he was asked: "Ronnie, what would you do if you knew you were going to die next week?"

He replied: "I would carry on in exactly the same manner, partaking in the sacrament of the present moment."

And I believe he made his final exit in that spirit.

I can still see the twinkle in his eye when, at the end of a party, before 'sloping off', as he used to say, he'd come out with a riddle: "What is lower on the scale, a first grade arsehole or a second grade arsehole?"

"Life is a sexually transmitted disease with one hundred percent mortality," he'd chuckle, and break into Fred Astaire's version of *'Puttin' on the Ritz'*:

If you're blue and don't know where to go to
Why don't you
Go where the fashion sits
Puttin' on the Ritz

One day my phone rings and it is Ronnie: "I'm working on my book *Do you love me? An entertainment in conversation and verse*. May I try out an idea on you?"

"Yes."

"Do you love me?"

I had to think before I replied; I was becoming conscious of the fact that I still didn't really know how to love or be loved, but felt I was coming closer to it; therefore it was almost honest of me to say: "Yes, I love you."

"Do you believe me?"

"Yes, I believe you."

"Believe me, you don't love me."

"Maybe I don't have to believe you in order to love you?" I worked out.

Ronnie laughed: "Good for you, Mina."

Oh yes, believe me, I loved Ronnie, and it had nothing to do with me being a woman and him a man; I would have loved him if I were a goat.

Meditation retreat in southern Thailand

After Ronnie's death, Kira invited me to go back to Thailand for a ten day silent meditation retreat in a Buddhist monastery in Chiaya, a market town 600km south of Bangkok. It was a timely invitation, giving me a chance to let my mind settle down and see if I could stand my own ground, as Ronnie encouraged me to do.

The first test of my emotional stamina came on the platform at Bangkok railway station when Kira, who had just completed her ten-day silent retreat, was trying to put me on the night train for *my* solitary adventure. I hadn't realised just how deeply the war traumas were still lodged in my psyche until I found myself, in peace time, with my daughter seeing me off on my way to a tranquil sanctuary and planning to meet in Chiang Mai afterwards to go trekking in the hills. Sounds great – were it not for the fact that I panicked and refused to get on the train. The platform, crowded with people carrying children and bundles, triggered memories of the four-year-old during the war being passed onto a moving train into the arms of a soldier whilst my mother ran along side, desperately trying to catch up.

Now, as an adult, I feel embarrassed about making such a fuss about getting onto this blooming train, and try to find excuses: "I'm not going; there are floods in Chiaya, I'll get stuck there forever."

Kira, only too familiar with my anxieties, tries to reason: "Look, Mum, you have three choices ..."

"I don't feel I have any choices."

"Ok, let's take it one step at a time. We'll get on the train, find your seat and then see how you feel; you can always get off."

I let myself be led to my compartment where we find two jolly young English guys, drinking beer. They must have picked up on my reluctance to remain on the train because they ask: "What's the matter?"

Kira gives them an abridged version: "My mother was in Russia during the war and she's anxious about train journeys. She's on her way to Chiaya to a meditation retreat."

"Don't worry, we'll look after you," the guys say in unison and offer me a beer.

I'm still feeling like a lost four-year-old trying to act grown up, when Kira, who trusts I have enough skills by now to calm my mind, grabs the moment to get away: "Bye Mum, see you in ten days." The train moves out of the station and gathers speed on its way to the south of Thailand, whether I like it or not.

I try to breathe and calm myself; after all, I've been practicing Yoga and meditation for twenty years and somewhere inside I'm aware that right now there's no cause for panic.

The attendant makes my bed and gives me a tall glass of cool, freshly-squeezed orange juice – a far cry from Second World War cattle trains and the one orange from Odessa shared by my cousin, my mother, my stepfather and me. The main lights are switched off for the night, I get under the covers and start reading my book, *The hundred thousand songs of Milarepa*, the Tibetan Yogi. He is easier to identify with than other spiritual teachers who seem to have *always* been perfect. He comes through as an ordinary human being who has committed some unwholesome acts. He took revenge; he killed, had many problems, but rose above the miseries of his early life through faithful devotion and perseverance, and became a fully awakened spiritual master.

As long as I'm reading, his words inspire and resonate with the dormant wisdom in my own heart, but as soon as I put the book down, I start obsessing that I'll miss Chiaya. How am I supposed to know when to get off if the names of all the stations we pass are in Thai script? I stick my head out from behind the curtain of my sleeper and ask the attendant, who doesn't speak a word of English, "Chiaya?' and point to my watch.

He looks at me as if I'm nuts, which I am, and says: "*Noh* Chiaya."

Am I on the wrong train? Can't be, Kira and the 'cool' guys would have known. I read some more of Milarepa's songs:

The essence of Mind is like the sky
Sometimes it is shadowed by the clouds of
thought-flow
Then the wind of the guru's teaching
Blows away the drifting clouds

That instantly calms me down.

A while later, I stick my head out again: "Chiaya?" and point to my watch.

He says: "*Noh* Chiaya", and chuckles.

Oh dear. I try my best to stay mindful, breathe and let go of my thoughts, after all I'm on my way to practice *Vipassana* meditation for ten days.

Eventually I fall asleep. When I wake up and open the

curtain, the sun is rising behind the mountains. After my toiletries, I fold my bed and sit there, not taking my eyes off the attendant, waiting for a sign from him. Breakfast is served: more freshly squeezed orange juice, coffee and toast. I eat, keeping an eye on the guy. Finally he announces: "Chiaya", and laughs, his whole body shaking.

Wat Suan Mokkh, the 'Garden of Liberation', is a forest monastery, founded in 1932 by one of Thailand's most revered monks, The Venerable Buddhadasa Bhikku. He established the centre as a sanctuary for laypeople, who wished to practise *Vipassana*-Insight meditation,

On arrival, a young American woman gives me a guided tour of the premises and shows me to my quarters: a cell with a cement block for a bed, a paper-thin straw mat, a wooden block for a pillow, a thin blanket, and a mosquito net.

"Here is the bucket for scorpions," she tells me matter-of-factly, "the shovel is for scooping them up. You throw them in the bucket and secure the lid. In the morning somebody will take them out to the edge of the jungle."

Although I'm not at all happy with having to trap scorpions, at least they're not mice.

"Men and women are segregated into separate parts of the grounds at all times," she continues, "These two cisterns are for washing, you wash in your sarong." She gives me half a smile and leaves, handing me a list of instructions:

4 am: the gong chimes: wake up, bathe, two hour meditation in the open air meditation hall, yoga and then private meditation.

7.30 am: breakfast, chores, Dharma talk, meditate, walking meditation, sitting group meditation.

12:30 pm: lunch (last meal of the day), chores, meditate, walking meditation, meditate, chanting.

6 pm: cup of tea or a sweet Soya drink, hot spring swim, two hour meditation

9 pm: bed.

No reading, no writing, no smoking, no drinking, no sexual thoughts or activities, no talking at any time. Stay mindful of your breathing while you are washing and eating and doing your daily chores. Each volunteer at the retreat must help with the upkeep of the monastery. Chores include raking leaves, scrubbing pots, and cleaning toilets. Observe your breathing and watch your mind during all these activities.

We sit in the open air meditation hall, ready for our introductory Dharma talk. The meditation master emerges from the forest in his saffron robe, walks mindfully into the hall, sits down on a cushion on the floor, and taps the small bell three times, which awakens and focuses everyone's attention. His kind face melts into a smile as he starts to talk, telling us that he empathises with the difficulties of the novice meditators. He was born over fifty years ago in England and, as a musician and artist, spent the sixties and seventies living a hippy lifestyle in India before becoming a Theravada Buddhist monk in the mid-eighties. He chuckles as he tells us that he has no regrets and doesn't miss the 'real world'.

"Life is suffering," he says with a mischievous grin, "it's nothing to be miserable about. We suffer because of our wrong thinking. We can become free of suffering if we understand profoundly enough that it is our state of mind that creates the suffering."

As I sit there in the meditation hall listening to the monk, I try to identify what's stopping me from being present with a quiet mind and an open heart in that moment; it's the constant commentary running through my mind: 'I like, I dislike, I want, I don't want'. It's the unease of constant craving. I remember the instructions, 'feel the unease and return to the breath'. I hear the monk say: "The Five Hindrances to effective meditation are: Desire, Restlessness, Sloth, Ill-will, and Doubt."

I remember Ronnie telling us about the obstacles to meditation at the Palazzo in Italy and how new and unfamiliar it sounded then. Now I understand it a little deeper.

The monk continues: "Anyone who breathes can practise Anapanasati meditation. It's good for your health and has no side effects. It's simple: feel your breath entering and leaving your nostrils, observe the thoughts in your mind, notice any physical sensations, let them pass and keep observing the breath."

Without speaking, reading or writing, I'm confronted more intimately with my own mind, which continually keeps wandering back to the past, or into the future. I observe it, let go of the thoughts and follow my breath.

"Try not to kill mosquitoes, just feel a mosquito land on you, observe the sensation, relax and breathe ... they won't bite," he shows us his bare shoulder, "See? No bites."

I feel a mosquito land on my arm and try to follow the monk's instructions: 'Feel the sensations, acknowledge the urge to slap it, breathe ....' and I must admit it works; I observe the surge of venom and anger and, instead of slapping the mosquito, I brush it gently away.

The monk strikes the gong and it's time for walking meditation. He gives instructions: "Walk silently and mindfully around the grounds, aware of your breathing. Notice the thoughts and come back to your breath and your feet touching the ground. Don't panic if you come across a snake on the path, they're mostly harmless." Mostly?

The chanting monk is like a jester; he guides us in a chant in Pali about taking refuge in the Buddha, the Dharma and the Sangha in a profound and at the same time playful manner. His expression, as if he knows some uproarious universal joke that the rest of us don't quite get, definitely helps me to lighten my heart and drop my habitual mental melodrama.

Every night we swim in the sulphur pond, in the moonlight, in silence. It is restful not to *have* to be sociable, not to *have* to greet anyone or even smile, but, in this blissful setting, smiles on everybody's faces are as bright as the moon.

Not speaking at all for ten days makes my thoughts so clear, that I feel I'm watching a private show in my head; at times painful, at other times amusing. One morning, during the group sitting meditation, I feel pain in my hips and keep moving and changing position. I catch myself having an imaginary conversation with the guy behind me, explaining to him that this restlessness is unusual for me; I'm a Yoga teacher and can usually sit comfortably in full lotus for an hour. Next, I am imagining telling my friend John back in London how I tried to justify my restlessness to a guy behind me, who was obviously also sitting with eyes closed, and John and I have a laugh; I nearly burst out with actual uncontrollable laughter.

Another morning we set off to hear the Dharma talk by the eighty-nine-year-old Master of the monastery, given in his garden – a half-an-hour of mindful walking to arrive there at 5 am. The Master, who can barely walk, is helped to his seat by a young monk; he sits in full lotus for two hours talking about mindfulness in Thai, translated by the American monk. In the garden chickens strut around with their new chicks; cats nurse their kittens, dogs sniff for food, birds sing and flowers open. From time to time a rooster alights on the old Master's shoulder; he just continues talking about the power of mindfulness overcoming suffering, or '*dukkha*' in Pali.

"*Dukkha* is the pervasive unsatisfactory nature of existence due to our wrong thinking. It is our underlying constant craving for something. For instance, to have to sit next to someone who appears to us unpleasant is *dukkha;* being separated from someone we want to be with is *dukkha.* Through mindfulness and investigation of reality we begin to understand that *dukkha* is not personal. Changing old habits is painful, but with practice, compassion starts to grow in our hearts."

At the end of the talk the Master says in his broken English: "On way back, walk without walker and, when come back to your country, remember magic of 5 am; introduce to your neighbours.

Walking back through rice fields with the sun rising, I try to follow the Master's advice to 'walk without a walker'. I walk mindfully, feeling my feet on the ground, breathing, noticing the thoughts, returning back to the breath, at the same time aware of other people.

For the first time in my life I have literally not spoken a word in ten days. I feel calm, happy and full of energy, so I make an enthusiastic resolution: from now on to be mindful of my eating and speaking. But at the end of the retreat when we begin to talk, straight away the issue of being with others and not reacting emotionally starts up all over again. With my background of starvation and later eating food for comfort, overeating has become an issue and has an unbalancing effect on me physically and emotionally.

Patanjali says in the *Yoga Sutras*: "Yoga is not for him who eats too much or eats too little, sleeps too much or sleeps too little".

Max Freedom Long says in his book *The Huna* or *Hidden Secret Code in Religions:* "Kahunas, the ancient Polynesians, believed that the seat of the low self was in the intestinal tract and the low self is the place where fixations and convictions of unworthiness and guilt must be sought and removed".

I am also inspired by the hexagram in The I Ching: 'Providing nourishment':

> *Mad pursuit of pleasure for the satisfaction of the senses never brings one to the goal. One should never follow this path, for nothing good can come of it.*
> *Words are a movement going from within outward.*
> *Eating and drinking are movements from without inward.*
> *Both kinds of movement can be modified by tranquillity.*
> *For tranquillity keeps the words that come out of the mouth*
> *from exceeding proper measure*
> *and keeps the food that goes into the mouth from exceeding proper measure.*
> *Thus character is cultivated.*

These texts inspired me to start letting go of the issues relating to early deprivation and my old habit of gulping my food down.

After the silent retreat, I take the train from Chaiya back to Bangkok, and then fly to Chiang Mai, where Kira picks me up at the airport. We are happy to see each other, hugging and laughing and talking about *'dukkha'* and how we create our own suffering. She takes me to the guest house, where we relax on the veranda in the gentle breeze.

I feel a different woman from the one who held back from hugging Kira after my first meditation retreat in Sussex twenty years ago, afraid to lose the fragments of balance I'd found. I feel so close to her now. We keep eulogising about how clear we feel, mentally and physically, full of joy and happiness, but keep wondering 'why can't we stay mindful of the breath, body, thoughts and eating, in every moment?'

We visit Chiang Mai's most sacred Temple and sit in front of the statue of the Buddha silently, feeling peace and harmony between us. We leave the Temple arm-in-arm, joking and laughing all the way to our favourite vegetarian restaurant.

I wish you love

I first met Eduardo Niebla in 1975, when he was twenty-one, and I, thirty-seven. We were neighbours. I was living in Little Venice and he was living with his girlfriend Montse in Bristol Gardens, a squat around the corner. To supplement his few poorly paid gigs and earn him time to compose, he gave me and a few other people guitar lessons.

Now he is an internationally acclaimed guitarist, composer and performer, playing all over the world to standing ovations. I had the good fortune to be his student, friend, and lover. It's one of the ironies of fate that I've always wanted to be with an older man and always ended up with younger men.

We lived together for a couple of years. Once, when Eduardo had a concert booked in Cape Town, he took my mother and I out to lunch at a fantastic restaurant on a hilltop overlooking the whole expanse of the Atlantic Ocean, only for my mother to put her elbows on the table, lean towards him and pronounce, "You are *much* too young, my dear."

At the time I would complain to my women friends: "He's younger than me, he never wants to come for a walk on Hampstead Heath, we hardly ever go to a concert or a show; it's just good food, good sex, good music and laughter."

My friends were flummoxed: "What else do you want?"

I think I was just too vain to be the older woman. Eduardo always was and still is a driving force, a mega power of musical creativity, composing original music and playing from morning to night. On top of all that he could make the most delicious paella and be a loving father and son, telling amusing stories about his father in Gerona, who would arrive on his scooter with vegetables grown on his allotment and a rose in his mouth, for his wife, Margarita.

Eduardo taught me music and rhythm, encouraging me to practice with a metronome every day. I came out of my relationship with him with more rhythm and more love in my heart than I went in. All those nights of love to Bach's *Cello Suites* played by Pablo Cassals!

Saint Exupery said: "Love is not sitting and gazing at each other but looking together in the same direction". Even though I always craved attention I couldn't stand too much of it focused exclusively on me. What made it possible with Eduardo was that for him music came first.

I was sad when we parted, but also relieved; it felt too strenuous to be the older woman and to have to look at every attractive, young woman in the street through his eyes. Well, I didn't have to, but I did.

Forever wishing to be on stage, I rehearsed a scene in my mind: at the door: as we are saying goodbye, I look into his eyes and sing the Charles Trenet song:

"I wish you shelter from the storm,
a cosy fire to keep you warm,
but most of all, when snowflakes fall,
I wish you love".

But, mercifully, tears choked my voice and stopped this melodramatic performance, sparing both of us a lot of embarrassment.

To mark our separation I bought myself a pair of red

silk pyjamas and, after the day's work was done, lounged around in them savouring the luxury of being alone, which lasted for about a month. Then I started feeling lonely again, falling back into that familiar pattern of my divided relationship with men: when I am alone I want to be with a man; yet when I am with a man I want to be alone.

I found it impossible "not alone to be, and yet free to be", the sentiment I so much admired in a song by the German *chanteuse*, the spirited Hildergard Kneff. She did the first nude scene in the history of German cinema, which caused a large scandal and protest from the Roman Catholic Church, to which she responded, "I can't understand all that tumult – five years after Auschwitz."

Eduardo Niebla is the last man I have lived with ... so far. Who knows, maybe, *"there's just enough libido in my plan for one... more... man"*, as my dear composer friend Mary Ann Ephgrave says in the song she wrote for me:

In Between Men

There are times when I'm in between men
At the moment I'm in between again
Enjoying my own company
All this space just to be me,
Which is fun
now and then.
Because it's good for the soul to be alone
To know for certain that no one will telephone
Another week's gone by
The sheets are clean and so am I
It's great
to watch blind date
Don't you know
it's my favourite show?

Quite enough to satisfy
My need for a partner or a mate.
So one more time
I try to convince myself that I'm
Through with all that
Think I'll buy me a cat
The price of a cuddle's too high
It's such a muddle
Who needs the angst?
no thanks,
not I
Well that's the story line I tell myself
But after a couple of months
Hanging out on the shelf
I breathe an exasperated groan
Call myself up on my mobile phone
The peace and quiet is getting me down
I want to dress up, go out on the town
When you reach the age of sixty-few
They tell you there's not a lot you can do
But there's quite enough libido in my plan
For one more
For one more man.

A path with heart

As for the first man I ever lived with, Arthur continued to search all his life for his true self, for his 'warrior nature'. He also wanted to break through a 'denseness' that was blocking his ears and his ability to hear a melody. He wanted to be able to sing a song.

He was mad about Carlos Castaneda, constantly quoting him on 'self- importance' and the idea that it was self-importance that obliges you to be constantly dissatisfied. Letting go of self-importance was high on Arthur's priority list, because feeling important makes one heavy, clumsy, and vain, and to quote Castaneda, "to be a man of knowledge one needs to be light and fluid." Despite apparently not being self-important, Arthur wanted to establish a commune with his extended family and 'followers'. There were Kira and I, Janet and her children Kim and Ias, and eventually there was also Maria, with whom he ran off the night before his friend, Menoles, was going to marry her.

Arthur and Maria were given a village in Greece that had been damaged by an earthquake, in exchange for renovating the houses. The village was going to be their commune. Before he left, Arthur asked me if I'd be wife Number Three in the hierarchy and come with Kira to live and train in their commune. Their motto was, 'a path with heart': to live free, to love unconditionally, to train physically, to learn to adapt to your own energy and to the energy of others for the sake of the integrity of the community.

To his request I simply said, "Arthur, I'm confused about quite a number of things in life, but this is not one of them."

At the time of his death Arthur and I had been divorced for twenty-five years. His journey was cut short when his lifestyle started to undermine his health, both physically and mentally. To put it simply, he took too many drugs, which did both his head and his health in. Dear, dear Arthur. It's amazing how he could be there for so many people, but in the end he couldn't be there for himself.

I remember how the African people working at Arthur's uncle's steakhouse, loved him as their friend, despite it being illegal for them to socialise at the time. I remember listening to him explaining the *Id, Ego* and *Superego* to me on our honeymoon, my whole being slowing down to a point of perfect happiness; and I remember how after Kira was born and I was lost in the grip of my own emotional pain, he would change her nappy, lay with her on his stomach, and the two of them would just look into each other's eyes. He gurgled and cooed with her when she was tiny, and when she got older he took her and all her friends to the zoo, to the park and bought them ice creams. He was such a lovely father. He loved children, and they adored him in return. For them, just to go and get an ice-cream with him was an adventure. Ronnie once commented that Arthur was the only adult he knew who could play with children until they had had enough.

Although Arthur's warrior nature eluded him, by the time he died he did manage to learn to sing a song pretty well. He always dreamed of singing Bob Dylan's *'Forever Young'* at Kira's wedding... while doing backflips all the way down the aisle. The dream did at least demonstrate his heart's blessings for Kira, even if it was in his own unconventional way.

May God bless and keep you always,
May your wishes all come true,
May you always do for others,
And let others do for you,
And may you stay forever young.

Thank you Arthur, for what you did for me, and for so many others.

We were divorced at the time but did a very harmonious trikonasana together.

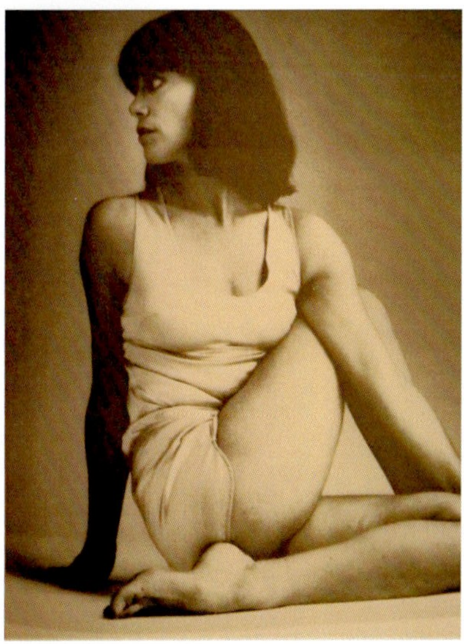

From Arthur's book *Every Body Knows.*

Arthur enthusiastically engages all his friends and family in the project, including the children.

The little yoginis doing very impressive, straight headstands!

Little Kira and I in baddhakonasana.

Trikonasana
with a twist for
Arthur's book.

A few years later, another photoshoot involved doing Yoga in my tango shoes ...

Theo.

In Theo's apartment in Amsterdam, on the canal.

Theo and I.

Nod.

Frankie the lurcher
who could run like
the wind!

The photograph of me with
Dzhulbars, our Alsatian,
who was tied up on a
chain by the gate, summer
and winter, in the suburb
of Moscow.

At a 'Psychiatry of the future' conference in Zaragosa with R. D. Laing. Our children joined us in concert, singing *'Stepping out with my baby'*.

From left: Natasha, Nina, Hannah, Kira.

Singing *'I was young and innocent and good'*.

With two musician friends, Jonathon Coudrille – an artist and an amazing guitarist, and John the saxophonist who also worked as a milkman. We called ourselves 'The Petersburg Connection'. We created the paper sign in this photograph and stuck it to the outside of London's Paddington Station.

I believe this is the 'languid' look I couldn't master at seventeen years old, when Volodya Tarasov asked me, 'Look languidly at me' when we were walking through the snow in the suburb of Moscow.

As The Petersburg Connection, we played in a couple of venues and hospices. I remember in one hospice, an old man with a heart condition put his hand inside his pyjamas and tapped his heart to the rhythm of '*Gari Gari*'.

'*Nu* I am going to sing you a song!'.

Items straight out of Fran's boudoir are all part of the stage set for 'Fran and Friends', a picture of decadent extravagance.

Eduardo Niebla providing an exquisite guitar accompaniment!

Beautiful Lolly, Janet and Mel joining in the chorus of *'Gari Gari – Burn Burn the love of the gypsy!'*

With ecstatic Kevin on the fiddle and handsome Greek accordionist whose name I have forgotten, may I be forgiven!

Our duo 'Mina and Kate' lasted for many years until Kate had a beautiful baby, Nancy, who now writes me letters about books she reads and songs she composes.

Gorgeous Kira with friends in Bali.

Ronnie playing the piano with his youngest child in Switzerland.

R. D. Laing (7th October 1927–23rd August 1989)
'Yes, believe me, I loved Ronnie, and it had nothing to do with me being a woman and him a man; I would have loved him if I were a goat.'

PART FIVE
My Yiddishe Mama

"You live, you learn and you die a fool"

– My Mother

My mother calls from Cape Town

I'm living in London on my own, after one divorce and four love affairs. I measure my progress by the degree of freedom I've achieved from the doctrine passed down generations that I can't survive without a man. I'm beginning to think I can, but my mother obviously doesn't.

She calls from South Africa: "Listen, I want that you should listen. I want to tell you something, don't get upset."

"What?" my heart starts beating faster. I prepare myself for the worst.

"Your Uncle Zalman died."

"When did he die?"

"*Ay*, seven years already ... *ay, ay*!"

"Seven years? Why didn't you tell me before?" I'm befuddled.

"I didn't want to upset you ... Sonya, his wife, died soon after him. It's already five years. Time flies! Do you remember Nekhamke?"

"Yes." My mind and body are on full alert.

"Smart she isn't, no brains, but even *she* found a husband, *nu*, every bottle has a top, every pot has a lid, may she be happy. And do you remember the young Gitke?"

"Yes."

"Gitke married a chemist, a good boy. They have a nice house, a new car and a swimming pool. And ... I also didn't want to upset you, Meishke, the youngest, poor boy."

"What happened to *him*?"

"He shot himself."

"*Shot* himself?"

"*Oy, oif puste felder* [may misfortune land on all the desolate fields, not on us], already five years ... yes ... he saw his girlfriend in the street with another boy, so he took out a revolver and shot himself in front of them ... but ... what can be done? ... may the dead bury the dead ... do you remember Mendel?"

"Of course I remember Mendel." I don't know where this is going, but somewhere even weirder, for sure.

"Mendel had hip replacement surgery, he inherited the house and he wants to marry you."

I'm stunned. I'm bewildered. My mind is boggled, my sense of reality challenged. I'm *shtum*.

"Why aren't you talking? This phone call costs money!"

"I don't know what to say."

"Say yes or no."

"No! Of course not!" I burst out in total exasperation.

"*Nu*," sigh, "all right, it's your life."

Kira refuses to be a buffer between me and my mother

Kira says: "I'll come with you to visit your mother on one condition, that you don't use me as a buffer." I look up the word in Webster's Dictionary: "a buffer is a small state between two possible belligerents, helping to diminish chances of hostility".

I am fifty-nine, a Yoga teacher for twenty-five years, and I am still afraid of totally losing control when faced with my mother. Every time I land in Cape Town I am on full alert like a prickly hedgehog. The best I can do is to pray for mercy. So I say to Kira: "I promise I'll try," but in my heart I know I can't vouch for it.

Mel, Kira's aunt, and her friend, Ario, meet us at Cape Town airport and we drive to the bungalow we've rented from my friends, Katinka and Ivan. On the way I make a plan: first a swim in the cold Atlantic Ocean, the quickest and most blissful way to recover from a long flight, so that we can arrive at my mother's refreshed and ready to face the music. I can hear my mother's voice in my head, 'I haven't seen you a whole year and what is the first thing you do? Go to the beach!'

When we arrive at her place she says: "Where have you been? I rang the airport and they told me, 'Mina and Kira arrived early in the morning.' It's four o'clock already. Come, sit down and eat, I made chicken and potatoes and apple cake."

"We had lunch, we are not hungry. Let's have tea and cake."

"You need food, not cake; *Ikh zol azoy lebn*." Which means 'if you want me alive', or in other words, our not eating equals our wishing her dead.

Mel suggests, "Let's say a prayer,":

"May this food nourish us on the path of love and understanding and greater expression of our divine nature."

This gratitude mantra is thousands of light years away from my mother's experience of famine and the unimaginable pain of having no food to give to her child, which in her mind, feels as if it happened only yesterday.

She ignores it: "Oy, why only cake? Eat, eat, you haven't eaten anything. What do you want to eat when you come tomorrow?"

I understand that she's stuck in her memories of starvation, but it still drives me mad. I notice the familiar symptoms: tightness in my abdomen, irritability and a total loss of the 'seventh sense' – my sense of humour. And of course Kira picks up on it instantly. Later, in the car, on the way to the restaurant in Sea Point, Kira becomes quiet and withdrawn. When we get out of the car at the sea front she says: "I'm not coming again to see Grandma with you; the way you behave with her makes me feel suffocated and brings out in me the same feelings your mother brings out in you."

I start on my old story again: "I'm sorry but I can't breathe. I'm trying to let go of the past and she pulls me back in. I'm sorry but I just can't control it."

"If you can't drop it now, I'm not coming with you."

Mel and Ario stand aside, obviously in total cahoots with Kira, which makes me feel outnumbered and defensive. But deep inside I know that I have to drop this old pattern of reacting to my mother and I'm grateful that my daughter doesn't let me get away with it.

I must admit it's easier to drop your negativity standing by the ocean with a full moon in the sky, anticipating a fresh seafood meal at a seafront restaurant. And if it weren't for my mother, I wouldn't be standing there at all, breathing this glorious Atlantic Ocean air.

The next day when we visit, I manage to see a woman who is my mother, who's been through the horrors of the Second World War, lost her husband and left alone with a little child in Kyrgyzstan – a land foreign to her. My heart opens and I feel love and compassion for her; what this woman only had to go through in her life in order to survive and protect me. It amazes me how much a heart can hold and bear; amongst other horrors, to have to see her child hungry and have no food to give her. My irritation at her telling me to eat all the time softens a little.

As if reading my thoughts, she says, out of the blue: "*Ay*, I don't know why; I suddenly remember how I used to stand at the market and sell *galoshen*."

"You sold *galoshen?* Where did you get them?"

"From Bertha," she says, as if it's obvious to the whole world except me.

"Where did she get them?"

"Don't you remember Liova? Her husband used to work at the shoe factory. He used to steal them."

"So it must have been dangerous selling them?"

"Dangerous, of course it was dangerous. I could get ten years in jail for it. Bertha used to give me fifty roubles for each pair I sold, so I sold them for a hundred roubles each and then I would buy chicken, bread, butter and even have some money left for sweets for you. One day a handsome, well-dressed man came up and asked 'how much for a pair?' so I told him. He said, 'Why so cheap?' I said, 'That's the price.' He bought a pair. The next day he was at the market again. I could see he was looking at me funny, my heart was beating fast, you can imagine, that guy could have been a plain clothes NKVD man. He came up to me and asked, 'How much are they today?' I said, 'The same price.' He said, 'Come with me, I want to talk to you.' I was nervous but I went. He showed me his passport. He was a metro engineer, the main one, no more no less. He said, 'Do you have any more at home?' I said, 'Yes', he said, 'Let's go ... I'll buy the lot.'"

"And you trusted him?"

"You have to trust sometimes, otherwise you don't eat. I took him to our room; you were alone at home with a sore throat. I told you to stay inside, but you didn't listen to me; you went sliding down in the snow on your belly and your coat looked as if you were attacked by dogs. He had a good look at you ... anyway what's there to talk much, he bought all the *galoshen*. He said, 'And you don't want to know what I'm going to do with them?' I said, 'It's not my place to ask.' He said, 'I'm going to sell them at Pushkino market for a hundred roubles more and I advise you to do the same.'"

"And did you?"

"No, I was afraid. Years later when I was already dressed in a smart coat with a silver fox around my shoulders and new boots, I saw him at the Komsomolskaya metro. He was with another man. He came up and said how pleased he was that I was looking so well. *Akh* ... those were some days."

The next day I notice my mother's neglected hair and ask her: "Would you like us to dye your hair?"

"What do you need to bother?"

"It's not a bother."

"*Akh*, what difference will a bit of dye make?"

"We'll see after we've done it."

"*Nu* ... all right."

We buy dark brown hair dye and Kira and I dye her hair. She actually enjoys the whole procedure.

"I need a haircut," she says after we finish.

"How do you want it?" asks the young hairdresser we take her to.

"I want a nice haircut, a little shorter, but not too short."

As I watch the hairdresser trim her hair, I can see it's beginning to look really nice; as usual, it doesn't take much to transform her from looking old and shrivelled to much brighter and younger. She's always had this ability to magically transform herself.

I ask her in Russian: "Are you pleased?"

"She still has quite a lot to learn ... but not on me," answers my mother nonchalantly.

When we take her home we bump into her friendly neighbour who greets us and says: "Mrs. Sher, I've never seen you on the other side of the gate. We often ask your mother to come with us to the park but she always says no."

My mother mumbles under her breath in Yiddish: "*Akh,* what do I need to go with them?"

"Why don't you want to?" I ask in Russian.

"I only like to go out with you."

As soon we come inside she says: "So, eat something?"

"We are not hungry."

"Why not?" she sighs the way she always sighs when food is being declined.

Before we leave she says: "At least an apple? Here, take it with you."

"We have apples."

"Where from?"

I want to kill her.

"Take at least one apple." She shoves an apple into my hand.

When we step outside, I put all my frustration into this apple and send it rolling down Derry Hill. Mel, Kira and I watch it roll all the way to the bottom of the hill and break into uncontrollable laughter.

OK, here I have to take a few deep breaths and do some urgent reasoning with myself. Yes, I feel sad that we live so far away from each other. I would love us to do nice things together more often. I'm not in a position to bring her to live with me and anyway, she'd be miserable in London. She likes the warm weather in Cape Town. I feel guilty, but I've been guilt-ridden all my life. Give me a break. It's not my fault!

On the plane I cry almost all the way back to London. If the human body is ninety percent water, mine seems to be ninety percent tears. When Kira sees that I've stopped crying for a moment, she asks in a sweet voice: "Having a little break?"

I don't even know why I'm crying anymore. Just an ocean of tears keeps welling up and up inside me.

How is the Greek?

Before we left Cape Town to go to the airport my mother took Kira aside and asked in a hushed tone: "Do you have a boyfriend?"

"Yes."

"Where is he from?"

"He's Greek."

"A Greek?" she repeats with non-comprehension and then remembers, "*Agh*, like your father."

A week after we come back to London mama calls.

"How is Kira?"

"She's fine."

"And how is the Greek?"

"He's fine."

"Fine is fine, but is there anything official?"

"Not official, but it seems serious."

"How serious is it if it's not official? Have you met him? What is he like?"

"He's very nice, good sense of humour."

"Sense of humour you can't live on. What does he do?"

"He does Thai Yoga massage. I don't know him very well, I only met him once."

"How many times do you have to meet him to know if he is a *mensch? Nu,* and what about you? Anybody on the horizon?"

"No," I snap.

"What happened to all those who were around?" and without waiting for an answer, she starts singing a plaintive

Russian song: *"everything that's been dear to my heart has flown under the bridge long ago …"*

After I put down the phone, I pour myself a shot of vodka in one of my new vodka shot glasses.

The Jewish old age home

When next Kira and I go to visit my mother she is at Highlands House old age home. We are escorted to the dining room where she is having lunch. There's a man in a wheel chair opposite her with his head on his chest and his glasses falling off the tip of his nose, asleep. She greets us and says, with her habitual sarcasm:

"Meet my conversationalist."

Sarcasm has become her survival technique; having endured a lifetime of pogroms, wars, starvation and loss, and having cried her eyes out, now she finds it easier to laugh than to cry.

"Why is my mother sitting at this table with a sleeping man, when there are all these people who are awake at other tables?" I ask a nurse.

"We put your mother and Moishe together because he speaks Russian."

My mother says in Russian: "*Nu*, they beat you and they don't let you cry."

After lunch we walk slowly to her room with her.

"Come to the window, have a look outside," I say.

"What do I need to look, I can smell the air."

The nurses tell me that she won't join in any activities.

"Why don't you ever go out of your room except for meals?"

"What do I need to go out for?"

The nurses are kind and caring. I feel slightly reassured that at least she's being taken care of and feel more secure that the nurse will give her the right insulin dose, as she no longer sees well enough to do it herself. We sit and hold hands and kiss. She seems more relaxed and enjoys our presence. For a moment there's a little space for Kira to feel she has a grandmother, not just her mother's mother with a terrible atmosphere between them.

"Do you have a doctor?"

"A doctor!" she exclaims as if I couldn't have asked a more ridiculous question.

"There are many doctors here, but they only wave at me, 'Hello Mrs. Sher.' Thank God, I don't need a doctor."

The next day when we come, she says: "*Akh*, I don't know why, where did I get it from, but I thought you had left already?"

Kira: "So it's a nice surprise?"

"Yes," she laughs, not at all bothered by her forgetfulness.

Every time we come, she says: "*Akh*, I don't know where I got it from, but I thought you left already."

I have to admit with a pang in my heart, that she's losing her wits. She has two pictures on opposite walls, one of me, twenty-seven years old, wearing the wig I bought in Mallorca, and another of Kira, five years old, sitting in full lotus, from Arthur's Yoga book, *Body Life*. She looks at the pictures and starts talking as if she is telling a fairy tale to a child:

"One day a man came in, I never saw him before, he took your picture and put it on this wall and then he took Kira's picture and put it on the other wall and walked out. I never saw him again."

"I tell you, some people even get married here. In the room across from me a 'young' couple got married. He is eighty-nine, she is eighty-eight. He asked the nurse to push the twin beds together, 'because,' he said, 'by the time I get to her bed I'll forget why I came.' *Akh*, if only the youth would know, if only the old would be able to."

Ben, who's had a stroke, is in the room across from her. He is seventy-five, my mother is ninety.

Mother says: "Come, let's go and say hello to Ben."

As we stand by his bed, she says to me in Russian: "I tell you, he wouldn't mind if I lay down next to him. His wife is also in the home but on another floor. They offered to move them together, but he didn't want to."

Ben smiles as if he understands what she's said. I feel a bit embarrassed and tell this man, who is paralysed on one side, that he looks like Fred Astaire.

"*Ah*, now I am not the full box of chocolates," he replies and looks flirtatiously at my mother: "Your mother is a beautiful woman."

Mother stands there *makhtsekh nisht visendikh* – pretending it doesn't concern her.

I ask her in Russian: "Did you hear what he said?"

"Yes, and he is not the only one."

Back in London I get a phone call from Highland House telling me that my mother has had a stroke, she can't walk anymore and her speech is slurred. She has to be taken to the bathroom in a wheel chair, the one thing she most dreaded. I phone and speak to her but she can't answer me. Then one day her speech is back.

"You sound better."

"I am better."

"Can you walk?"

"Of course I can walk. Where is there to go?"

That was the last time she made me laugh. Before we hung up, she said, for the last time: '*Vsio budiet khorosho*'. Everything will be all right, which is what she always said to me to comfort me, through all our terrible times.

On a number of occasions, I tried to thank her for

everything she'd done for me, but her response always was: "*Akh,* what do you need to thank me."

So, thank you, Mama.

My mother's death

My mother, Dina Sher, died on April 23rd 2003 at 12pm South African time – 11am London time – in Somerset Hospital, Green Point, Cape Town, South Africa, one month before her ninety-third birthday. I felt a few moments of panic, remembering: "Without me you are nothing!" What if she was right?

But, in a way I felt immunised against her death by her endless threats that she was going to drop dead any day now. I had lived in constant anticipation of that day all my life; when it arrived she was ninety-three. If I'd known she'd live so long I could have enjoyed myself more.

But what's there to say? Of course I felt very, very sad. Now the unimaginable has happened; our mother-daughter relationship is forever imprinted as a tiny part of the vast pattern of the Universe. It was what it was and can't be anything else anymore. This is it. This is the form our love took, take it or leave it.

We arrived in Cape Town in 1960. My mother was fifty years old, fifteen years younger than I am as I write this.

"You are difficult to love," my mother always told me.

She was right; I wouldn't allow myself to love and be loved. Being loved meant being totally engulfed by the other, and so I put a wall around myself; distanced myself. It took a long time to undo this knot of confusion.

The last time we spoke on the phone was the day before she died. "How are you?" I asked.

"I'm fine, my life, my world, my little dove. You must

eat and be healthy. Look after your health. Are you going to come over?"

"Yes," I said, not knowing when.

Now at last she was free. But was I?

Before flying to Cape Town for mother's funeral, I went to the hairdresser; she always told me I needed a haircut. Standing in the crowded tube on the way to the salon my heart was with her and I wished her to be free of her suffering. I recalled and recited a Tibetan Bardo teaching referring to the time after death:

> *"Do not be afraid of the dissolution of the life you have been attached to, and find Peace in God. Go, go, go towards the light, and don't look back."*

And I added, *'Don't be afraid, don't worry about me, I am alright.'*

But ironically I felt I was going to miss her all-encompassing concern about me, however oppressive it had been; now I was nobody's child. There also still lurked in me a fear that no matter how much Yoga and breathing I did, I'd still end up exactly like my mother.

We were bound by chronic emotional pain, worry and anxiety; victims of a life that, in my mother's words, dealt us an unfair hand; "I was young, beautiful, intelligent, the best cook in my village, and look at me now. Is this my neck, are these my eyes?" my mother would say scrutinising herself in the mirror.

Standing there in the subway train on the Jubilee line, her threats that plagued me throughout my life, come to mind: 'Wait till I die, then you'll know, then you'll taste it. You don't want *manna*, eat shit.'

On the subject of shit, I don't think my mother would mind me telling an amusing story:

A little bird was flying south for the winter. It was so cold that the bird froze and fell to the ground in a large field. While it was lying there, a cow came by and dropped some shit on it. As the frozen bird lay there in the pile of cow shit, it began to realise how warm it was; the shit was actually thawing him out! He lay there all warm and happy, and soon began to sing for joy. A passing cat heard the bird singing and came to investigate. Following the sound, the cat discovered the bird under the pile of cow dung, gently licked the cow shit off him and then promptly ate him. The three morals:

Not everyone who shits on you is your enemy.
Not everyone who gets you out of shit is your friend.
And, when you are in deep shit, it's best to keep your mouth shut!

On second thoughts, I don't think it's my mother's kind of story.

The funeral

27th April 2003

The words came to me in Russian: *Mamu pokhoronili* – My mother was buried. *Khoronits* – to commit into the safe keeping of God. *Pokoinitsa* –she, who is at peace.

I couldn't quite take in that the deceased person the burial people were talking about was my mother. They uncovered her and there she was. I leaned over her. She was so obviously an empty shell, her face almost unrecognisable, no lines at all, just slightly sunken in the mouth. I bent down closer and thanked her for everything, for bringing me into the world with all its suffering and pain, but also joy; for bringing me out of Russia to beautiful Cape Town. Then one of the attendants came in and asked me if I had finished saying my goodbyes. I said I had. He started banging nails into the coffin.

The young Rabbi surprised me with his openness and gentle support. When he tied a scarf around my neck, making an incision in the fabric, which I then had to tear further to express our heart-rending separation, a deep sob burst out of me. The Rabbi asked me to tell him our story about the war and how we left Russia, and retold it with real feeling and sensitivity later at the service.

It was a beautiful sunny day at the Jewish cemetery in Pinelands. The attendants wheeled the coffin slowly. Rosie, my mother's step-daughter-in-law and her two children and I, walked behind the coffin with the Rabbi walking behind us, singing prayers. I looked inside the grave before the two young black men, with their kind, open faces, lowered the coffin. Then they threw some earth onto the coffin and so did we. Everyone started to walk away. I didn't want to leave. I walked slowly, looking back for the last time as the two men filled the grave with earth.

I said quietly: "Mama, your soul flew away ... like the mother who turned into a bird in the story you told me that evening in the Tatar republic during the war, when we were alone in the snowed-in little house ..."

> *Once upon a time and far away there lived a mother with two little children, a boy and a girl. One day when she was ill in bed she asked them for a glass of water but they were so busy playing with their toys, they didn't hear her. So she turned into a bird and flew out through the window. Before she flew away she knocked on the window with her beak. The children looked up, startled by the sound, but she was gone.*

The stark finality of the mother's disappearance had sent me into uncontrollable sobs; outside a snowstorm raged, the wind rattled the little window and wolves howled in the distance.

I begged her through my tears: "Please don't turn into a bird and fly away."

She held me and consoled me: "Don't be silly, of course I won't fly away ... if you promise to be a good girl."

Finally I fell asleep holding onto her, resolved in my four-year-old heart to always be a good girl – a promise, which fortunately for me, I didn't keep.

Driving away from the cemetery, I looked up into the sky and saw a big bird, unlike any I've ever seen before, furiously flapping its wings, as if trying to follow us. I kept looking back till it disappeared into the distance.

The service at the synagogue in the old age home followed the burial. It is a requirement of Jewish Law to have ten men at the service for the dead. The organisers had done their best, but only managed to get five.

"We need five more men," says one of the women in the congregation.

"What about Shlomo in room 102?"

"He is not feeling well."

"Go and try."

A few minutes later she comes back with Shlomo, who is shuffling along, holding onto a Zimmer frame. He just about manages to drop into his seat.

"Now we need four more, have you tried Moshe from room 115?"

After half an hour, we have ten men. One arrives in shorts. The woman next to me says: "What a disgrace to come in shorts. And do I need to look at his legs all knock-kneed and the varicose veins?"

Somebody lets off a malodorous fart of such super-high intensity that the odour spreads to every corner of the synagogue within seconds. The same woman, who objected to the man in shorts and his varicose veins, jumps up and runs towards the exit, yelling: "I'm not staying with this putrid smell, not if you pay me."

So the mourners are Rosie, my mother's third husband's daughter-in-law; a friend of Rosie's, whom I've never met before, and the ten men who are barely able to sit up, keep falling asleep and every time the Rabbi says *'Amen'*, wake up with a jolt and say in unison *'Amen'*. I could just imagine my mother laughing and making her usual mocking wisecracks at the tragicomedy of it all.

At the end of the prayers everybody comes to shake

hands with us and to say the customary, 'I wish you long life.' The ten old men, with their heads bowed, take their time to shuffle through.

The next day I cleared my mother's wardrobe and put all her clothes in bags for charity. Her dresses with printed rims at the hems evoked vivid memories of how she always dreamed of this kind of design and how difficult it was to find in Russia. Amongst her things was a playing card of the ace of hearts, which she kept as a good fortune amulet for me to find a husband; a little leather bag with coins, as her own peculiar prayer for wealth for me; a pair of new leather gloves and the mink collar of which she was so proud. I put them all in my bag, except for the mink collar, which I left lying orphaned on the table.

The memories caught at my throat and tears started streaming down my face; tears for what was, and was no more, and mostly, for what had never been.

The night after my mother's funeral I had a dream:

The sun is setting in the desert. I see a ladder that extends right up to the clouds. I start climbing it. The ladder is leaning against a tall, narrow structure standing in the middle of nowhere. On the other side of the structure is another ladder. When I get to the top there is a man on the other ladder, encouraging me to climb over to his side. It looks impossible and I'm petrified, but he seems so sure it's safe that I start climbing over. Sure enough, as soon as I do, both the ladders begin to move and topple over to one side. It is certain death – we are falling from above the clouds. But then, during the fall, I feel my wings open. I land on my feet and so does he.

Honouring her memory

So, what about the Jewish tradition of honouring my mother's memory by setting a stone on her grave? She always told me that she felt a heavy stone on her heart, so why would I put a stone on her grave? But I feel pressured by this tradition. I need to think it through for myself. I'd rather plant a tree for her and gather a few friends together to remember her. But I'm torn by the 'but what will people say' syndrome.

I remember those desolate evenings with just the two of us, when my mother would start singing the song: *"I'll die and be buried and nobody will even know where my grave is."* I felt her tugging at my heart strings, prophesying that I would forget her after she died. She knew she'd have me in floods of tears, but she'd go on delivering the song with a lot of emotion, until my sobbing got out of control and then she'd make pancakes to console me.

I suppose there's still a part of me that believes my mother's words: that I am an unruly *vilde khaya* (a wild beast), just because I question tradition and want to discover for myself how to live an authentic life. But this *vilde khaya* is transforming into a centred 'wild woman'; true to herself, filled with wonder and ageless knowing, not holding her breath for anybody or waiting for anybody to make her happy, free to dance and sing, laugh with joy and howl with sorrow.

In the Jewish tradition, people don't bring flowers to the grave as you are not supposed to cut down living things to honour the dead. Isaak Babel, the Russian Jewish writer, said that when he first ventured into his writing career the only tree he could recognise was the lilac and even then, only when it was in blossom. He felt there was something odd about the way Jewish people, unlike gentiles, didn't know the names of trees or birds. A tree is a tree, a bird is a bird, a dog is a dog, and that's it. It certainly seems like it when I think of my mother, who never pointed out a tree and said its name, except a birch tree perhaps and that mainly because it would get her singing a song about a lonely birch tree standing in the field, swaying in the wind, longing for the oak tree on the other side of the river.

So it seems more appropriate to plant a tree – a birch tree – in my mother's memory and let her spirit fly beyond tradition. Hilmar Schonauer, whose 'Getting to Know Ourselves' workshops I have attended for a number of years, said to me: "Stone setting, or whatever other religions do, is all about keeping the old family traditions alive and not really setting the spirit of the person free. The tradition of burning the body and letting the ashes blow in the wind, or at sea, is much more in accord with setting the spirit free, letting it go beyond its cultural and family limitations."

And, yes, I *am* sad that I didn't get on the plane to Cape Town in time to hold her hand before she died. I have to live with that. But do I have to go on feeling the traditional guilt, instead of enjoying the loving connection with my mother I now feel in my heart?

As for me, I hope whoever is around when I am dead will find a place to cremate me and scatter my ashes over the ocean, with one chrysanthemum floating on the waves. No graves, no stones, no waste of space. And that's it. There goes Mina with all her *mishugaes.* Although my lifelong dream of finding an older, wiser man is still not totally relinquished, it better be soon... because I'm well on my way to becoming older than any wise old man alive.

My mother, Dina Sher.

My mother's family.
She is in the top left, at eighteen years old. Her mother, my grandmother in the centre.

In South Africa for a visit. From left: Me, Kira, my mother, and Theo.

My mother in Cape Town.

I'm not singing because I'm happy;
I'm happy because I'm singing!

EPILOGUE

I'm not singing because I'm happy I'm happy because I'm singing!

Maya Angelou's grandma taught her how to sing:

> *"In order to lift your voice you've got to lift your head*
> *And if you lift your head you are looking at heaven."*

Sometimes I sing a song while my students are changing into their Yoga clothes. Someone inevitably says with a tinge of envy, 'You *are* happy,' and I reply, and really mean it, 'I'm not singing because I'm happy, I'm happy because I'm singing.'

From 1976 to this day I have never been without a singing teacher. I've enjoyed their company and their colourful personalities and learnt a lot from their life experiences, but not so much about why my voice continued to be stifled by inhibitions and how to release them.

My lucky stars guided me to find, on the internet, my current singing teacher Guillermo Rozenthuler, a greatly gifted Argentinean tango singer and teacher who, quite simply *relaxed* me into singing by telling me to stop dramatising the early memories and let go of my attachment to the drama, 'You don't need to *try* and express the emotions of the song; those songs are in your genes. You'll have to give up the drama,' (I think he probably meant the melodrama) 'then you'll be able to sing. The area at the root of the tongue is connected with the unsaid, but you don't need to analyse it anymore; it needs to be deprogrammed. Make a conscious decision not to give any more energy to those old stories, but let the negativity neutralise itself here and now, so your voice can recover and express the wisdom it had before it got side-tracked.'

That resonated with what Ronnie Laing had said to me: "If you realise profoundly enough that your life does not depend on what happened in your childhood anymore, then you are free to remember it, instead of being haunted by it." The brilliant African American actress and singer, Pearl Bailey, also once said: 'There is a way to look at the past. Don't hide from it, it won't catch you if you don't repeat it.'

It took forty years of Yoga, numerous fasts and brown rice diets, sensory deprivation tanks, singing lessons, swimming in the freezing cold pond on Hampstead Heath right through the year, and therapy, to exorcise the Soviet psyche and my Yiddishe Mama. The hardest thing to give up was the need to be amazing, and simply live and love, without the old illusions.

Periodically I lose my confidence, which is not a bad thing. Confidence, based on being surrendered to the Source, or God, cannot be lost; what we can lose is the connection to it. Every time we realise we're disconnected is an opportunity to become more humble, go even deeper and allow the reconnection to happen.

Why is it so difficult for us humans to be present with love in our hearts, without a break in continuity? Humans get tired of being mindful and present and need a break, like it's a chore to be a real human being. I don't know! It is as if God said, 'Here ... you will have clinging, craving, possessiveness, attachment, fear, greed, pride, anger, aggression, blame, competitiveness, self-deception ... and your task on this earth is to let it go, surrender to Me, and learn to love one another.' Difficult, but not impossible; in the words of R. D. Laing: 'It's easy when you know how.' When we get fully in touch with what it means to be a unified human; mind, body, breath, spirit – it stops being a chore.

For me, the scariest thing in the world is a hardened heart. Again I am reminded of the story from my childhood, which I mentioned in my first ever story 'Mice on the Day of Victory', *The Snow Queen*, where the little brother and sister are sitting playing in the snow, making snowmen. Suddenly the Snow Queen swoops through the air and tries to seduce the little boy to come to her palace, with promises of tempting treasures. The little boy is won over by her and the Snow Queen sweeps him off into her Ice Palace. The sister goes looking for him and when she finds him sitting in the palace playing with magical ice toys, he doesn't recognise her.

I found that the scariest thing in the world, scarier than all the fairy story monsters. Because this is how I felt when my mother would disconnect from me, become hysterical and shout at me and curse me. I felt she didn't know who I was. In the story, when eventually the sister cries, her tears melt the boy's heart and the two of them run away.

My mother's heart would also melt after I shed many tears. In order to make a gentle loving heart our priority at all times, we need to practice going through life and all that it presents, without exception, without disconnecting.

Everything that happens is an opportunity to keep opening the heart.

The most famous and beloved Russian ballerina Galina Ulanova, known for her exceptional humility and gentleness, told a story about a young ballerina she was teaching, who was going through a crisis in her personal life and felt she could not possibly dance in the coming performance. Ulanova told her, "You have many performances before you. Start now. Take into each and every performance whatever is happening inside of you." The ballerina said she carried that advice with her all through her life. That story reminds me of the image of water that flows through all obstacles without skipping anything, every nook and cranny.

I am a work in progress. The howling wolf of my childhood, which I associated with fear and poverty, turns out to be my birth totem, a symbol of free spirit, giving me powers of endurance, reminding me to listen to my inner voice and trust that I can open my heart.

And what is the Royal Jelly of all my life's practice?

The Spirit of Love.

The End